C0-AXQ-793

RANCE CO. DOMINION C
GH PROPERTIES LTD. THE GLOBE & MAIL
TELEGRAPH THE SCOTSMAN SOUTH
ND BUYER THOMAS NELSON & SONS LTD.
USTRATED LONDON NEWS COMPUTER
CIANS' DESK REFERENCE CABLE VISION
ORLD AUSTRALIAN ADVERTISING RATE
RAILWAYS OF SOUTHERN AFRICA SOUTH
NSTRUCTION IN SOUTH AFRICA THOMSON
EUROPEAN LAW DIGEST PORTLAND
BRITANNIA AIRWAYS LTD. THOMSON
THOMSON NORTH SEA LTD. HAMISH
HUDSON'S BAY CO. SCOTTISH & YORK
ATED TRUCK LINES SIMPSONS LTD.
GLOBE & MAIL THE CANTON, OHIO
THE SCOTSMAN SOUTH WALES ECHO
THOMAS NELSON & SONS LTD. DRAPERS
TRATED LONDON NEWS COMPUTER
CIANS' DESK REFERENCE CABLE VISION
WORLD AUSTRALIAN ADVERTISING
ING RAILWAYS OF SOUTHERN AFRICA
BOOK CONSTRUCTION IN SOUTH AFRICA
A) A/S EUROPEAN LAW DIGEST
LIDAYS LTD. BRITANNIA AIRWAYS LTD.
ATIONS THOMSON NORTH SEA LTD.
TD. HUDSON'S BAY CO. SCOTTISH
LIDATED TRUCK LINES SIMPSONS LTD.
GLOBE & MAIL THE CANTON, OHIO

THE THOMSON EMPIRE

THE THOMSON EMPIRE

SUSAN GOLDENBERG

BEAUFORT BOOKS, INC.

New York

Copyright © 1984 by Susan Goldenberg

All rights reserved. No part of this publication may be reproduced or transmitted in any form or by any means, electronic or mechanical, including photocopy, recording, or any information storage and retrieval system now known or to be invented, without permission in writing from the publisher, except by a reviewer who wishes to quote brief passages in connection with a review written for inclusion in a magazine, newspaper, or broadcast.

ISBN 0-8253-0259-5

Published in the United States by Beaufort Books, Inc., 9 East 40th Street, New York, N.Y. 10016

Published in Canada by Methuen Publications, 2330 Midland Avenue, Agincourt, Ontario M1S 1P7

Excerpt from After I Was Sixty by Roy Thomson is reprinted with permission from Hamish Hamilton Limited, London, England.

First American edition

Printed and bound in Canada
10 9 8 7 6 5 4 3 2 1

To My Parents

IN APPRECIATION

My deep thanks and appreciation to the many people within and without the Thomson companies in Canada, the United Kingdom and the United States who generously gave me interviews for this book.   S.G. (June 1984)

CONTENTS

I

THE EMPIRE

1

THE EMPIRE

EVEN IN 1966, when he was just starting to patch together one of the world's largest family fortunes, Roy Thomson was confident he would someday own a worldwide business empire. So when the builders of the Toronto-Dominion Centre, Toronto's first major downtown development project, asked the Toronto-born Roy, who was by then Lord Thomson of Fleet and living in London, to move his Canadian operations into the Centre, he laid down certain conditions. The first stipulation was quickly accepted by the builders: one of the three office towers in the complex would be named the Thomson Building. But the second condition took the developers aback: Roy wanted to have the flags of every country where he did business flying from a flagpole in front of his building.

At that point, the Centre's developers decided that, really, Roy's businesses would be occupying very little space in the tower and therefore the tower should not bear his name. Roy suddenly began to see the advantages in being located a few blocks north, across from Toronto's city hall, especially as the builder of a new building at the corner of Queen and Bay streets was willing to name it after Thomson as the main tenant. Unfortunately, unlike the Toronto-Dominion Centre's towers, which front on a square, the building is right at the sidewalk and there was no room for a flagpole.

Nineteen eighty-four marks the fiftieth anniversary of the start of the Thomson empire. From the outset, when Roy Thomson bought his first paper, the Timmins, Ontario, *Daily Press*, it has been an empire primarily built through acquisition. Today, it controls assets worth more than $10 billion on four continents—Europe, North America, Africa and Australia—and in fourteen countries—Canada, the United States, England, Scotland, Wales, Ireland, France, Germany, Holland, Denmark, Norway, Australia, South Africa and Nigeria. If the revenue from all the empire's business were lumped together, it would total more than $8 billion, making it fifth, in terms of revenue, among Canadian companies.*

That places the empire on a par with such U.S. giants as General Foods, Xerox, and PepsiCo and significantly ahead of such well-known firms as Coca-Cola, Johnson & Johnson, Gulf & Western Industries, and General Mills. The empire's revenue is equivalent to that of the General Electric Company in the U.K. and is $1 to $3 billion more than what such major U.K. firms as British Steel, British Airways, and Marks & Spencer make.

All this has made Kenneth Thomson, who has headed the empire since his father's death in 1976, Canada's only billionaire. His personal fortune would place him at least on a par with the richest man in the United States, Gordon Getty (son of the late Jean Paul Getty, a partner of Roy Thomson in North Sea oil development), who is estimated to be worth more than $2 billion. Kenneth's net worth would exceed that of such U.S. media-based family fortunes as the Hearst, Cox and Newhouse ones, each estimated to be worth between $1 and $2 billion. And if all the employees who work for Kenneth Thomson around the globe were added together, they would number close to 100,000—a total that, if all were in Canada, would make Kenneth Canada's second-largest business employer, after Canadian Pacific (about 127,000 employees).

On a comparative basis with U.S. firms, the empire employs one and a half times as many people as Proctor and Gamble and twice as many as the large oil company Atlantic Richfield. In comparison with U.K. firms, it employs twice as many people as Marks & Spencer, three times as many as Cadbury Schweppes, and five times as many as British Petroleum.

The empire started out in newspapers and they still constitute a major portion of its business, although it is now also involved in many other fields. In terms of the number of newspapers owned, it ranks first in Canada and second in the United States, after the Gannett Company. It is the leading publisher in the United Kingdom of regional

---

*Canada's largest company, in terms of sales, is General Motors of Canada Limited, with revenue of $13.8 billion in 1983.

(non-London) newspapers. It owns the "national" paper of Canada, the *Globe and Mail* of Toronto, as well as of Scotland, the *Scotsman*, and of Northern Ireland, the *Belfast Telegraph*. All told, it owns 200 newspapers. At the average rate of 250 trees chopped daily for one newspaper's newsprint, about 50,000 trees are felled each day for the Thomson papers.

Newspapers are just one segment of the Thomson media empire. It is the largest trade (nonconsumer) magazine publisher in both Australia and South Africa and the second largest in the United Kingdom. In total, it owns more than 140 magazines. One South African magazine alone, the *South African Industrial Week*, grosses about $143,000 a month. In addition to newspapers and magazines, the Thomson empire also owns fourteen general and professional book publishers in the U.K., U.S., Canada and Australia. In the last five years, it has bought more magazine and book publishers than the rest of the industry in the U.S., spending more than $400 million. This shopping spree has already made it the fourth-largest U.S. magazine publisher. In the fast-growing telecommunications field, it ranks first among U.S. magazine publishers.

In recent years, the empire has also branched into computer-databank information services companies and now owns ten in the U.K. and U.S. One of these companies, Thomson & Thomson, a Boston firm that, despite its name, had no prior connection to the family, produces 50,000 customized trademark searches annually. Another firm, Research Publications Incorporated of Connecticut, is involved in the largest micropublishing project ever: a listing of all the works printed in English anywhere in the world during the Age of Enlightenment between 1700 and 1800. It is estimated it will contain 10 million frames of microfilm and take fifteen years to complete.

But the Thomson empire has become far more than a media empire. In the last twenty years, it has expanded into travel, oil and gas, retailing and real estate. In the U.K., Thomson Travel is the largest package tour operator, with about one-fifth of the country's total business. The company operates its own charter airline, Britannia Airways, whose fleet of thirty-three planes is equivalent in number to the size of CP Air, Canada's second-largest airline. Thomson Travel moved into the U.S. market four years ago and is already the country's third-largest tour operator. It has also recently entered the Canadian market.

The empire now has oil and gas operations in the North Sea, whose gusher of revenue in the past six years has made possible the expansion of the empire into information services and also into oil and travel in

Canada and the United States. The purchase in 1979 of the Hudson's Bay Company made the empire the owner of Canada's oldest and largest department store chain as well as the owner of two other major retailers previously bought by The Bay—Simpsons Limited and Zellers Incorporated. Together, the three chains account for 45 percent of department store sales in Canada. In addition, The Bay owns Markborough Properties Limited, a major residential and commercial real estate developer in Canada and the United States. Its projects include the 3,000-acre community of Meadowvale, just west of Toronto, where about 28,000 people now live.

The Thomson empire has five main divisions: Thomson Newspapers, based in Toronto, runs the newspapers in Canada and the United States; the Hudson's Bay Company oversees the retailing operations; International Thomson Organisation Limited (ITOL), with nominal corporate headquarters in Toronto but its chief operating executives in London, looks after the newspapers in the United Kingdom and the worldwide magazine, book-publishing, information services, travel, and oil and gas operations; Scottish and York Insurance Limited takes care of the insurance business, which is flourishing in Canada but on hold in the United States; and Dominion-Consolidated Truck Lines runs the trucking operations, which are solely in Canada. The Thomson family, of which Kenneth is the largest shareholder, controls these businesses through a series of holding companies: The Bay and Thomson Newspapers by the Woodbridge Company; ITOL by Thomson Equitable Corporation; Scottish and York by the Standard St. Lawrence Company; and the trucking by Dominion-Consolidated Holdings.

Although the empire was founded five decades ago, the family has realized most of its wealth in the last twenty years as the empire diversified. In 1959, six years after Roy Thomson moved to the U.K., the predecessor company of ITOL had sales of £30 million. In 1976, the year Roy Thomson died, the sales were £285 million. Impressive as these gains were, they have been surpassed; in 1983 ITOL's sales reached £1.5 billion. While Thomson Newspapers has not recorded as steep a climb, its revenue has more than tripled since 1976.

That the Thomson empire *is* an empire is due as much to luck and circumstance as to any grand design. Roy Thomson originally started in the communications business in radio, first trying to sell radios and then owning a small northern Ontario radio station. He moved into newspapers because the Timmins paper happened to be in the same building as another struggling radio station he owned. In what would become something of a hallmark for later ventures, Roy plunged into the newspaper business without much advance study of the industry, simply because it was an additional way of making money. This tendency to decide to enter a business because it seemed like a good idea often resulted in the purchase of financially or managerially troubled companies that more cautious people would have avoided. In the long run—a decade or longer—these investments sometimes turned out to be astute. This was true with the U.K. travel business, for instance, but much less so with the U.K. book companies. Happenstance was a major factor in the empire's diversification. The ideas for the insurance and trucking businesses came from Roy's longtime friend and accountant, Sidney Chapman. The North Sea oil bonanza was due to three American oil companies needing a British partner to facilitate getting exploration licenses from the government.

In some ways, the empire has gone full circle. It started in Canada, branched into the U.S. as Roy bought some newspapers there in the 1950s, and moved to the U.K. when Roy settled there in the fifties and where he expanded into travel, book publishing, and oil and gas in the 1960s and 1970s. Then, in the late 1970s and early 1980s, under Kenneth, the emphasis switched back to North America with the purchase of eight major Canadian papers, including the *Globe and Mail*, and of The Bay in Canada, and with the slew of magazine and book firm acquisitions in the U.S. Kenneth is also responsible for the sale in 1981 of the crown jewels in Roy's portfolio: the *Times* (of London) and its sister paper, the *Sunday Times*. Kenneth sold them because of financial losses and constant labor unrest.

Just as it has returned geographically to where it started, the empire is also again placing its hopes for the future on the media. This time, however, the stress is on high-technology electronic information services and publications aimed at the professions, rather than newspapers, although the newspaper field is not being ignored, with an average of four U.S. papers being purchased annually. The decision to build up an information services business makes sense considering that the market for electronic programming for business and professional uses is said to be growing by an astounding 75 percent annually. Moreover, profit margins can be as high as 35 percent, and the Thomson empire seeks high profit margins like a cat chases a mouse.

Other basic features of the empire also remain ballasts and contradictions, as they have been throughout the years. The stringent penny-pinching, in which every box of pens and every paste pot is included in the budgeting of most newspapers and supplies are doled out grudgingly to reporters, is counterbalanced by acquisitions costing millions of dollars. Most of the small town Thomson papers are objects of virulent contempt within the journalism profession for their stiff budget controls, a perceived emphasis on service club news, and their efforts to remain nonunionized. Yet the quality of the *Times* and the *Sunday Times* did not decline under the Thomsons, nor has that of the *Globe and Mail*. The Thomson small town papers do not differ in their type of content or antiunionism from other small town newspaper chains, such as that of the Gannett Company.

There are other paradoxes, too, in the Thomson empire. While many of its newspapers are monopolies as the only paper in a town, in other businesses the empire does not steer clear of competition. Travel, book and magazine publishing, as well as oil and gas, are all fiercely competitive fields and crowded with rivals—yet the empire has not hesitated to move into them. There are contradictions in the management style, too. Highly intelligent, entrepreneurial people are eagerly sought and given considerable leeway in daily operations, but are reined in by the knowledge that the empire demands, on average, 20 percent profit margins, much higher than what most of its competitors achieve. Most of the employees of the empire have never met Kenneth Thomson because despite his efforts to visit different operations, the empire's vastness would require years for him to see every company. Consequently, managers feel very much like their own boss, rarely remembering that Kenneth, and not themselves, holds the ultimate control.

Not only does he have the ultimate control, but the Thomson empire will remain a Thomson empire. Roy Thomson did not make the same decision as William Randolph Hearst, who diluted family control by naming eleven warring members to the board of trustees for his estate. Hearst's five sons were outnumbered by the six trustees who were managers of the Hearst business, and consequently, while the sons held the titles, the managers had the power. Roy Thomson's will made it very plain that Kenneth, then Kenneth's eldest son, David, and eventually David's son, would run the empire he founded. Already David is being groomed to take over one day. Even his full name—David Kenneth Roy—shows that he is the latest generation in an intended dynasty. Unlike many business empires that have crumbled because of family dissension and corporate lack of purpose, the Thomson empire is firmly entrenched as it marks its golden anniversary.

II

BUILDING THE EMPIRE

CHAPTER

2

THE TWO SIDES OF ROY THOMSON

THE *TIMES* (OF LONDON) boasts of having more prewritten obituaries than any other newspaper: 6,000 are ready at any one time. On 4 August 1976 Sir Denis Hamilton, editor-in-chief and chairman of Times Newspapers Limited, faced a particularly sad task when he had to print the obituary he had personally written about his boss, Roy Thomson.

The eighty-two-year-old barber's son, school dropout, and self-made millionaire, for whom Hamilton had both deep admiration and affection, died on August 4 following a chest infection and severe stroke. The death of the owner of the prestigious daily *Times* and *Sunday Times*, a string of far less respected small town newspapers in Canada and the United States, several book companies, and travel, insurance, trucking and oil businesses, was front-page news in papers around the world. Thomson had attracted the public's fancy as a late bloomer who, at the age of fifty-five, became a millionaire after several false starts in deadbeat businesses, twenty-five years behind his self-imposed schedule. He bought the *Sunday Times* when he was sixty-eight, the *Times* at seventy-three, and struck it rich in North Sea oil when he was seventy-nine.

Determination and an unshaken belief that he would somehow become a millionaire kept Thomson going through years of setbacks, undisturbed by the snubs he encountered en route from the pillars of high society. However, Thomson was fortunate in that he could count on the support of his wife and children, who always believed in him. Their faith was justified because Roy's disappointments in various

11

endeavors eventually led to something better. He failed in early career attempts at farming and selling automobile parts, but he eventually became an international newspaper tycoon. He was defeated in an attempt to be elected to the Canadian House of Commons, but became a member of the British House of Lords in 1964.

His dogged determination and magnetic personality were his key assets in conquering hardship, for in appearance Roy Thomson was unprepossessing. His trademark was his glasses, with lenses as thick as the bottom of glass jars. His eyesight was so poor that he had to read everything close to his face and could not drive a car. In the early days of his career, his wife had to drive him. "She was so short she could hardly see over the steering wheel," says Robert Marshall, who knew the Thomsons during the time when Roy launched his career in North Bay, Ontario. Thomson was five feet, ten inches in height and had a bulky frame. He went on at least forty diets in his lifetime, but his weight would always shoot back to around two hundred pounds. His fluctuating weight contributed to his suits looking ill-fitting, even though they were tailored on Savile Row. He was a nonsmoker and a nondrinker, possibly because his father had had a drinking problem. At parties, he drank orange juice.

Photographs taken over the years show him growing increasingly relaxed and smiling more as he became wealthier and began to lead an interesting life of meeting royalty, as well as the Chinese premier, Chou En-Lai, and Russian leader Nikita Khrushchev. (For the rest of his life, he carried a photograph in his breast pocket, taken in 1972, of himself with Chou En-Lai.) Still, the official portrait of Thomson—done after he had achieved wealth, fame and his title by leading British portrait painter Sir William Coldstream over a long stretch of fifty sittings— shows an unsmiling Thomson with downturned mouth, sitting in a chair with his legs tightly crossed. The portrait focuses on the determination in Thomson's ruddy, broad, square face and his pale blue eyes.

It could be said that there were two Roy Thomsons. There was the younger Roy Thomson who made his wealth in Canada through stringent cost-cutting at his chain of small town newspapers, where the emphasis of management was more on money-making from advertising than on editorial content. As Thomson once said, "Editorial content is the stuff you separate the ads with." This Roy Thomson became known for tough financial controls on office supplies, with reporters told to use scrap paper instead of notepads for interviews, and with pens or pencils doled out one at a time.

There also is resentment among some residents in Timmins, where Thomson bought his first paper, that he did not make financial contributions for community improvements even though he laid the foundation of his newspaper empire there. Leo Del Villano, a former eleven-term mayor of Timmins—from the 1950s through the 1970s—says he asked Thomson many times to "pick his own contribution" to Timmins. He never received a reply. "When he visited Timmins in the 1960s, I asked him why he hadn't answered and he said that if he didn't answer, it meant he wasn't interested in doing anything." However, while Thomson did not care to donate to Timmins, he did give $250,000 towards a YMCA building and another $110,000 for a swimming pool to North Bay where he lived before going to Timmins. This unusual burst of generosity occurred during a special celebration for Thomson in North Bay in 1967, Canada's centennial year.

Then there was the older Roy Thomson who started the most rewarding part of his life, in terms of money and prestige, at fifty-nine in another country, where he knew few people. At an age when most people are planning their retirement, Thomson was just getting started, buying the *Times* and *Sunday Times*, both regarded as among the world's greatest newspapers, and venturing for the first time in his career out of the media business into such risky fields as oil and gas and travel. While the Canadian Roy Thomson had been snubbed by the newspaper establishment for regarding his papers solely as cash boxes and not as instruments for shaping public policy, the U.K. Roy Thomson had bought prestige when he purchased the *Times* papers. They helped gain him the title of Lord Thomson of Fleet, as well as his oil and gas riches, since he was selected as the British-based partner by several prominent U.S. firms because of the entrée to the halls of power his ownership of the papers gave him. This access enabled the quick granting of oil exploration licenses.

This Roy Thomson did not flinch over reporters spending thousands of pounds chasing a story around the world or buying "exclusives," such as the £2,000 given Francis Chichester in 1966 for the serial rights to his journey by sailboat from England to Australia. This Roy Thomson accepted a £1-million loss in 1962 when the *Sunday Times* introduced the first color magazine supplement in the United Kingdom, and he poured millions of dollars of his own money into the daily *Times*, which was never profitable during his nine years of ownership. In a luxury sense, the *Times* was for him what yachts, racehorses and a fleet of antique cars are for other wealthy men. Moreover, in London, Thomson news executives appreciated his detailed budgeting. "He shook up the whole newspaper industry in the United Kingdom, where budgeting had hardly existed, by forcing all his newspapers to go into the most detailed budgeting procedures," Sir Denis says. "He always had a series of black books with him and knew the revenue and expenditure of every department in any of his papers."

Both the Canadian-based Roy Thomson and the British-based Lord Thomson of Fleet maintained that they never dictated editorial policies, as other media magnates such as Lord Beaverbrook and Henry Luce did. But his detractors said that any opinion would have been better than the bland editorials in North American Thomson newspapers and his noninterference with the segregationist views of the southern United States papers he owned. But overseas at the *Times* and *Sunday Times*, famous for their forthright editorials, there was pleasure at Thomson's breaking the long-standing tradition of British newspaper owners trying to sway public opinion.

"People claimed it was just public relations when we said how Roy gave us complete freedom," Sir Denis says. "But he gave us no instructions about the content of the papers. This isn't to say that he didn't have a personality or mind of his own—he had robust opinions favoring the restoration of capital punishment and reducing defense budgets. The advantage to us was that he became popular in such a short time, that he was soon walking with the great. If you walk with kings and queens and industrial barons and trade union leaders, you learn a lot and Roy was a great listener. I believe that if you can't get information firsthand, you should get it secondhand and I was always interested to hear what a prime minister or archbishop had told Roy."

The difference between the admiring, yet critical, North American view and the laudatory British opinion of Thomson is striking and has not gone unnoticed by Sir Denis, who does all he can to polish Thomson's North American image: "I resent the fact that Toronto is inclined to write off Roy Thomson as a 'little man.' Whenever I speak to industrialists in Toronto about Roy, I tell them they're jealous, and there is a stunned silence. Within a short time of Roy's coming to London, he became very greatly loved and respected and in terms of commercial success, he was a colossus.

"Every single newspaper Roy bought in the United Kingdom was bigger than any he had had in Canada. What chance is there for spectacular judgment in news coverage in a place like Moose Jaw?"

Obviously, Sir Denis is not impartial about Roy Thomson, nor does he pretend to be. The British obituaries of Thomson in the two *Times* publications were in the same laudatory vein. Both Sir Denis and Alastair Dunnett, the commissioned author of a two-page *Sunday Times* article and former editor of the *Scotsman*, had high praise for their late friend and employer. Wrote Dunnett: "Nothing can take away the thought of the indomitable heart of him, an adventurous man from nowhere, ennobled by the great virtues of courage and integrity and faithfulness." Hamilton's article about Thomson's tenure at the *Times* said: "There was no false pride about him, no power complex. Unlike so many other tycoons in the history of Fleet Street, he never issued directives, sacked editorial or managerial staff, or sought to be flattered as 'the Chief.'"

In North America, though, where there had been mixed views about Thomson, there was nervousness in the Thomson ranks about the possible slant of the obituaries. The *Times* and *Sunday Times* both referred to Thomson's legendary thriftiness, as did major North American newspapers, and although Thomson himself enjoyed cultivating a tightwad image, his North American papers presented a sanitized account of his life. Managing editors at Thomson newspapers in the United States recall receiving several telephone calls from Thomson Newspapers' American headquarters outside Chicago on how to run the obituary being sent out by the Associated Press wire service. The editors were told to chop out any references to Thomson's stinginess and to exclude his famous comment that owning the franchise for the independent, nongovernment Scottish Television (STV) network was "a license to print your own money."

That was Roy Thomson's most famous quote, but over the years he had honed a slew of quotable comments about his love of money, with his frankness and sheer zest for wealth endearing him in a way to the public. Here is the gospel according to Roy:

- "For enough money, I'd work in hell."

- "I'd rather read a balance sheet than a book."

- "The most beautiful music to me is a spot commercial at ten dollars a whack."

- Commenting on a gold lamé gown worn by a model at a fashion show: "My favorite color—gold."

- And when asked to sign the guest book during the centennial celebration in North Bay: "I'll sign anything but a check."

Many rich people build up a reputation for being eccentric penny-pinchers. They own several houses, a yacht, a racing stable and jewels but still save pieces of string or shop in discount stores. Roy Thomson was a champion penny-pincher. There was the Roy Thomson who freely spent his money on a villa in France that he rarely used, a flat in Grosvenor Square in London, and a Spanish-style house with four reception rooms, six bedrooms, four bathrooms, a staff flat, and an indoor swimming pool on about twenty-two acres in Buckinghamshire outside London. When the house was sold eight months after Thomson's death, it was valued at £250,000 (about $465,000 Canadian), up considerably from the £15,000 Thomson had paid for it. A chauffeured Rolls Royce took him to and from the railway station where he took the London commuter train.

Conversely, there was the stingy Roy Thomson who, on a trip to Italy, sent postcards to his grandchildren by sea mail because the postal rate was half that of airmail. He also booked economy class on planes (although he would often be upgraded to first class without charge when he checked in); weighed his luggage before he left home to avoid paying excess baggage charges; carried his luggage, even in his seventies, to escape tipping porters; ate breakfast in inexpensive cafeterias in lieu of more expensive hotel dining rooms; celebrated buying another paper in the United States over a hamburger at McDonald's; and happily accepted free press junkets.

One such excursion occurred in April 1968 at the Hilton Hotel in Paris. Everything during the week-long junket, including air fare from London, was free except for one evening set aside for a charity event. On that particular evening, there was only a skeleton staff at the hotel because all the guests had gone. "Eight of us reporters had gathered in the coffee shop for our free meal and we eventually noticed there was one other person there—Roy Thomson," says John Carter, then the travel writer for the *Times* and now a British Broadcasting Corporation (BBC) television commentator on travel and industry. "He kidded us about 'cooking' our expenses, and a journalist from the *Daily Mirror* replied that Lord Thomson had such a cheap reputation, he would pick up a franc if he saw it on the pavement." While many would regard stooping to such a prank as demeaning, Thomson chose to view it as a publicity stunt and agreed to pose for a picture. A *Mirror* photographer set up the shot, putting a franc on the sidewalk, and Thomson came out and picked it up.

Because he thought it a waste of money to pay extra for first class just to be served champagne, Thomson insisted that his employees travel economy. But his edict was not always heeded. "When we owned Scottish Television, Roy and I flew tourist class from Glasgow to London," says James Coltart, the retired deputy chairman of the Thomson Organisation and now head of the Thomson Foundation, which trains aspiring journalists from developing countries. "Roy was shortsighted, but he thought he recognized some of the people in first class. They were STV cameramen who, according to their union agreement, could travel first class."

These manifestations of what Thomson himself described as his stinginess are entertaining, but his parsimony over employees' wages was not amusing. In the early struggling days, employees would have understood getting fifteen dollars a week and not receiving raises or fringe benefits if Thomson had not come into the office wearing an expensive, new two-hundred-dollar suit, or had he not just bought himself a new car. Nevertheless, employees, caught in the web of Thomson's almost hypnotic salesmanship, did not quit in those early days, even after he cut their pay. One such instance occurred when a reporter asked for a raise, explaining he could not otherwise repay money he had borrowed from Thomson. Thomson agreed to cancel the debt, but did not give a raise; instead he deducted a small amount each week from the reporter's salary until the loan was repaid. The way Thomson explained the procedure at the time, the reporter felt it sounded like a plan benefiting him and not Thomson.

In later years, with Thomson's magnetic personality no longer there to squelch rebellions, low salaries at his North American newspapers, such as a five-year reporter earning $225 a week (less than half the normal salary at other papers for such experience), prompted several strikes.

Roy Thomson wanted to become rich, but so do most people. What motivated him just as much was an obsession with the game of business, the thrill of acquiring more and more, not for the sake of power but because he was essentially a collector of businesses. "Why do you want to buy more papers?" he was once asked. "To make more money." "Why do you want to make more money?" "To buy more papers."

Other press lords have poured their money into lavish estates. William Randolph Hearst forced his newspapers to provide funds for the construction of his castle, San Simeon, 1,600 feet above the sea near San Francisco. Thomson's Buckinghamshire home would have fit into a corner of San Simeon with its hundred rooms, two swimming pools and two libraries (one for Hearst, the other for his guests). So hungry was Hearst for money to pay for San Simeon that he would send collectors to terrorize his own management into giving more.

While Hearst plundered his newspapers' tills to the point where they bordered on bankruptcy, Roy Thomson preferred to spend his money on acquiring new businesses rather than on lavish personal possessions. His personal tastes were simple. He did not spend his fortune frivolously, philanthropically—unless convinced that it was opportune to do so—or culturally on an art collection, as his son, Kenneth, has. He did collect some antique silver, however, as well as some jewelry, albeit purely on the basis of what attracted him and not necessarily for the value. However, his biggest collection was a vast library of cheap detective novels. His taste in entertainment was similarly plebian— vaudeville and burlesque shows in his younger days and Doris Day movies when he was older.

While he enjoyed meeting the rich and famous, such meetings were in the course of the business day and never at home. Home was a private sanctuary and not the scene of glittering dinner parties or salons of intellectuals such as other media moguls like Hearst and *Time* magazine founder Henry Luce held. While Hearst would never reinvite a dinner companion he had found boring, Roy Thomson, gregarious in public life but solitary in private, dined alone.

His family stayed out of the public eye, too. While Luce's wife, Clare, was a star in her own right as a playwright and ambassador to Italy, and Hearst's thirty-year romance with showgirl Marion Davies was well known, Thomson's wife, Edna, always stayed in the background and died before Roy went to England. Her main hobbies were betting on bridge games in which she played, and on the horses, the latter to such an extent that her husband eventually put her on a strict allowance.

Unlike other tycoons, such as the Rockefellers and the Fords, who used part of their fortunes to set up philanthropic foundations, Roy Thomson never felt the urge to give to charity either out of a genuine desire to help or a desire to soften his stingy reputation, a motive sometimes behind other moguls' philanthropies. That there *is* a Thomson Foundation is due instead to James Coltart, Roy's number two man in the U.K., serving as deputy chairman of the Thomson Organisation. Coltart, now eighty, had always been interested in the development of Third World countries, and in 1963 he persuaded Roy to establish a foundation to instruct journalists from these nations in news gathering as well as to train others to become television technicians. He made his case at a good time because Roy was at the height of his campaign to gain a peerage, which he received one year later.

The foundation has trained thousands over the past two decades, but that it has is due only to the tenacity of Coltart and his assistant, Don Rowlands, because they must manage on a shoestring. Their headquarters are in a cramped, converted house in a somewhat seedy district of London. Roy Thomson endowed the foundation with £5 million, not in an outright donation, as is often done, but from shares and dividends earmarked for that purpose. To date, the foundation has spent £6 million. Like most foundations, it existed on the interest from the endowment, but in recent years it has had to start dipping into the principal. Kenneth Thomson has chosen not to contribute any more money and so the foundation has had to make do with tuition fees, which are deliberately low to enable the students to attend, and payments from governments for training the television technicians, for which the often financially troubled countries cannot pay.

Giving money away did not interest Roy Thomson, but making it gave him joy. What really made him glow with enthusiasm was the strategy and exhilaration of a successful deal. "He once said about himself, when asked what his motives were, that after he had made one million dollars, he could buy anything his family wanted and at that point he was no longer making money to change their standard of living," says Sir William Rees-Mogg, who was editor of the *Times* while the Thomsons owned it. "He liked setting up deals and bargaining, which he did well. He was like a Wimbledon tennis player who is playing not just for the score, but for the enjoyment of doing something well. He gave a lunch one time for Jean Paul Getty, his partner in North Sea oil exploration, when both were over eighty, and in an after-lunch speech said that 'Paul's richer than I am, but then I'm six months younger than he is.'"

It is an interesting twist of fate that two of the most prominent names in the twentieth-century British newspaper world were both Canadian-born: William Maxwell Aitken, who received the title of Lord Beaverbrook, and Roy Thomson. Beaverbrook, who was born in 1879, fifteen years before Thomson, died in 1964, just fifteen days after a glittering eighty-fifth birthday party given him in London by Thomson. Like Thomson, Beaverbrook bounced around from job to job in his youth, but by the time he was thirty, he had become a multimillionaire from the merging of eleven eastern Canada cement mills into the Canada Cement Company. At the age of thirty-one, Beaverbrook left Canada for England, became active in politics, and bought the then-ailing *Daily Express*, originally as a political platform for his friends, for £42,000. Later, his newspaper empire expanded to include the *Evening Standard* and *Sunday Express*.

Unlike Thomson, Beaverbrook used his papers to make or break political careers and took pleasure in humiliating or firing reporters and editors. Also unlike Thomson, he used his papers for his personal campaigns to promote free trade within the British Empire and heap scorn on public figures whom he disliked. All his papers were breezy tabloids that leaned to sensationalism and gossip rather than in-depth analysis of the news. In addition, Beaverbrook became a cabinet minister. During World War I he was minister of information, and during World War II he served as minister of aircraft production.

When Beaverbrook was asked about Thomson as the latter built up his newspaper empire, he dismissed the younger man as "a little guy who owns a lot of newspapers." But although it took Thomson longer to get rich and obtain a title, he eventually duplicated these achievements of Beaverbrook's.

Thomas Wilson, the retired publisher of the Thomson-owned *Oshawa Times*, says that when he once asked Thomson what tips he would give a youngster who wanted to become a millionaire, "Thomson did not suggest going to business school or investing in blue-chip stocks. Instead, he had homespun advice: 'Each time you get a two-dollar bill, set aside one dollar and by the time you're fifty, you'll be a millionaire.'"

Thomson was often asked what his magic formula was for becoming rich. His answer put more demands on people than what he told Wilson: "Hard work. You can't make money just because you would like to be rich," he said. "You've got to work at it all the time. It must come ahead of everything else." He expected similar dedication from his staff. "If you arrived at Heathrow Airport at 7:30 a.m. after a trip to India and Nigeria, Roy expected you in by 8:30," says James Coltart.

The two distinct phases of Roy Thomson's career—the early years of struggle and failure in Canada, and the last twenty-three years in England during which he achieved enormous wealth and the glory of a peerage—were mirrored by distinct sides of his personality. In the years of glory, it was naturally easier for him to be the jolly Roy Thomson, giving his employees carte blanche, than in the early years when his survival, and that of his family, depended on tough financial controls. Roy Thomson's legacy is that both sides of his nature live on today within the empire he built.

3

THE EARLY YEARS

THE LOWER MIDDLE CLASS district in which Roy Thomson lived in his youth and the exclusive area in which his son, Kenneth, now resides are only a few blocks apart. But those few streets symbolize the distance the Thomson family has climbed since its humble beginnings.

Roy Herbert Thomson was born in Toronto on 5 June 1894, the older of two boys. His parents lived in a row house on Mulock Avenue (now known as Monteith Street) just north of Yonge and Wellesley streets in midtown Toronto. The block-long street, today renovated as trendy town houses, is about a mile from the mansion in Rosedale where Kenneth Thomson lives.

Thomson dropped out of Jarvis Collegiate at the age of thirteen and then studied bookkeeping for a year at a business school, working as a janitor to pay the fee. From the age of fourteen to twenty-four, he worked for a cordage firm, first as its bookkeeper and then its manager. In 1916 he married a shy, attractive neighborhood girl, Edna Irvine.

In 1919, with two young daughters increasing his family responsibilities, Thomson plunged into the first of a series of business failures, chucking the security of his job for a farm in Saskatchewan because he was attracted by a billboard showing a farmer driving a tractor through wheat fields. A year later he was back in Ontario, having lost most of the $15,000 he had invested.

Thomson next became a distributor of automotive parts. That was not successful either. "Roy had suggested to his brother-in-law, Ed Bilton, that they switch jobs and Roy would become the salesman and

Ed the bookkeeper," says Sidney Chapman, the chief financial officer at Thomson Newspapers for close to forty years, starting in 1940. "Roy sold far more tires than Ed had, but when the Depression hit, most gasoline service stations closed down, so Roy and Ed went broke. Ed said it wouldn't have happened if they hadn't changed jobs."

As Roy was nearing forty, the age at which most people have settled on their choice of career, he was seemingly going nowhere fast. He was trying to sell radios in northern Ontario in the face of insurmountable obstacles. The Depression left few people with money to buy radios, and even if they did have the money, few would buy because the reception of programs was poor. Roy was growing older and paunchier, and it appeared as if he would never be able to pull himself out of the isolated northern Ontario towns for the big time of Toronto. Then Thomson stumbled into the newspaper business through the back door of first owning small radio stations, a business he had also stumbled into.

In 1930, seven years after the birth of his last child, Kenneth, Thomson obtained a franchise to sell radios in North Bay, about five hundred miles north of Toronto. Only someone with Thomson's optimism, stamina and ebullient salesmanship would have accepted such an assignment under the odds he faced. In addition to the Depression and poor radio reception, the single transmitter in North Bay was decrepit. Thomson decided the only way to improve the sale of his radios was to open his own radio station in North Bay, CFCH. Borrowing all the money, he bought a secondhand transmitter for $500, then had to spend another $169 for missing parts. As he could not afford employees, Thomson became a one-man show: selling advertising time, introducing programs, conducting interviews, and still selling radios.

Like other owners of small stations, Thomson hired eager-beaver youngsters whose lack of experience made them willing to accept low salaries. For young people interested in advertising, Thomson provided a useful example for selling in a dry market: "He introduced a Christmas-in-July campaign, playing Christmas music on July 25 along with a safety theme that the carols were being played for those who would be killed in traffic accidents at Christmas time," recalls Bryan Manson, a salesman then, as well as today, for CFCH, which is now owned by Telemedia. "The culmination of the day was Santa arriving with free soft drinks and hot dogs. One year Santa came by pony cart and another year by motorboat."

Not only could Thomson not afford staff, he found it hard to find the money to pay bills. Some he never paid, even when he became wealthy.

Timmins resident Mac Cochrane recalls that Thomson's twenty-eight-dollar check to his now dead brother, Ian, who helped build the North Bay station, bounced. "Thomson didn't have a nickel then," Cochrane says. "The check wore out in my brother's pocket."

But if he did not pay others, Thomson also did not spend on himself in those days. He dressed neatly but shabbily, even after being elected as an alderman in North Bay. "I was the only reporter covering city council and sat behind Roy Thomson, and when he stood up to speak, I noticed a patch on the backside of his pants," says Mort Fellman, who later became publisher of the *North Bay Nugget*. Fellman says Thomson's election as alderman was not a sign of popularity, as "election to the council then was no great thing, since it used to be hard to get candidates." Events bear out this contention, for Thomson was defeated in 1932 when he ran for mayor.

Some people prefer not to gamble their few savings because they might be lost; others, like Thomson, are willing to take the risk in the belief that it is the only way to make money. He believed the way to make money was to use very little of his own and borrow the rest from the banks. He made sure that even if he could not repay other creditors, he would be able to repay the banks so that they would be willing to lend to him again. In between his political campaigns, Thomson proceeded to buy two more radio stations, mostly on borrowed money, in gold-mining towns north of North Bay: Kirkland Lake, about 185 miles north, and Timmins, about 250 miles north. In the saga of the development of the Thomson empire, the Timmins station was more significant, as it was located in the same building as the Timmins newspaper, the *Daily Press*. Again, Thomson made his purchase with very little money down. He made a $200 down payment for the paper and pledged the rest of the $6,000 purchase cost in twenty-eight promissory notes.

As Thomson's main motive in buying the *Press* was that it was another way of selling advertising space, he makes an intriguing comparison with another poor boy who became a leading newspaper figure. Adolph Ochs, who also worked as a youngster, first sweeping floors at the age of fourteen at the *Knoxville* (Tennessee) *Chronicle*, started out as a newspaper owner by buying one of the world's best newspapers, the *New York Times*, in 1896 when he was thirty-eight, two years younger than Roy Thomson was when he bought the Timmins paper. By contrast, Roy Thomson did not become the owner of a world-renowned newspaper until he bought the *Sunday Times* in London in his late sixties. The *New York Times* was losing money when Ochs bought it, but unlike Thomson, Ochs believed that emphasizing editorial quality, rather than placing the stress on advertising, was the key to the paper becoming successful. His approach was as lucrative as Roy Thomson's and had the added benefit of giving him worldwide respect in the newspaper industry, which Thomson lacked. While Thomson's North American newspapers worried about the Associated Press's obituary on him, the Ochs family had no such concerns. Instead, the news service paid tribute to Ochs on his death by a worldwide silencing of its wires for two minutes.

Although Roy Thomson had the ambition and drive to become rich, he would probably not have succeeded if he had not attracted gifted employees to work for him. Of the two people who helped most in the early days, Jack Kent Cooke, now a multimillionaire communications and sports tycoon living in the United States, is the best known. But he worked only a few years for Thomson and was more significant as a confidant and buddy than for his contributions in building the empire. That role was filled by Sidney Chapman, who developed the careful— some would say stingy—financial controls that enabled the infant empire to survive.

Cooke was involved almost from the creation. In 1936, when he was twenty-three and a salesman for Colgate-Palmolive, Cooke decided he wanted a career in radio management and applied to Roy Thomson for a job. Thomson paid Cooke $25 a week, less than his previous salary, and made him manager of the Stratford, Ontario, station he had bought in 1934, even though there already was a manager there. Thomson told Cooke it was up to him to ease out the existing manager, which Thomson was reluctant to do because the manager owned the station's transmitter. Two months later, the manager was gone and the transmitter had been purchased for $300.

Cooke and Thomson had a lot in common. Cooke had also worked while in his teens. Born in Hamilton, Ontario, as a teenager he had sold encyclopedias and played saxophone in a dance band to earn money. Both also enjoyed the art of salesmanship. Cooke, like Thomson, was a salesman to his toes, who would even help salesmen sell to him. The two men spent the workday together, then went to vaudeville shows in the evening. Thomson's family grew to resent and dislike Cooke for Roy's spending more time with him than with them.

The two men also shared the characteristic of hating to part with their money. They both dressed snappily, with Cooke turning Roy into a nattier dresser, but would not spend on employees. One of the few employees who outwitted Cooke was actor Lorne Greene, who worked for Toronto's CKEY, the radio station that Cooke ran after parting with Thomson. "I asked him for a large sum of money, which he said was too much," Greene says. "About four months later, he called me back and suggested that instead of his original terms of my doing four newscasts of five minutes each, I do two, with one to run fifteen minutes and the other five minutes." Greene, no slouch at arithmetic, pointed out that he would still be broadcasting for a total of twenty minutes. "I asked for the same fee that I had the first time and Jack again said it was too much. I told him that he sold time and so did I. I think I was the only person who ever got Cooke to give in about money."

Like Thomson, Cooke could switch from Mr. Congeniality to Tough Guy if he was crossed. Former employees describe him as having a "killer shark" smile and "ruthless, killer gray eyes that disappear when he smiles." Acquaintances remember his telling off his brother Hal, a "go-fer" for Jack, in front of others for misjudging where to stop Jack's Cadillac when he fetched it for him. He respected toughness in others, though. Greene recalls once telling Cooke he would not be in on a certain Saturday but instead would be taking it as one of his five days off per month in order to host a party at his house. Cooke first argued over the day off and then avoided Greene's telephone calls. But the next day he was all smiles, said to forget about the argument, and gave Greene the time off.

Cooke's genius at selling was invaluable in obtaining advertising for Thomson's radio stations, and his later management of the stations left Thomson free to expand his newspaper interests. He also was responsible for Thomson buying what turned out to be a broadcasting gold mine, a radio station in Rouyn, Quebec. The station cost $21,000, and Thomson and Cooke put down a deposit of $2,000. The purchase was astute because Rouyn was located in the heart of iron deposits, which kept out radio signals from other places and resulted in the Rouyn station having a lock on listenership in the area. A gifted programmer, Cooke reprogrammed the station with new shows, and within a year, it was worth about $100,000.

Thomson and Cooke got along so well that they formed a partnership in 1940, with Thomson owning two-thirds and Cooke the other third. They went on to buy a chain of outdoor movie theaters, which were later sold, and a prominent Canadian magazine, *Canadian Liberty*, which was also subsequently sold. Nevertheless, their David and Jonathan relationship began to splinter in 1945 when Cooke bought CKEY, a far bigger venture than any Thomson had, with his share of the proceeds from the 1944 sale of the Rouyn station (Thomson declined Cooke's offer to join him in buying CKEY). Then, in 1949, the partnership and friendship dissolved when Cooke obtained a $100,000-a-year contract from Southam Press to manage its Ottawa station on the proviso that Thomson be excluded. Cooke accepted the terms even though he and Thomson had agreed to split everything.

With hindsight, while Cooke's departure hurt Thomson deeply for a long time, it probably was for the best, since Cooke was not the type to stay in the background. Even though he just had a one-third interest, had he continued with Thomson, it could have caused problems over control of Thomson's business both before and after Roy died, and Cooke most likely would have wanted his interest enlarged as the business grew. Also, he was veering more towards radio, while Roy Thomson was putting his emphasis on newspapers. In addition to CKEY, Cooke later purchased the Toronto Maple Leafs baseball team and more than a dozen magazines. But he lost out in a bid for the *Globe and Mail*, now owned by Kenneth.

The parting did not affect the success of either man in making a fortune. Cooke, unlike Thomson, made his first million dollars by the time he was thirty, and did so by concentrating on radio. He is now estimated to be worth more than $600 million. That is substantially less than Kenneth has, but still enough to make him one of the 400 richest people in the United States.

In 1960 Cooke moved to the U.S.; President Dwight Eisenhower had used his influence to get Congress to pass a special act making Cooke an American citizen overnight. He invested in cable television and real estate, and built the sumptuous, $16.5-million Forum in Los Angeles. He also bought the Los Angeles Lakers basketball team, the Los Angeles Kings hockey team, and a huge California ranch. The Kings, Lakers, Forum and ranch were sold in 1979 for $67.5 million, with $50 million going towards Cooke's divorce settlement to his former wife of forty-one years. Cooke then moved to Virginia, where he lives on a fifty-acre estate. He now owns the Washington Redskins football team, the 1983 Super Bowl champions. In 1980 he remarried, with Judge Sirica of Watergate fame performing the ceremony.

Cooke and Thomson were reunited occasionally after their rupture. Cooke hosted dinners at the Forum for Thomson, and the two were filmed joking together in a 1966 Canadian National Film Board documentary on Thomson.

Cooke, flashy and glib, had been essential in obtaining the lifeblood of advertising revenue for the Thomson businesses, but when he left, they went on to grow, rather than flounder. Much of the credit for this goes to Sidney Chapman. He provided the financial wizardry to pull the fledgling empire through its shaky days. He was so reliable that Thomson put him in charge of his northern businesses at the end of 1940, less than a year after he hired Chapman.

Chapman is just as energetic and fleet of mind at seventy-four as he was when he joined Thomson at the age of thirty. He is so pleasant a raconteur and host that it is hard to believe this nice, rosy-cheeked, mild-mannered, harmless-seeming man was a steely bargainer who outmaneuvered wily Roy Thomson in salary negotiations, closed a company partly because it became unionized, and developed the "count every pencil" accounting of Thomson Newspapers.

Chapman is a realist with an astute eye for a business's long-term potential, and these qualities made him ditch a secure but dead-end job as an accountant at Silverwood's Dairies for the uncertain early days of Roy Thomson's business. "I didn't have any equity in Silverwood's; I was just an employee and my superiors were not old," he says. "I wanted to join something that was going somewhere and have equity in it." Two days after Chapman got his five-years-of-service medal at Silverwood's, he saw an ad Roy Thomson had placed for a financial man. Roy, Jack Kent Cooke and a secretary then shared one room in the Victory Building located behind the site of today's Thomson Newspapers' head office in Toronto. "Roy was so busy on the telephone, he could hardly talk to me. I had been making $40 a week at Silverwood's and Roy agreed to pay me $45." This was quite an accomplishment, since Thomson usually convinced employees to take a cut in pay from what they had made elsewhere.

Next came a battle over Chapman's insistence on buying $10,000 worth of stock in the company. "Roy had said he would discuss this at the end of my first month. At that time, he asked if I had the cash and said, 'That settles it,' when I said I didn't. But I was determined to have that stock. I went to the Bank of Nova Scotia manager in Timmins, where I was then working, and asked for a $10,000 loan. For collateral, I offered my group insurance." The investment took more than two decades to make Chapman's determination to get the stock worthwhile. "I didn't get any dividends for twenty-two years but when the company went public, there was a thirty to one split."

Roy Thomson's acquiescence to Chapman's demands was unusual but practical because of Chapman's financial adroitness in keeping the young business going. Every day was a balancing act, a demonstration of survival accounting. If a draft came in for $5,000, Chapman would pay $500 down and the rest in $100 notes. "I called them 'blue notes' because their fate was up in the air. When they were returned, I would renegotiate them. I used to say about Roy's motto of 'Never a backward step,' that he had better not step backwards or he would fall in a hole."

Once Thomson's business was rolling along, it was indeed easy to borrow from the banks. But in the early days, with overdrafts common, Thomson was not as welcome in bank managers' offices. The Bank of Nova Scotia was the business's banker in its first years, but a rift developed in 1946 when Thomson sought to buy newspapers in Guelph and Chatham, Ontario, for $800,000, just two years after spending the same sum for four other Ontario papers in Sarnia, Woodstock, Galt and Welland. "The Bank of Nova Scotia felt we were going too fast, so we moved over to the Royal Bank, and the Bank of Nova Scotia has been sorry ever since," Chapman says. "Shortly after we switched, we put out our first $1-million bond issue and paid off the Royal Bank."

Chapman's financial skill was not limited to balance sheets. He also saved the company money in other ways. He suggested that the company form its own purchasing division, Replacement Sales Limited, for bulk purchasing of standardized forms, such as petty-cash vouchers and personnel record cards, for all the newspapers. The volume buying enabled the company to get discount prices.

It was Chapman, not Roy Thomson, who was responsible for the Thomson empire adding on trucking and insurance. Dominion-Consolidated Truck Lines, now a $60-million-a-year business, is one of Canada's top five truckers and is number one in car hauling. It owes its origin to Chapman's habit of eating breakfast at Kresge's, a five-and-ten-cent chain, when he lived in Timmins in the 1940s. "I used to sit at the counter beside a trucker named Barney Quinn who wanted my advice on buying the trucking business of Ford cars from a Windsor widow. Although the trucks were rusty, with bald tires, and business was slow because of the war, I expected a revival in business and decided to go in on the venture. Roy gave me four reasons for not joining Quinn in the venture: I didn't know that business, didn't have the money, was too busy, and he didn't like Quinn. I told him I trusted Quinn and wanted to start my own business, as he had, and he would own more than I would. We paid the widow $125,000, with Quinn owning 51 percent and Roy and I the rest, with Roy's share about double mine. In two years, we paid off the loan for that purchase and I heard that another Ontario trucker, Bob McAnally, was retiring and wanted to sell his business. We negotiated from 8:00 p.m. until 1:00 a.m., with McAnally keeping on his hat and smoking a pipe, and I couldn't get him to agree to my offer of $230,000. Finally, I said I was going to the washroom but first wanted a yes or no and he said yes. Subsequently, McCallum Transport of Oshawa, one of Canada's largest car haulers with close to 500 trailers, was bought for $425,000. We also bought seven smaller firms and consolidated them under the name, Dominion-Consolidated." Quinn decided he wanted to confine himself to the original Windsor company and exchanged his Dominion-Consolidated shares for Thomson's and Chapman's in that first acquisition.

Scottish and York Insurance (named after the Scottish and York regiment to which Thomson belonged) was also instigated by Chapman, born out of his passion for consolidating, and thus lowering, expenses. "There were about 150 different insurance policies for the newspapers and I could see that it would be worthwhile to save the premium paid to an outside insurance agency. Moreover, our then agent had misplaced some of our policies. With Roy's permission, Kenneth Doyle, who worked for our insurance company, and I bought a number of small agencies." As Chapman and Doyle each owned 15 percent, they were eager for Scottish and York to expand, but Roy Thomson wanted to put his money into newspaper growth instead. Consequently, in 1961 Chapman and Doyle decided to make Scottish and York publicly owned in the hope that by publicly showing a record of profits, they could borrow more easily to expand the firm. Scottish and York was the first Thomson-controlled company to go public. Thomson Newspapers did not make its first common share offer until 1965.

Chapman retired from the position of senior financial vice-president at Thomson Newspapers in 1975, but remained as senior vice-president of the Woodbridge Company and as a director of Thomson Newspapers until 1982. His ties with the empire were never entirely severed, however. In addition to being a trustee of Roy Thomson's will, he continues as a director of Scottish and York.

Still, despite Chapman guiding Thomson into new businesses, the heart of the empire was still newspapers. As he bought more papers, Thomson developed a technique that kept newspaper owners from being tipped off about his interest in acquiring their paper. Much of the scouting was delegated to Thomas Wilson, who was given the sort of instructions an undercover agent might receive. "I was told to go by train rather than by car because my license plates might give me away. I was also told at which hotel to stay, and to meet the publisher some place other than the hotel so his employees would not know about the negotiations. One time, however, I blew my cover. I had gone to Cornwall, and since it was some distance from the train station to the hotel, I grabbed a taxi. But when I got in it, the taxi driver recognized me because he had previously lived in Oshawa. In order not to disclose the purpose of my visit, I got out at another hotel and then walked back to mine."

Thomson also taught salesmen to pitch the "benefits" of advertising to merchants. "Our approach was that a client was making an invest-ment when he placed an ad and that the benefit to him was that he could talk to the public about his pride and joy," recalls Ronald Hedley, who worked for the Thomson chain between 1936 and 1948 before moving to the U.S. where he became the publisher of a Detroit-area paper. "We would suggest ways of writing advertising copy and doing layouts."

Another strategy was special issues pegged to the openings of new stores or railway-line extensions and relying often on strong-arm tactics by the Thomson salespeople. "One outstanding success was a special issue connected with the construction of a new section of the Temiskaming and Northern Ontario Railroad, which took the line to Hudson Bay. The three Thomson-owned newspapers in the area at North Bay, Timmins and Kirkland Lake put out a common special section, with ads obtained from suppliers to the railroad. The secret of our success was our getting the general manager of the railroad to write the suppliers, too. It was like holding a gun to their heads.

"Another big success was a one hundred–page section in the Vancou-ver *Herald* [now defunct] when the British Columbia government extended its railway north. The other two papers, the *Sun* and the *Province*, got only twenty-four pages each. We beat them by selling the transport minister on the idea of a special issue and having him give us official government stationery on which we typed up solicitation letters for the railroad's suppliers and had him sign them. That got us lots of advertising. We used to think of ideas like this because ideas sell advertising."

The end of the 1940s marked a close to the first phase of the Thomson empire. Roy had found that the cornerstone of the empire he envisaged was small newspapers, and he already owned eight. Nine-teen forty-nine marked the first tentative step he took to expand outside of Ontario when he bought the Moose Jaw, Saskatchewan, *Times-Herald*. The year was also a personal turning point because Roy had split with his partner and main pal of the early days, Jack Kent Cooke, and was once again on his own in determining in which direction he should go next.

4

REACHING THE TOP

THE 1950s MARKED a crossroads for Roy Thomson. The decade started off well, with his family settled in a large home just west of Toronto, but then he encountered a series of traumas.

His wife died of cancer in 1951, and in 1952 he was defeated as a Conservative candidate for the House of Commons. Although comfortably off, he could not shake the tendency to acquire anything just so long as it increased the size of his business. This led him to make several bad purchases.

The first flop evolved from getting the Canadian franchise for Toni hair-do kits. A plant was rented in Toronto to mix and package the kits, but Thomson got into the business as the fad was dying out. He closed up and stored the unsold inventory in a warehouse. A while later when the warehouse was checked, all the Toni kits had gone—the truck drivers had given them to their wives.

Later, at a creditors' sale, Thomson bought a firm called Modern Planned Kitchens in Neustadt, Ontario (near Kitchener), which made kitchen cabinets, coffee tables, television cabinets, and bedroom suites. It was the only manufacturing plant in town, and Thomson had it renovated and electrified. That venture was also short-lived. The plant was closed because of attempts to unionize it, which would have made the plant uncompetitive with nonunionized Quebec furniture-makers.

Other problem ventures included a method of making cream from vegetable oil for cakes and pastries, and a shoe-polish distribution system. The cream business failed when the cream producers got cake stores to put signs in their windows saying they used only pure cream.

The shoe-polish distribution system ended with the firing of the lone salesman after Roy asked him to name one person he had seen and he could name none.

The Thomson empire does, however, still own one business dating from those trial-and-error days: Veri Best Products Limited of Hamilton, Ontario. Although it could make nine ice-cream cones at a time, production was quickly stopped because the cones came out with fins. So Veri Best switched into the carton business, starting with the boxes intended for the cones. Although Veri Best still loses money, and although the Thomson empire is known for its bottom-line mentality, out of sentiment Veri Best has been kept and even a new building foundation was recently installed.

The early setbacks were short-lived, however. Instead, the 1950s marked the expansion of the business outside Canada, first into the United States and then, a year later, into the United Kingdom. Although Thomson was looking for growth, both excursions were, just like the purchase of the Timmins paper, due to chance rather than advance strategy. The first U.S. newspaper, the *Independent* of St. Petersburg, Florida, was bought because Thomson berthed the boat he owned for a short time near St. Petersburg. Buying the paper allowed him to write off the boat as a tax expense, and also brought him into the U.S. market.

By the 1950s, Thomson was able to consider expansion outside Canada because his Canadian newspaper operations were being ably run by the Galt Gang, a group of employees who had all started out at the Galt, Ontario, paper. Chief among them was St. Clair McCabe, who rose up through the ranks because his expertise in advertising techniques had made the Galt paper first in advertising lineage. Gruff and taciturn with strangers, McCabe was skillful in motivating staff to produce, and he was a very good idea-man. He was helped in having a talented right-hand man, Ed Mannion, who developed training clinics and a manual on layout, illustrations, special editions, and selling techniques. The twelve-week program, the first of its kind at Canadian newspapers, was capped by an examination, with graduates receiving diplomas. The system is still used by the Thomson papers and was given on request to other newspapers, including the *Toronto Star*.

Mannion points out that Roy Thomson only owned twelve Canadian newspapers in 1953, the year he moved to the United Kingdom, and gives McCabe most of the credit for the expansion of the North American newspaper chain of which he eventually became executive vice-president. "Mac was an excellent negotiator, who put people at ease, had lots of patience, and was able to get people to sell who didn't know this is what they wanted."

McCabe now is president of Thomson Newspapers Incorporated, the U.S. branch, but in effect is retired, the daily operations being run by executive vice-president Frank Miles. In 1981, his retirement year, McCabe, having divorced his first wife, married Margaret Hamilton, a longtime colleague dating back more than thirty years to when they were both at the Galt paper. It was her first marriage.

Although she rose to be number three in the Thomson newspapers hierarchy as its senior vice-president, Margaret Hamilton maintained a very low profile. Her position gave her wide-ranging authority over advertising, circulation, news coverage, and production in both Canada and the United States. "She was very efficient, a detailed thinker with a very good mind, who was a good right arm to McCabe," Mannion says. There was no doubt of her toughness, but it was covered by a gloss of femininity. A stylish dresser, with a liking for broad-brimmed hats, she decorated her office with antiques and dainty Dresden figurines. Margaret Hamilton is the only woman to have reached the Thomson executive suite, although the chain has women publishers, general managers, editors, production supervisors, and advertising managers.

Born in Galt, she joined the *Galt Evening Reporter* in 1949, after high school, as an accountant and business manager, but her duties extended to writing stories and advertisements and delivering newspapers to local farmers. She was the first woman to hold the position of business manager in the Canadian newspaper industry, but she was not the first member of her family to hold the job—her brother, later publisher of the *Reporter*, preceded her in the post. She joined head office as executive assistant to the managing director, became a director in 1972, and senior vice-president in 1975.

She also set a number of firsts for women in business in Canada. She was the only woman on a seven-member advisory committee to the federal government on the status of women in industry, and she was also the first woman to join the Council of the Board of Trade of Metropolitan Toronto.

With McCabe, Hamilton and Mannion capably running the Canadian operation under Kenneth as president, Thomson was free to turn his attention to expansion in England. The United Kingdom whetted his appetite because the number of papers for sale in Canada came nowhere near his insatiable desire for new ones. In 1953 he started a weekly paper for Canadians living in the U.K., the *Canadian Review*, as a foothold in the market. But the purchase that really marked the beginning of the U.K. phase of his life was the result of a chance encounter at a dinner in 1950 with an executive of the *Scotsman*, Scotland's national newspaper. At that time, Thomson, who had a habit of asking newspaper owners if they would sell to him, asked the executive to keep him in mind if shares of the *Scotsman* ever went on the market. The *Scotsman* directors and management, as heads of a venerable paper, had scant regard for the colonial owner of small papers. But in 1953, when the *Scotsman* was in severe financial difficulty and there were no other buyers, the paper was willing to sell 100 percent to Thomson. In an exchange that would be paralleled later in his purchase of the *Sunday Times* and the *Times*, Thomson exchanged his dollars for the respectability of owning a national institution.

Besides its editorial quality, the *Scotsman*, founded in 1817, is also known for its own blend of whisky ("Here's a bottle and an honest friend," the label reads) and for having once employed actor Sean Connery as a mechanic. When Thomson bought the *Scotsman*, he not only got a newspaper but also a Scottish landmark. The *Scotsman* building resembles a castle, with the bottom three floors on Market Street and the top fourteen, including the building's entrance, on High Street near Edinburgh's famous Royal Mile containing Holyroodhouse Palace, the residence of Mary Queen of Scots, and John Knox's church. Inside, the building has a magnificent marble staircase with a circular gold-leaf design overhead and, at the landing, a stained-glass window with the city crests of Edinburgh, Glasgow and Aberdeen. In the fourth-floor boardroom, called the Walnut Hall because it contains carvings from Scottish walnut, portraits of editors since the paper's establishment line the walls. Roy Thomson's former huge corner office was so big that the present occupant has split it into an office and a boardroom separated by a curtain. Although Thomson did not change the content of the paper, he did move the advertisements covering the front page—a tradition in the United Kingdom—inside the paper, as is common in North America. However, the *Scotsman* continues to have one big ad on the front page, usually in the bottom-right corner.

Those purchases made by Thomson that were not accidental often seemed foolhardy, but Thomson's gambling paid off. In 1957, when others thought investing in television was like throwing money down a drain, Thomson obtained the license for Scottish commercial television. He was convinced that despite the early failure of commercial television in England, TV would become popular and profitable in Scotland, just as it already had in North America. He was right. The

£40,000 in shares owned both by Thomson and his company swelled so quickly in value that within two years, in 1959, he was able to buy the Kemsley publishing empire, then the largest group of newspapers in the United Kingdom. The group included the *Sunday Times* and twenty-two other Sunday, daily and weekly papers for which Thomson paid $31.5 million (Canadian). Kemsley had previously treated Thomson with calculated contempt, deliberately jacking up the price of an Aberdeen paper he owned beyond the affordable limit when Thomson made a bid in 1952. But by the late 1950s, Kemsley, just like the *Scotsman*'s owners, became more interested in Thomson's money than his pedigree. Again Thomson was willing to overlook insulting treatment in order to gain the prestige that ownership of the *Sunday Times* automatically bestowed. It also helped lay the groundwork in his campaign to get a peerage.

Thomson would not have been able to meet Kemsley's steep price without the ingenuity of his investment dealer, Henry Grunfeld of S. G. Warburg. Grunfeld pioneered the reverse takeover to enable Thomson to buy the Kemsley newspapers. Under this formula, the Kemsley chain bought Thomson's STV Company, paying Thomson with Kemsley shares of such voting power that he would then control both the Kemsley chain and STV and thus be able to raise the money to buy out Lord Kemsley. This procedure was necessary because STV on its own could not afford to buy the Kemsley papers.

Grunfeld brought thirty years of experience in high finance to the Thomson-Kemsley deal. Born in Germany to a well-to-do steel family, he went to England in 1934 and joined a new merchant banking firm started by Siegmund Warburg, a descendant of one of the leading Hamburg banking families. Grunfeld eventually became chairman of Warburg, which mixes what *Institutional Investor* has called "a track record second to none in the world of international finance" with some eccentric business practices. Prospective employees must undergo handwriting analysis, and interviews deal with interests other than business because it is taken for granted applicants must know business and it is felt staff should have outside interests.

Warburg employees say Grunfeld pays "tremendous attention to detail, likes to act as a kind of teacher, and has a photographic memory. He tolerates mistakes if people admit they were wrong." That was one of the qualities that Grunfeld admired in Roy Thomson. "He was one of the rare people in a very important position who was still prepared to listen and possibly change his mind," Grunfeld says. "Only people of strong character are willing to change their mind."

To reporters used to Lord Kemsley's aristocratic behavior, Roy

Thomson's approachability was startling. Lord Kemsley lived on a two hundred–acre estate with thirty-six bedrooms and servants who handed him ticker-tape wire-service stories on silver dishes. To his staff, he was a remote figure. "When he arrived at work, the back hall would be cleared and the elevator held for him. He was very aware of his importance," says ex-*Times* man John Carter. "About three days after the sale of the Kemsley papers, this chubby person turned up in the newsroom, sat on the edge of a desk, introduced himself as Roy Thomson, and asked people their names. There was no 'side' to him, no need to be deferential because he was the boss."

As soon as he owned the *Sunday Times*, Thomson began to search for a daily paper that could be run in conjunction with it in order to share the cost of machinery, since the same amount of equipment is needed for once-a-week as for daily production. The most similar paper, which also had a stellar reputation, was the *Times*. Of equal attraction at the time were its financial troubles, making the owners, the wealthy Astor family, willing to discuss its sale. Again, Thomson was in the position of being able to exchange his money for more prestige. Shortly after the purchase in 1967, the *Times* and *Sunday Times* were amalgamated under the newly formed Times Newspapers Limited. As England's most influential newspaper, the *Times* made Roy the nation's leading publisher and saddled him with a financial and managerial nightmare. The paper steadily lost money and erupted in strikes until a thoroughly disenchanted Kenneth sold it in 1981 to this generation's Roy Thomson, Rupert Murdoch.

Newspaper owners and editors in England sooner or later become "Lord" or "Sir" and Roy Thomson was no exception. In 1964 he was made Lord Thomson of Fleet, of Northbridge in the City of Edinburgh, for which he had to give up his Canadian citizenship. Nevertheless, Thomson remained as down to earth as he had been on the other side of the Atlantic.

Whereas most tycoons equivocate or refuse to answer questions about their fortunes, Thomson would literally tell any visitor to the *Times* all about himself, with no prodding. "If a stranger on the lift asked him how things were going, he would pull out the week's balance sheet and often take the chap to his office to give him more details," Denis Hamilton recalls. "For a long time, he answered his telephone calls, until the volume, as well as the crank calls, became too much."

But while he did not crave flattery as the *New York Times'* Ochs did in his later years, and while he did not become a snob, his Horatio Alger story gave Thomson so much pleasure that he would tell it again and again in speeches and at social events, as well as in two books. The first, a biography, *Roy Thomson of Fleet Street*, was published in 1965 by Collins Publishers, since owners of publishing houses traditionally did not publish books about themselves. Thomson took a keen interest in the book's sales. "The day before I was to be interviewed by Roy for a job, I decided to brief myself by checking with Collins on the book's success and was told 20,000 copies had been sold," recalls George Rainbird, who later sold his book firm, bearing his name, to Thomson. "At the beginning of my interview, I mentioned this and said he must be pleased and he answered that up to the night before the book had sold 21,863 copies. He got a daily report."

A decade later as he saw Thomson "growing frail," Denis Hamilton persuaded him to write an account of his years in the United Kingdom. Thomson did it himself, without the assistance of a ghost writer. In this case, the book was published by a Thomson company, although not without some internal battles. Michael Joseph, the most successful of the Thomson book companies, refused to publish the autobiography, and it wound up being published by a sister firm, Hamish Hamilton Limited.

Unlike many people who become wealthy, Roy Thomson did not become autocratic, nor did he abandon either his habit of speaking candidly to anyone, regardless of their rank, or his store of off-color traveling salesman's stories as he climbed the social ladder. "Roy used to dislike people starting sentences with the word 'frankly' because he believed that if you were really frank you didn't have to say 'frankly,'" says Sidney Chapman.

Thomson certainly was frank when asked in a 1974 television interview about what he did in the House of Lords. "Very little," he replied. "I can't spare the time from my business to attend sessions and I don't like to talk superficially. If I stand up to make a speech there, I want to have something to say."

Although a tough, shrewd wheeler-dealer, Thomson had a knack of being very friendly with all levels of his staff and of society in the United Kingdom, which endeared him to the Britons. "One of the first things he said to me when I met him in 1970 was that the most important person in a company is the switchboard operator, because she is the first contact with the public," says Edmund Fisher, a former senior book-publishing executive in the British side of the Thomson empire. Thomson also made a point of remembering people's names. "On his seventy-fifth birthday, he held a party for five hundred guests, including Princess Margaret, at the Dorchester Hotel in London and greeted everyone by name and often by their first name," says J. H. B. Monroe, who was financial controller of the *Scotsman* under Thomson.

To his employees and trade unionists, Thomson was known as "Lord T" or "Uncle Roy." "He was very charming to women in a paternal way, wanting to be sure that arrangements at a dinner were all right," says Trevor Davies, a former Thomson Travel executive and now a senior executive at American Express's London office.

The same friendliness was evident on Thomson's trips to his empire. "Since he had none of his family in England, he would go to the Thomson hotels in Europe on bank holidays," says Davies, who accompanied Thomson on these trips. "He would greet people in his shirt-sleeves, ask them to call him Roy, put his arm around the hotelier's shoulders, and compliment him on the meal. He came across as very human. His reputed meanness, grasp of business, and the vast profits he made were not apparent on his surface."

In daily business life, Thomson rarely lost his temper. One time his staff feared he would be furious was in 1968 when the *Sunday Times* paid £100,000 as a down payment for what was thought to be Mussolini's diaries but were actually fakes. As Thomson executives recall, when Gordon Brunton, Thomson's chief assistant, went to tell him what had happened, Thomson was in a foul mood because his chauffeur had been playing cards with some other drivers when Thomson had wanted his services. He greeted Brunton with a stream of complaints about the lack of control over the chauffeur's time. After ten minutes, Brunton gingerly broke the news about the £100,000 loss of money. Thomson asked a few questions, unconcernedly said, "Oh well, you win some, you lose some," and then resumed his tirade about his chauffeur.

Nobody lost their job over the fake diaries, but Thomson did not hesitate to fire people if they "were not bringing in their corn," as he put it. "Roy thought it was a positive unkindness to keep a square peg in a round hole," Monroe says. Despite the jolly Santa Claus image the public saw, Thomson was still bottom-line oriented.

When Thomson bought the *Scotsman*, it was in such bad shape financially that its survival was in doubt. One step taken to cut expenses was to eliminate 300 jobs in the first eighteen months of ownership. It was decided to keep people not on the basis of seniority, but on their ability "to save the paper," Chapman says. During the first six months of Thomson's ownership, staff were graded and those who were felt lacking were let go with several months severance pay.

In addition, if ambitious employees found better opportunities elsewhere, Thomson did not try to keep them through a promotion or wage increase. Instead, he encouraged them to strike out on their own. "I had worked for the Thomson organization for seven years, mostly as

Gordon Brunton's assistant, and had previously worked for their London law firm, so my decision to leave was traumatic for me," recalls Robert Smith, now president of Talcorp Limited of Toronto. "I wasn't looking forward to telling Roy Thomson I was going to leave, but when I did, he congratulated me and said there was nothing better I could do than go to Canada. I didn't know whether to be pleased or displeased," However, Smith and Thomson did not make a total split; the Thomson family is the largest individual shareholder in Talcorp, which is involved in oil and gas development in Canada, as well as chemicals and printing inks.

Just as Sidney Chapman was responsible for Thomson branching into new businesses in Canada, Roy was fortunate in having gifted employees in the U.K. who suggested avenues other than newspapers to make money. While the 1950s marked his newspaper expansion, the 1960s kicked off the moves into the new ventures of book publishing and travel in the U.K.

Since 1961, when he joined the Thomson businesses in the U.K. at the age of forty, the chief architect of this diversification has been Gordon Brunton, a complex mixture of potent charm, extreme intelligence, and testiness with those who run counter to his wishes. The testiness is usually submerged, though, and so amiable does he seem with his genial smile, so pleasant and so relaxed, that he is the empire's ultimate weapon when all else has failed in convincing a reluctant company to sell to Thomson. More than one former owner says his fatal mistake was agreeing to a meeting with Brunton.

Brunton enjoyed his pivotal role in the development of the Thomson empire, and his position seemed Rock of Gibraltar secure. Moreover, he seemed to have no plans to retire. "There is no mandatory retirement at ITOL and Kenneth Thomson wants me to go on," he said in 1983. In a comment indicating he planned to stay for several years, Brunton added: "You can be young at seventy and old at thirty-two." Yet in the spring of 1984, it was announced that he had decided to take early retirement at the age of sixty-three in December 1984. Health reasons can be ruled out, since his retirement was announced months in advance, ITOL executives said he was in good health, and he was active in Hong Kong on ITOL business the week of the announcement.

Brunton does not deny saying what he did in 1983 regarding retirement. The official reason for his early departure, as stated by Brunton, and echoed by Thomson executives, is that "sixty-three in today's environment is a perfectly reasonable age at which to retire from full-time executive responsibilities, particularly when very able successors have been well-seasoned over many years and are able to take up the reins. . . . I have always been determined to go when I was still in good form and my health was good." He says he plans to continue to "support the company in any way they think I can be helpful" as well as remain a director of Sotheby Parke Bernet and Company, the world's biggest fine art auctioneer. He had been chairman until 1983 when Sotheby's was acquired by Americans. He will also remain chairman of Bemrose Corporation, a major U.K. printing firm.

Since he apparently does not feel, nor is regarded as too old for these other positions, age may not be the prime reason for his earlier than expected departure from ITOL. Despite a statement by Kenneth praising Brunton when the coming retirement was announced, several factors indicate that behind the scenes the situation may not have been as pleasant. While Brunton had a very close relationship with Roy Thomson because Roy was based in the U.K., he has been across the ocean from Kenneth and even further distanced from Kenneth by the placement of John Tory as deputy chairman of ITOL. The relationship between Brunton and Tory has always been somewhat uneasy.

In addition, during the last six years ITOL has become more of a North American than a U.K. company, with the head office moved from London to Toronto and most of its growth now occurring in the U.S. rather than the U.K. Brunton has been a key player in this refocusing, and he placed his protégé, Michael Brown, in the top executive slot in New York. But since Brown has been on the spot to do acquisitions, there has been no need for Brunton to fly over frequently, like he did in ITOL's early days in the U.S., especially as the company built up a management team there and slowed down its acquisition binge in 1984. Thus, there has been less for Brunton to do and he is an entrepreneur at heart. Now, however, ITOL is in a consolidation period and needs people with an operational bent, such as Brown, who will succeed Brunton as president of ITOL. In recognition of ITOL's North American tilt, Brown will continue to be based in New York and will also be chief executive officer of the U.S. wing, International Thomson Holdings Incorporated. Before, he was executive vice-president of that division and Brunton was chief executive officer. International Thomson Organisation PLC, the British arm, will be headed by James Evans, now its joint deputy managing director as well as the head of Thomson Regional Newspapers in the U.K.

Brunton was born in 1921, two years before Kenneth Thomson, and their appearance is somewhat alike. Both are tall and wear glasses, and the similarities prompted Roy Thomson to treat Brunton as a second son, especially as Kenneth was based in Toronto. Brunton's office has the aura of a gracious drawing room, with soft colors, comfortable sofa and chairs, sash-tied drapes and a lovely floral arrangement on the coffee table. There are few pictures—a portrait of Roy Thomson hangs on one wall and a painting of a horse over Brunton's work-filled desk. The only jarring modern touch is a desk-top computer terminal.

In conversation, Brunton is a mixture of the understated, upper-crust British manner along with a touch of vanity, a strong streak of social conscience, and an analytical, penetrating incisiveness about companies and people. He is responsible for the company's involvement in projects to help depressed areas with high unemployment in the United Kingdom. The word Brunton uses most frequently is "honest," which is what he says he looks for most in people.

Like Roy Thomson, Brunton did not have a wealthy background; his father was a theater box office manager. And like Roy's, Brunton's career path was accidental rather than intentional. "After serving in the army during World War II, I needed a job desperately," he says. "I was married, with a baby on the way, and this concentrates the mind. I had an allowance of under ten pounds a week and as this wasn't enough for rent or food, I had to get a job. My first job was selling advertising at two not terribly high-quality publications, but we had to eat and I was going to university at night. I grew up quickly in that environment. The circulated figures of the magazines were a figment of their imagination because there was no Audit Bureau of Circulation verification. Later, when I was running trade publications, I said we should be straightforward and honest and if we claimed a certain circulation, it should actually be that amount. I was asked what would happen if we were honest, and I said it would work out, which it did."

Later, Brunton joined Odhams Press, a major newspaper and magazine publisher for which Roy Thomson bid unsuccessfully in 1961, one of his few failures at a takeover. During the negotiations, Thomson met Brunton, who by then was executive director at Odhams. They hit it off well. "At Odhams I was regarded as someone who would have a high function in the future, but I didn't like the concepts or way of doing things of the owner, Cecil King. Money has never been as important to me as job satisfaction, and I was prepared to take the risk of making less money in the short term with Roy Thomson because I had a feeling of empathy with him.

"We were 100 percent different. If you asked Roy and me six questions about the way society was organized, you would have got six different answers. But Roy was straight and honest and we had one of the most remarkable business relationships not only in British publishing, but in British industry. If similar people get together, they lack the strength they would have if they were different. Roy and I disagreed fundamentally on social issues, but had mutual respect. I was a Harold Lasky student at the London School of Economics, and although I am not a raging socialist, I believed in the need for a welfare state and Roy didn't. I believe my view was more representative of the world that was emerging, and I hope I will have the wisdom to have the same understanding about the world that will emerge in the next few years."

Thus, while Roy Thomson yearned and campaigned for a title, Brunton has shunned the peerage, unlike most British press lords. "I disagree totally with the concept of honors; to me they are an irrelevancy at this stage of history, so whether I was offered a title is irrelevant. I have a young child and it is hard enough to keep our feet on the ground with my lifestyle, and handles make it more difficult."

Brunton's lifestyle includes an estate in Surrey and racing and breeding horses. At one time, he owned a boat converted from an ex-naval craft. His interest in horseracing dates back to when he was eighteen. "I backed a horse at Newmarket during the war for a bet of two shillings each way, for win and place, which paid off at thirteen pounds, seven shillings, and six pence. The odds were in excess of sixty to one." Brunton also has a bittersweet tale about his interest in horses. "One Christmas I bought a horse for my second wife [Gillian, whom Brunton married in 1966]. It was an ex-racehorse I had had debriefed by a riding hack. I gave it to my wife with a ribbon around its neck and when she got on, it bolted. So I consulted my gardener about what to do, sent it to the cheapest stallion, and its offspring have won nine ribbons. I have had about twenty horses since, and one day I will have a brilliant horse. People need follies and diversions that are totally unrelated to business."

Not totally unrelated, however, for Brunton regards inviting authors and their agents to sit in the Thomson box at Ascot races as "a civilized way of entertaining." Sometimes, however, authors have been underwhelmed. "Brunton took H. E. Bates, a well-known British author, to the race that the famous Canadian horse Njinsky won at Ascot, and said to Bates, 'H. E., you've just seen one of the country's best horses win the race of the year,'" says Edmund Fisher, another guest at the event. "Bates replied he was glad to see it but the race looked like a bunch of different-colored mice running around a billiard table."

In addition to his responsibilities at Thomson, Brunton has been chairman of two prominent United Kingdom companies, Sotheby's and Bemrose Corporation. He has steered both firms through difficult times. "I was invited to join Sotheby's board because it lacked businessmen. When Sotheby's ran into serious problems in the late 1970s [attributed by critics to overexpansion and poor management], I was asked for my advice. I said I would help, provided I could have access to everybody on a totally frank basis and submit my report directly to the president. I spent evenings and weekends interviewing eighty senior people at Sotheby's and submitted the toughest report I've ever done. It called for the resignation of six directors and the appointment of a group of young talented people. To my utter surprise, I was asked to become chairman to ensure that the recommendations were carried through." However, unlike Kenneth Thomson, Brunton does not collect art. "I can't afford it. I didn't inherit wealth; I earned everything."

In 1983 Brunton helped Sotheby's stave off an unwelcome takeover bid from two wealthy Americans in favor of a third bid from another American, who was a regular customer. It was also a good deal for shareholders, as the final offer was substantially above Sotheby's stock market valuation. The Sotheby takeover battle followed Brunton's success in fighting off a takeover of Bemrose a year earlier. "It was a classic defense of a small company against a competitor," Brunton says. The defense included persuading another company to buy Bemrose shares temporarily to frustrate the original bidder and then sell them, which it did at a gain because Bemrose's profits increased in 1982.

Most present and ex-Thomson executives have high praise for Brunton. "Gordon has the ability to delegate and yet get involved if it is required," Richard Groves says. "He has made a standing offer that if I feel his presence in negotiations will help, he will fly over on the Concorde." Adds Jack Fleming, president of the Toronto-based Thomas Nelson International book-publishing firm: "Gordon is very brilliant. It's not often that a man like that surfaces. He grasps the point very quickly. I find it amazing that he can deal with such a variety of companies with complete understanding."

Says George Rainbird: "Gordon is as straight as a gun barrel. He is kind, considerate and generous, and looks for loyalty more than anything else." Edmund Fisher praises Brunton for "trusting me enough to put me in charge of Michael Joseph when I was just twenty-nine, and never interfering. He is a man of proven honesty with a great retentive memory and a tremendous dialectic mind. Although I would lose arguments with him, his fine arguments made me better equipped for the next argument."

There are those, however, who regard Brunton less fondly for his hard-nosed realism and his talent for surviving company power politics. "Gordon believes in fighting hard until the investment is no longer justified and then writing it off," says William Rees-Mogg, who was "annoyed" at Brunton taking this approach during the 1978–79 dispute at Times Newspapers. "Gordon is supposed to be Kenneth's hatchet man, but you never knew in which direction his hatchet would descend." Such is Brunton's enigmatic nature that George Rainbird says he "hated firing people," while Robert Smith, his former executive assistant, says Brunton "could be very firm when he wanted to be and made the firing decisions." However, generous settlements with clauses that prevent the public washing of dirty linen have prevented bad publicity.

This was the case with Brunton's main rival, Bryan Llewelyn, whose talent and ambition earned him promotion after promotion until his success and aspiration for further power put him in range of Brunton's position. Their jockeying for power occurred in the 1960s and 1970s as Roy Thomson grew older, although Llewelyn held on until 1980. Llewelyn, born in 1927, was an anomaly in the conservatively dressed, self-controlled Thomson executive lineup. Instead, he was a casual dresser and encouraged informality. A heavy smoker who still bites his fingernails down to nothing, Llewelyn is described by former acquaintances as "very emotional and high-strung" but also as excellent in administration and marketing.

Llewelyn started at Thomson Regional Newspapers in 1962 as a regional marketing manager and four years later became chief marketing director. His success led to his appointment as managing director and then chairman of the Thomson travel division where, by all accounts, he did a first-rate job erasing its problems. His efforts won him an effusive article in the 13 April 1976 *Financial Times* (of London):

> There was a time when Thomson Organisation executives regarded a posting to the group's travel activities like being sent to the corporate stocks. Bright young men tended to end their first few weeks with a deal of egg on their face. When Llewelyn was made head of tour-operating activities in 1969, he was the fifth to have the job in less than two years, but he has been more than a survivor. In 1975 Thomson Travel turned in more than half of the profits of the Thomson Organisation. Now he is the darling of the group. . . . An apocryphal story, which Llewelyn does not deny, has it that when he joined the company he was so alarmed by the lack of management/staff contact that he threatened to fire any executive found at his desk at tea break. They had to circulate while sipping. ·

Llewelyn next was appointed the first head of Thomson Publications in the U.K., a newly formed group aimed at bringing unity to ventures in book publishing, information services, and directories. It was a daunting task for Llewelyn, who felt at sea with book publishing and faced the added complication of the brutal warfare at the various companies. Those familiar with the warfare between Brunton and Llewelyn claim Brunton engineered Llewelyn's transfer, much as King David dispatched Bathsheba's husband to the warfront.

And so in the 19 June 1980 *Financial Times*, there was this brief item: "David Cole has been appointed chairman of Thomson Books in succession of Bryan Llewelyn who is taking up other business activities but will continue as a consultant to the group." Llewelyn now works in a shabby one-room office that he shares with a secretary in a building in the Covent Garden district. He owns a kitchen supplies shop in the Covent Garden market, built on the site of World War II bombings, and does occasional consultancy work for the Thomson Organisation, most recently for Thomson Regional Newspapers.

The travel and book businesses were both internally generated businesses, but Thomson's entry into North Sea oil development was again due to happenstance rather than deliberate planning. Yet without the cash generated by North Sea oil, the empire could not have moved into its nonnewspaper businesses in the U.S. in recent years, nor bought the Hudson's Bay Company, nor withstood the losses of the London *Times*.

The matchmaker in the oil deal was Warburg's Henry Grunfeld, who had been so instrumental in the Kemsley newspaper chain purchase. Warburg's was the U.K. investment firm used by Occidental Petroleum, headed by Armand Hammer, and brought Occidental, Getty Oil, and Allied Chemical together as a consortium to drill in the North Sea. As the trio were all American, they needed a British partner who could help them get the exploration licenses speedily from the U.K. government. As owner of the *Times* newspapers, Thomson had high visibility and impeccable credentials. So eager were the three firms to have Thomson involved that they offered to lend him $5 million to cover his share of the initial exploration program. It is phenomenal to strike it rich the first time in drilling for oil, but that is what happened to the consortium. Not only did they strike oil, but it was a gusher containing 700 million barrels.

At that point, the Americans tried to buy out Thomson, offering $10 million, twice their original loan. Most of the directors of the Thomson organization in the U.K. wanted Thomson to sell even though it was the Thomson family that had initially footed the North Sea bills in order not to involve the business in risk taking at a time of heavy spending on modernizing its U.K. newspapers and travel division's aircraft. Roy Thomson, however, decided to hold on to his 20 percent interest, and his decision was justified within months when drilling twenty miles from the first well discovered a field with 400 million barrels of recoverable oil. In his first two wildcat ventures, Thomson had struck two major discoveries the size of which most companies never find.

Thomson's involvement in North Sea oil came when he was in his seventies, proving once again that advancing age does not slow down thinking power. Despite his age, Thomson was very much on top of things. "I had just been at Michael Joseph for a week, when I was invited to join the whole brass on a trip to New York," Edmund Fisher recalls. "Lord Thomson, who was drinking milk, and Gordon Brunton asked me to join them in the hotel bar. Lord Thomson then asked me questions about our stock depreciation system, which he emphasized should be rigorous and conservative, and losses at Sphere Books (Thomson's paperback division), whose board I had just joined. After Thomson left, I asked Brunton if this type of questioning was normal and he said, 'This is like social conversation, my boy.'"

In the last years of his life, Thomson slowed down his pace and only came into the office twice a week. In addition, he would phone Gordon Brunton and ask him what was new. "I would often invent something," Brunton says. "I was playing a game, but Roy appreciated what I was doing." Yet up until these years, Thomson was the leading disciple of his philosophy that hard work pays off—literally in dollars or pounds or francs. He worked full days and at the age of eighty-one visited a storm-tossed oil rig, in which he had a financial interest, in the North Sea. His thirst to expand into new territories and acquire more companies did not wane as he grew older. "Roy was about eighty-one when I visited him in London and the Thomson organization was already a big empire. I remember him banging his hand on the table for emphasis and telling me that his organization must do more in the United States and that North America was the best place to invest money," says Robert Smith. "Even at that age, he was still thinking of expansion."

At a meeting with Khrushchev in 1963 when he took a group of tycoons to Moscow to celebrate the first birthday of the Sunday Times' color magazine, Khrushchev asked him what use his money was, "since you can't take it with you." "Then I'm not going," Thomson said. He could not avoid death, but Thomson was able to structure his estate so that as little as possible went to the government in estate taxes and as much as possible to his beneficiaries. Like most wealthy people, he transferred as much money as he could in the form of trusts to his children while he was alive. Thus, his will reveals little of his fortune. According to probate records, Thomson left assets of only $236,744.64 (Canadian), although his personal worth at his death was estimated at more than $100 million and his businesses' assets exceeded $750 million (Canadian).

The will has several other interesting features. As the rich frequently do, Thomson in his will skipped a generation and divided the bulk of the estate, after $1,000 bequests to his two brothers-in-law and one sister-in-law and twenty-three nieces and nephews, to his seven grand-children in equal amounts. The shares are to be administered by the four trustees appointed in the will until each child reaches the age of thirty and gets his or her money outright. By skipping a generation, the will removes the prospect of Roy Thomson's children paying estate taxes.

The will also differs from the norm in having four trustees: Kenneth Thomson, his surviving sister, Phyllis Audrey Campbell (his other sister, Irma, died in 1966), Sidney Chapman and John Tory, a lawyer who is now deputy chairman of the Thomson businesses. According to estate lawyers, the large size of Thomson's estate probably required this many trustees. All would have to agree on any action taken regarding the estate, but if one died, the other three could carry on.

But the structure of the will and trust funds had another purpose, too: that the family would carry on the business. Roy Thomson spelled this out in his autobiography:

> David, my grandson, will have to take his part in the running of the Organisation, and David's son, too. For the business is now all tied up in trusts for those future Thomsons, so that death duties will not tear it apart.
>
> With the fortune that we will leave to them go also responsibili-ties. These Thomson boys that come after Ken are not going to be able, even if they want to, to shrug off these responsibilities. The conditions of the trusts ensure that control of the business will remain in Thomson hands for eighty years.

Roy Thomson had done more than build an empire: he had made certain that his legacy would be not only wealth and position, but also a Thomson dynasty.

CHAPTER

5

KEN

THE SECOND GENERATION to head the Thomson empire is as much a paradox as the first. Like his father, Kenneth Thomson has been a conqueror in the business world, buying both Canada's oldest and largest department store chain, the Hudson's Bay Company, and the country's equivalent of the *Times* (of London), the *Globe and Mail* of Toronto. Yet he is regarded by the public and business associates as a pale, somewhat disappointing version of his magnetic, dynamic father. Even though Roy depended to a large extent on the ideas of other people, such as Jack Kent Cooke, Sidney Chapman, James Coltart and Gordon Brunton, he always received the glory. But, with Kenneth, the credit instead goes mostly to his right-hand man, John Tory, who is deputy chairman of each of the two main wings of the empire—Thomson Newspapers and ITOL—and is regarded as Kenneth's *éminence grise*.

While Roy Thomson craved and enjoyed publicity, Kenneth avoids the spotlight. Just as there were two sides to Roy Thomson, Kenneth's personality also is a conflicting mixture. It ranges from sentiment to insensitivity, a homespun diffidence to haughtiness, generosity to stinginess, and enjoyment of the good things of life to penny-pinching. The dichotomy extends even further in regard to his cultural activities. He is the major donor to Toronto's newest concert hall, named as a result after his father, but apparently cares little for classical music, since he has no season's ticket to the concerts.

He is proud of owning the world's largest collection of paintings by

48

Dutch-Canadian artist Cornelius Krieghoff. However, there is a practical side to having the collection: his monopoly helps keep the price of Krieghoffs high, and should he decide to give some to a gallery, he would be able to make a tax deduction equal to the current market value. In addition, in return for allowing Hallmark Cards to reproduce a different painting each year on their Christmas cards, Kenneth receives a large number of the cards free.

Like many people with a domineering and hugely successful father, Kenneth was eclipsed by Roy. Although he was in charge of the empire in North America for twenty-three years before his father's death, Kenneth did not really come into his own until after Roy died. At first, he seemed content merely to take his father's place as head of the empire, but in recent years he has moved from being a perpetuator of Roy's achievements to being a builder of his own empire through the acquisition of the eight-newspaper FP chain (for $130 million) and the Hudson's Bay Company (for $640 million). In acquiring the *Globe and Mail* as part of the FP purchase, Kenneth succeeded where his father had failed, Roy having lost out on a bid for the paper in 1955.

At six feet, one inch, Kenneth is taller than his father and slimmer. Like his father, he wears glasses and is a nonsmoker, but he does take the occasional drink. Kenneth Roy Thomson was born 1 September 1923. His childhood appears to have been lonely. He was quiet, not athletic, and his mother would select the youngsters to attend his birthday parties. Like his sisters and mother, he was retiring, living in the shadow of the extroverted Roy. Kenneth adored and respected his father, and they were very close and fond of each other. But, in public, the introverted Kenneth showed his affection more than the extroverted Roy. Each was always genuinely interested in the comments and reactions of the other to business proposals.

In his youth, Kenneth saw little of his father, as Roy traveled around northern Ontario, scratching for a living, and spending any spare time with Jack Kent Cooke. As a result, Kenneth spent much of his boyhood with the Robert Marshall family, especially with Robert Junior, who later became a football player and teacher in Toronto. Kenneth and the Marshalls would go fishing and hunt rabbits and partridges. Marshall treasures Kenneth telling him in later life that the Marshalls had been his "North Bay parents."

Although his life in North Bay was lonely, Kenneth's art collection seems a throwback to those days, with Krieghoff's confectionery-like landscapes of nineteenth-century Quebec reminiscent of the similar scenery of northern Ontario. While many art patrons house their collections in especially constructed museums, Kenneth has chosen to hang his 157 Krieghoffs in a more unusual location—in a gallery adjacent to his office on the twenty-fifth floor of the fourteen-year-old Thomson Building.

Placing the gallery next to his office makes it readily accessible to Kenneth, but it also has had an odd repercussion. Kenneth has opened the collection to public viewing two afternoons a week, but because the tour starts in his Krieghoff-lined office, the head of the Thomson empire must vacate the office in order to make room for the visitors. Sometimes, however, he elects to put aside his work and lead the tour himself.

As a result, the public gets a chance to see where Canada's wealthiest man works. The office is far smaller than the battleship size of most bank presidents' suites, and is no larger than Gordon Brunton's office. The high-backed black leather chair behind Kenneth's neat desk imparts an aura of regal power, but the thirty Krieghoffs around the room and a grandfather clock with a spade-size pendulum offset this by giving the room a warm, pleasant atmosphere. The credenza behind the desk is lined with magnificent wildlife sculptures by Jonathan Kenworthy, a British sculptor whose huge bronze sculpture of elephants grazing in Kenya greets visitors when they step off Kenneth's private elevator between the twenty-fourth and twenty-fifth floors. The most unusual object in the office, however, is a photograph on the windowsill of a relaxed, pullover-clad Kenneth holding a gorilla. There are no family photographs, though in the foyer of the twenty-fourth floor there is a large photograph of Roy Thomson in profile taken by Cavouk.

The gallery is arranged in the inviting style of a living room rather than a formal museum. In addition to the Krieghoffs, there is an outstanding collection of ivory miniatures and a wooden bust of the head of Michelangelo's David. One of Kenneth's pleasures is to arrange and rearrange the crowded glass cases of miniatures himself.

The collection of Kenworthy's bronzes reveals Kenneth's discernment in spotting an up-and-coming artist. They met in 1967 when Kenworthy, then just twenty-four, had a display at the Royal Academy Summer Exhibition in London. Kenworthy's pieces are based on extensive travels to Africa, dating back to 1965, to study wildlife, as well as on animal anatomy through dissection, and on nomadic tribesmen he met in such places as Kenya and Afghanistan. Kenworthy says Kenneth has never specifically commissioned any of the pieces, which he has also bought for his home, but has placed orders after seeing preliminary models in Kenworthy's studio. Kenneth is not the only well-known person to have recognized Kenworthy's talent. Ernest Hemingway's widow, Mary, commissioned the artist to sculpt an impala in bronze for a memorial in Idaho to her husband, and the Carnegie Museum in Pittsburgh and the Smithsonian Institute in Washington have also bought his works.

Like his interest in Krieghoff paintings, Kenneth's interest in country music and westerns dates back to his days in North Bay. When he was sixteen, he worked as a disc jockey at CFCH, his father's radio station in North Bay. Roy had ingrained in him the importance of advertising revenue, and so, despite his youth, Kenneth did not hesitate to telephone an announcer to correct him for mispronouncing the name of the station's biggest advertiser. Much of the music played by the young Kenneth was country music, and he became a fan of Canada's leading country performer, Hank Snow.

About twenty years ago, when he was in his forties, Kenneth finally met Snow. Unlike the usual fan who waits outside the star's door on the off-chance he might get an autograph, Kenneth could afford to stage the meeting in grander style. "I was performing at the Peterborough, Ontario, auditorium and after the show, I was told a fan wanted to see me in the 'green' room, where entertainers relax before and after their show," Snow recalls. "Kenneth had laid out a spread of sandwiches on a big conference table for me and my backup group." The meeting led to a lasting friendship. A few years later, after Snow's show at Toronto's Massey Hall, Kenneth gave him a gold Hamilton pocket watch, the type used by railways because of its accuracy, that had been handed down for generations in the Thomson family.

After Snow moved to Nashville, home of the Grand Ole Opry, he exchanged letters frequently with Kenneth. Then in the fall of 1983, Kenneth and his friend Robert Gimlin, chairman of Abitibi-Price Incorporated, the world's largest newsprint producer, and also a country music fan, flew to Nashville in Abitibi's private jet (the main purpose of Gimlin's trip was to meet with newspaper publishers who are Abitibi customers; Kenneth was going to the site of his U.S. oil operations in Texas). They toured the Grand Ole Opry and an adjacent park, and Kenneth visited with Snow at his home. Snow is also an amateur painter, and he wanted to give Kenneth a memento of the visit. "I stuck a landscape I had done in the trunk of my car and asked Kenneth's daughter Lynne whether, despite Kenneth collecting paintings worth $250,000 and up, he might like my painting. She said he would love it, and I presented it to him in Opryland's TV studios."

In addition to country music, Kenneth is a western movie buff. Because few westerns are filmed anymore, he has bought a collection of taped movies to view in his home.

When Roy Thomson moved his family back to Toronto, Kenneth was enrolled in Upper Canada College, a prestigious boys' school for the rich and upwardly mobile. He was just as low profile there as in North Bay. His housemaster, W. G. Bassett, recalls Kenneth as "an adequate student, in the seventies range in marks, not terribly interested in games, not athletic, and not involved in the school's annual Gilbert and Sullivan productions."

Following Upper Canada College, there is the mysterious case of Kenneth Thomson's college education. In *Who's Who*, he lists himself as graduating from the University of Cambridge in 1947 with a B.A. and M.A. But a Cambridge M.A., according to the university's registrar's office, is not earned, but instead "conferred as a mark of status to those Bachelors of Arts who request the conferment of the degree six years after their first term of matriculation." This is done by Cambridge, as well as by Oxford University, because they regard their B.A. (honours) degree as the equivalent of an M.A. degree elsewhere. Kenneth Thomson attended Cambridge for two years and received a first-class honors degree in law.

This is something of which to be justifiably proud, but what makes it even more exceptional is that Kenneth failed his first year at the University of Toronto. The University of Toronto does not disclose marks; but it stresses that only passing students' names are listed annually in the newspapers, and Kenneth was not listed in the published results for 1942–43, the one year he attended the university. One might wonder how Kenneth then managed to get into Cambridge, which he attended after joining the Royal Canadian Air Force in World War II, serving in London on an RCAF publication. The answer to the Cambridge puzzle is in Russell Braddon's biography of Roy Thomson. Braddon does not mention Kenneth's failing at the University of Toronto, but he does explain that Roy got Kenneth into Cambridge by saying his son was the heir to a publishing empire and, therefore, needed a British education. This is not the only time Cambridge has bent the rules. In 1983, the admission of Prince Edward, a C and D student, caused an uproar.

Following his days at Cambridge, Kenneth returned to the family business in Canada, working first in the editorial department of the cornerstone of the newspaper empire, the Timmins *Daily Press*, and later as an advertising salesman for the *Galt Evening Reporter* for two years from 1948 until 1950. At the *Reporter*, he shared a desk with another advertising salesman, Ed Mannion, who had joined Thomson Newspapers in 1948. Mannion, now chairman of Southam Communications Limited, remembers Kenneth as "quiet, very serious, and a hard worker who made lots of sales calls." Between 1950 and 1953, Kenneth was general manager of the Galt paper, where his tenure was undistinguished. "He didn't introduce anything outstanding," Mannion says.

Timmins and Galt were selected as the best training ground for Kenneth because at that time within Thomson Newspapers Timmins was regarded as the best editorially and Galt the best in salesmanship. Roy and Kenneth later plucked most of the senior Thomson Newspaper executives from the Galt paper, including Mannion, McCabe, and Margaret Hamilton.

Kenneth's ties to Timmins appear to be less strong, just as his father apparently had little affection in his later years for the community. The appearance of the *Daily Press* building, a showplace when it opened, is now disgraceful. The blue paint on the inside walls is peeling, and torn pieces of plastic are used instead of blinds or curtains over the windows. In an age of computerized video display terminals in the newsrooms, the *Press*'s ten reporters have manual typewriters and sit at desks that look as if they date back to the time of Charles Dickens. The *Press*'s current publisher and general manager, Maurice Switzer, says that following rumors a few years ago that the paper would get new quarters on property it owns a block away from its existing premises, no money was spent on refurbishing. He says a new *Press* building is high on the list of Thomson Newspapers' priorities. But, with few people likely to travel to Timmins to see the paper, head office will not likely rush to replace the *Press*'s rundown quarters.

In 1953, when his father moved to England, Kenneth became the head of the North American operations. He also began to think about marriage. According to Robert Marshall, in his youth Kenneth bet him that he would not marry until he was older than the age Marshall had been—twenty-four—when he had got married. Marshall says that Kenneth did not even date until after he was twenty. In 1956, when he was thirty-three, Kenneth found the girl of his dreams, Nora Marilyn Lavis, who modeled dresses for clothing manufacturers when they showed their merchandise to department stores. Acquaintances describe the vivacious Mrs. Thomson, who is seven years younger than her husband, as having "a nice upbringing and good sense of humor," as well as "being very intelligent" and holding a teacher's degree in piano. They emphasize that Kenneth is a faithful husband, unlike his father, who admitted to cheating on his wife in his younger days.

Like her husband, Mrs. Thomson maintains a low profile. Her name does not appear in the social columns, and she is not prominent either in community or cultural activities, as is John Tory's wife, Liz. Her invisibility was momentarily broken in July 1983 when she and the younger of the two Thomson sons, Peter, were in a car accident on Highway 401 between Toronto and Kingston, Ontario, as they were driving to a nearby racetrack. Police said Mrs. Thomson lost control of her red 1982 Porsche when she tried to pass another car using a lane leading to an exit ramp. Her car hit an embankment and rolled across the road before coming to rest upside down near the median. Neither Mrs. Thomson nor Peter were injured, but $5,000 damage was done to the car. She was charged with careless driving, which carries a fine of $128 and six driving demerit points. That is the minimum number of demerits at which an Ontario license may be suspended for that particular offense, but hers was not lifted.

The newspaper coverage, or rather, noncoverage, of this incident was interesting. The Thomson-owned *Globe and Mail* of Toronto, which has written about car crashes involving other prominent people, wrote nothing. The rival *Toronto Star* had a three-paragraph wire service story in the middle of its front section. The *Cobourg Daily Star*, an independently owned paper in the community nearest the site of the accident, did have a front-page story. But the headline gave no indication as to who was involved. It said: "Escape injury in 401 accident."

Kenneth maintains residences in both Toronto and London. In London, he lives on Kensington Palace Gardens, a wide, tree-lined street of embassies and business tycoons' residences with driveways filled with Jaguars or Rolls Royces. Known to Londoners as "Millionaires Row," Kensington Palace Gardens has black latticed iron-grille gates, with locks, for both pedestrians and motorists, and security guards at each end. Kenneth Thomson lives in a rectangular, granite five-storey building that has only five tenants plus a porter. Across the street is the $50-million home of King Fahd of Saudi Arabia, who lives there for about a month a year. Nearby neighbors include the Prince and Princess of Wales and Princess Margaret in Kensington Palace.

In Toronto's still mostly "Old Money" Rosedale district, Thomson lives in a red-brick Georgian mansion, with ivy around the ground-floor windows and thick trees and bushes. Privacy is ensured by a black fence, and safety by a privately hired security firm, which maintains a car watch over the home at night. The architecture of the house is impressive. The roof is concealed by a stone and brick parapet with ornamental acorn-shaped standards that match similar decorations on the pillars at the twin entrances to the circular driveway. On the pediment at the top center of the house, there is a carved stone plaque inscribed "A.D. 1926," the year construction was started on the house. The grounds also contain a three-car garage and separate guest house.

The house and its lot have an interesting background. Today's mansion is predated by humble beginnings. In the early 1900s, the site was the home of a coachman named John Holder, according to Toronto city hall records. In 1926 his house was torn down and adjoining lots were purchased by Gerald Larkin, president of the Salada Tea Company of Canada. Larkin spent $50,000 to build the house, a large sum in those days and, considering inflation, the equivalent of several million dollars today.

It is not only its history that makes the house interesting, but also its present form of ownership. Instead of Kenneth Thomson, the owner, according to the city hall registry office, is the Woodbridge Company, one of the two major Thomson family holding companies of which Kenneth is the largest shareholder. Lawyers say that although such a procedure is unusual, sometimes a corporation does buy a house, and if it is used for business purposes, it can get a tax deduction. The same practicality extends to Thomson's housing his Krieghoff collection at the office, as it allows him to depreciate the paintings as a business expense.

The Thomsons' lifestyle exemplifies the peculiar ways in which the wealthy are budget conscious. Kenneth walks his dog and sometimes does the family shopping himself at a Loblaws supermarket and a Becker's milk and bread corner store. He usually drives an Oldsmobile or Pontiac, rather than a Cadillac, haggling over the price. His latest purchase, however, was a turbo-charged Porsche that he got after trying out and liking the one he had bought for his wife at the suggestion of their older son, David.

The twin Porsche purchase was a flamboyant exception, however. Mrs. Thomson waited, for example, to buy an air conditioner at Simpsons until it was on sale. In London, Kenneth refused to use the black and white Rolls Royce which the *Times* had for its owner, leaving it in a garage. Mrs. Thomson often cuts her husband's hair, saving him a trip to the barber, and when he bought FP Publications, Kenneth was photographed with a huge hole in the sole of his shoe. Similarly, he has been seen asking for a doggie bag after taking his daughter to lunch at the Arcadian Court in the downtown Simpsons store across the street from his office.

While Roy reveled in his title, Kenneth uses it only in England. In Canada, he prefers to be called "Mister" and often answers his telephone directly. Because he is unwilling to surrender his Canadian citizenship, he has not taken his seat in the House of Lords. While his father had to abandon his Canadian citizenship for the title, heirs do not have to do so.

The three Thomson children—David Kenneth Roy (born 1957), Lesley Lynne (born 1959) and Peter John (born 1965)—are strong-willed, but acquaintances say they have not been overindulged by their parents. The family is close-knit, often eating together at Toronto's Granite Club. Unlike many young people these days who live away from home even though in the same city as their family, David, Lynne and Peter still live with their parents. When the children were young and Kenneth and Marilyn went away, they would leave the youngsters in the care of Mrs. Thomson's parents, who live in the guest house adjacent to the main house at the Rosedale estate, rather than rely on servants.

The emphasis on family probably results in large measure from Kenneth's lonely childhood. In addition, while Roy felt he had to travel to build up his business, Kenneth does not have to do this. "Roy Thomson had few regrets in his life, but one of them was that he had not spent more time with his family," William Rees-Mogg says. "He didn't delude himself about anything and he did not regard himself as a good husband or father, believing he had devoted himself too much to the creation of his business. One of the few pieces of advice he gave me was to have a large family, which he said was crucially important and all that mattered in the end."

Like Kenneth, both boys were educated at Upper Canada College, with Kenneth overriding his father's suggestion that David attend Eton College in England. David later studied history at Cambridge, graduating in 1978 with a bachelor of arts degree and class II results, according to the university's registrar's office. Like his father, David is an art collector, although his taste runs to modern abstract expressionism. He is particularly interested in the surrealist paintings of Swiss-German artist Paul Klee.

Unlike many scions of rich men who spend their lives with a highball in their hand, Kenneth has been conscientious in carrying on for Roy. He has not been an absentee owner like Huntingdon Hartford, who ignored his family's business, the Great Atlantic and Pacific Tea Company (A&P supermarkets), and instead poured his $65-million inheritance into exotic, money-losing ventures and jet-setting. Nor has Kenneth imitated Tommy Manville, the heir to the Johns-Manville asbestos fortune, who was best known for marrying eleven wives in thirteen marriages. Manville, who died in 1967, spent more than $1.25 million of his $10-million inheritance on divorce settlements.

It is difficult for any inheritor to live up to the pioneering accomplishments of the founding father, and Kenneth faces an extra obstacle in that he lacks his father's colorful personality. He is typical of the paradox of many second generations who, despite possessing great wealth and power, are regarded as bleached out compared with the forceful patriarch.

Since Roy's death in 1976, the revenue of Thomson Newspapers in North America has tripled and the revenue of ITOL quadrupled. Nevertheless, despite this rapid growth, Kenneth is not regarded as a trailblazer like his father. If this bothers him, he gives no sign of it, because he is his father's biggest admirer. While employees and associates praise Kenneth for his elaborate courtesy in conversation and his letters, and for the autonomy he gives, they believe he lacks the risk-taking, entrepreneurial daring of his father.

Denis Hamilton, who has no difficulty in expressing his enthusiasm about Roy Thomson, lapses into one of his well-known pauses, the length of time it takes to eat a sandwich, before carefully answering: "In my journalistic life, I have seen many great fathers succeeded by irresponsible playboys with no thought for the employees at the business created by their father. Kenneth Thomson works very hard and takes the line his father did of decentralizing management authority as much as possible. He is a man of high moral character. However, either in battle or history, there are no two dynamos in a row."

Sidney Chapman, who has a lode of stories about Roy Thomson, shows the same strange reticence as Hamilton when asked for a comparison. "That's a delicate question. Ken has high integrity. He lacks the financial finesse of his father but can speak well and has stepped into the breach. He has administered the companies without being unfair to the executives."

Rees-Mogg reiterates Hamilton's comment about Kenneth Thomson's lack of dynamism, but his views are tinged by his opposition to Kenneth's shutting down the *Times* (of London) in 1979 and then selling it in 1981 because he was fed up with the labor problems and demands that plague the British newspaper industry. "Kenneth Thomson would never conceivably have become a tycoon if he had not been born into it. He has a basically kind but diffident nature which he had to turn into the nature of a successful businessman. His roots are in Canada and he resented, in his straightforward Canadian way, some of the aspects of industrial life in the United Kingdom. His father hated the unions, too, but he lived in London and took part in the battle. Roy Thomson had the ability to change situations by his own presence. Ken is honorable and likable, but he doesn't inspire fear."

That Roy was more of an entrepreneur is also the opinion of Ed Mannion, who helped train Ken Thomson. "Roy was a crapshooter, a gambler, a hard-nosed diamond in the rough. Ken is a good guy to inherit and expand the empire and more polished than his father, but he probably couldn't have built the empire."

Current Thomson executives emphasize that Kenneth Thomson gives them a free hand. "I have never had a fundamental disagreement with him," Gordon Brunton says. "One of the most marvelous things since Roy Thomson died is that we have been able to continue and develop the business and that Ken has had the courage to give authority and support to people he trusts, most of whom were there when his father was alive and whom his father also trusted."

But his close working relationship with father and son has also made Brunton well aware that their main common characteristic is their surname. "Roy wasn't an interventionist but could have been. He epitomized the Victorian concept that the wasting of money is immoral. He believed the purpose of money was to build business and more business. He was a tough, hard-hitting risk taker. Ken is a quiet, humane person interested in the world of art and willing to let people he trusts run his businesses."

Executives who have joined the Thomson empire in the 1970s and 1980s also assess Kenneth as noninterventionist. "He is the nonoperating owner," says Richard Groves of International Thomson Business Press. "He runs a huge empire that he has allowed to flourish."

Another U.S.-based Thomson executive, requesting anonymity, sees the two Thomsons in military-campaign terms. "Roy built the empire and had the confidence that comes from winning the skirmishes required to construct that empire. Kenneth is more reserved and cautious. His task is to preserve and protect the empire. He has lieutenants and he doesn't even have to give them commands."

The sheer size of the empire keeps Thomson from getting personally involved with all the details, and heads of various major Thomson companies say they see Kenneth Thomson perhaps once a year and, often, less frequently. It took four years until Thomson visited Thomson Book Service Limited's new computerized, centralized warehouse for the British book companies, located outside London. "I have heard from him perhaps two dozen times in the past four years when he sent possible deals related to energy," says Edward Monteith, president of Thomson-Monteith of Dallas, the U.S. branch of the Thomson oil and gas business. "On 90 percent of them, he'll tell me to handle them directly but keep him advised about them."

Occasionally, Kenneth does ask his executives to consider a proposal of his, but will back off if they say it is unsound. One such case occurred a few years ago following the sensational press coverage of a "sex and chains" case in the United States involving a Mormon youth and his female captor. "Kenneth Thomson was an admirer of the Mormons and was very concerned about the impact of the case on them," Edmund Fisher recalls. "He suggested that Sphere publish a book on the Mormon faith. He asked me as a favor to see some Mormons who would explain their religion to me. I told him I would publish such a book if he, as my boss, wanted me to but that it would not sell. He thanked me with incredible courtesy for calling back and said my advice was fine with him and to think no more about it." (Thomson's own religious affiliation is Baptist.)

Although he is more remote from the daily operations than his father was, Kenneth is readily accessible to people who have a good deal. "When I heard recently of a magazine for sale that I thought would be of interest to International Thomson Business Press, I called Thomson Newspapers in Toronto and asked to whom I should speak and was put right through to him," says Leroy Keller, a New York media broker.

Kenneth is capable both of great sentiment and thoughtfulness, as well as insensitivity. His love for his white Shetland terrier, Gonzo, matches that for his family. A staunch supporter of the Humane Society, Kenneth got Gonzo at the society's kennels and bathes and walks him faithfully. Although normally reticent in public, Kenneth will walk up to almost anybody with a dog and swap pet talk. He also tries to persuade his friends to adopt Humane Society animals.

Another example of his softer side is his replacement of Krieghoff's tombstone in Chicago, on which the inscription had faded beyond recognition, with a duplicate on which Krieghoff's name is clearly engraved. He was given the original tombstone, which he keeps in the basement of the Thomson Building, having decided against putting it in his gallery.

Kenneth can also be a considerate and thoughtful acquaintance. One recipient of this kindness was Bill Kennedy of Burlington, Ontario, from whom Thomson buys cars. In one of those "small world" coincidences, Kennedy is the brother-in-law of broadcaster Betty Kennedy, his brother's widow, who then wed Allan Burton when he was chairman of Simpsons. Burton retired after Kenneth acquired the company as part of the package when he bought its owner, the Hudson's Bay Company. Twelve years ago, Kennedy's young son, Bill, got Hodgkin's disease. "Ken would phone every week when he was in Toronto to ask how Billy was," Kennedy says. "At that time, Ken spent half the year in London and within twenty-four hours of his return to Toronto, he would phone about Billy. Later, he made it possible for Billy to get several thousand dollars worth of books for college at the cost price."

Kennedy tells another story about Kenneth's thoughtfulness. "When Roy died, I asked Ken if I could buy something that belonged to his father [which Kennedy will not identify]. Every time I saw him I asked when I could buy it and finally in the summer of 1983, Ken called me that he had had the item appraised. He asked me what I would be willing to pay and then said to write out the check to my son Danny, who attends a school for the hearing disabled in Washington." But since Danny's education is covered by government vocational rehabilitation grants, Kennedy instead applied the money to his daughter's education.

Other Thomson philanthropy, however, has been more controversial. This was the case with Roy Thomson Hall. Although hall officials claimed that the $4.5-million Thomson donation did not carry the proviso that the hall be named after Roy Thomson, who had no liking for music, that is what happened. The decision to do so was remarkable in that the Thomsons had paid for well under half the cost of the $42-million hall, with $25.5 million of the cost being paid for by the taxpayers, many of whom had suggested names based on classical music. The other $12 million came from private donations, all smaller than the Thomsons'.

It was the first occasion in Toronto that a concert hall was named after a major contributor who had not paid at least half the cost. The hall's predecessor, Massey Hall, was 100 percent paid for by the Massey family. In addition, because arrangements were made for all the private contributions, including those by the Thomsons, to be paid over a five-year period, inflation will dilute their value considerably.

Just as Kenneth's interest in Roy Thomson Hall has not led to his attending regularly, so does his attraction to Krieghoff's landscapes not seem to extend to the real thing. This, at least, was the impression gained by Vladimir Raitz, a Londoner who helped Roy Thomson get into the travel business. "The year that Thomson Travel flew its inaugural flight to Yugoslavia, it took a group of eighty people including Roy Thomson, Kenneth Thomson and his wife, Gordon Brunton and me to Dubrovnic. The festivities included a bus tour of the countryside and I was on the same bus as Kenneth. The scenery was breathtaking, but Kenneth spent the entire time reading a detective story. He had obviously followed in his father's footsteps as an avid crime fiction reader. He didn't once look out the window." This also was like Roy, who had once rejected a four-day conducted tour of Israel, following a business trip there, so he could return to work in London.

Moreover, while the Krieghoff art brings back memories of the countryside near North Bay, the city itself does not have a magic hold on Thomson when it comes to charitable contributions. In 1981, when North Bay's Empire Hotel, where Roy Thomson often met with other businessmen, ran into financial difficulties and had its gas supply cut off, Robert Marshall called Kenneth and asked if he would help bail out the hotel. "He said that with the cost of money, that was the way of doing business and gave nothing," Marshall says. Of course, Kenneth cannot donate to every supplicant and the Empire Hotel managed without his help and is still in business.

Outside of the Roy Thomson Hall donation, which may have been motivated as much by the desire to have a monument to his father as to civic duty, Kenneth is as tightfisted as Roy regarding public charity. Just as the Thomson Foundation was not the creation of Roy Thomson, the main manifestation of the empire's community spirit today—the re-building of the economy of a highly depressed city in Wales—is due to Gordon Brunton's belief in a welfare state. That Brunton was able to involve ITOL in assisting the city of Neath, located near Cardiff, is a testament to his determination to pursue his beliefs despite their being opposite to the Thomsons', as well as to his power within the empire. The project also demonstrates his ingeniousness in structuring deals.

Although Neath does not look poor because the house-proud owners paint their window frames in bright colors and cover the windowpanes with starched, white lace curtains, nearly one out of five of its labor force was unemployed in 1981 when Brunton decided ITOL should help its 66,000 residents. To sell Kenneth Thomson on the idea of helping out, Brunton noted that the empire had some ties to Neath, since it owned the small local paper. More importantly, he devised ITOL's assistance in the form of on-the-scene advice from just one employee, whose salary ITOL pays, rather than one huge outright donation. This was also to Neath's benefit because it desperately needed guidance on how to create jobs. The ITOL employee now on loan is Jeremy Filmer-Bennett, previously personnel director of Thomson Directories, and a dynamo of ideas. Working with a cooperative council, eager to help their city, he has prompted the development of small-business work-shops, most of them doing carpentry, in a converted vacant factory, as well as a high-technology center, and a budding tourism program centered around the city's canals and a twelfth-century abbey. By 1986, he expects 1,500 new jobs will have been created—equal to more than one-third the number of jobs that have disappeared in Neath since 1981.

The success of the program has brought the lion's share of publicity to ITOL because although several firms are involved, it is the best known and its representative is in charge. But Filmer-Bennett, and especially Neath, deserve the credit; unlike other self-help projects that have done poorly, none of the workshops have gone bankrupt, compared with a 60 percent failure rate elsewhere, and Neath's council, at Filmer-Bennett's urging, moved more quickly than competing cities in getting U.K. government approval for its high-technology center. This was essential, since only a limited number of centers are being backed by the government. In early 1984, ITOL extended its support of Neath through 1985, but with Brunton's earlier-than-expected departure, future ITOL backing is less assured.

But Neath was not Kenneth Thomson's idea and while there are those like Bill Kennedy who praise Kenneth as being generous, there are many who despise and hate him. One former reporter of a Thomson paper in the U.S. that went on strike over low wages, normally a soft-spoken model of self-control, describes Thomson's "cutthroat operation as something truly evil right in our community."

Canadian journalists remember his chilling comment that "each one has to find his own way in the world" after his closing of the *Ottawa Journal* in August 1980 put 375 people out of work. Thomson Newspapers made no head-office effort to find jobs for the paper's employees at its other newspapers. By contrast, Southam Incorporated, which closed its *Winnipeg Tribune* on the same day as Thomson closed its Ottawa paper, leaving Thomson as the sole newspaper publisher in Winnipeg and Southam as the single one in Ottawa, took a different tack. Southam officials pledged their assistance to their former Winnipeg employees in finding openings at their other papers and opened a temporary employment office in the *Tribune* building. Less than a month after the shock of the *Journal* and *Tribune* folding, Thomson Newspapers laid off another sixty-one employees when it merged its two Victoria, British Columbia, newspapers, the *Times* and the *Daily Colonist*, with no prior consultation with employees.

Because of the size of his newspaper empire in North America and the U.K., it would be impossible for Thomson to visit them often if he felt so inclined—which he doesn't. Moreover, he typifies the irritating habit of newspaper owners and editors of avoiding interviews, or saying very little if cornered, even though they would not be in business if the people they want interviewed were to have the same attitude. At the time of Thomson's suspension of publication of the *Sunday Times* and the *Times* in 1979 during a dispute with a number of newspaper unions, the *Sunday Times Reporter*, an internal staff publication, assigned *Sunday Times* magazine reporter Susan Raven to portray a day in Thomson's life, since she wrote a regular series of such profiles. He was in Toronto and she started by writing him, asking for a long-distance telephone interview, and subsequently called him. Here is her account of the conversation to the *Sunday Times Reporter* readers:

S.R.: "Is that Lord Thomson's office?"

MALE VOICE: "Yes, it is."

S.R.: "Is that by any chance Lord Thomson?"

MALE VOICE: "Yes, it is."

S.R.: "I was really ringing to find out from your office whether you got my letter. I wrote to ask if I could interview you over the telephone."

LORD THOMSON: "Yes, I did, and I have already written to you, Mrs. Raven, because I really am not seeking any personal publicity at this time."

S.R.: "Oh dear, it wouldn't be the story of your life or an analysis of your political views. I wouldn't ask you a single question about our present crisis, unless of course you wanted to say something. It is really meant to give the human side of the people involved."

LORD THOMSON: "Well, Mrs. Raven, I appreciate that and I would like to say how much I feel for all you journalists. It must be like being a painter and sitting in front of a blank canvas. I'm speaking from memory of what I said in my letter to you, but I don't mind saying it to you now—I would prefer to stay out of print as much as possible."

Only an art collector would speak of a blank page in a reporter's typewriter as being similar to an artist's canvas. But, however courteous the words, the upshot is the same. Whether he is courteously rejecting Susan Raven, or facing a hurricane of protests, Kenneth Thomson is perfectly capable of standing firm and speaking out forcefully on his own, rather than hiding behind Gordon Brunton or John Tory. "Kenneth Thomson is not really shy; he is able to speak instantaneously and spontaneously," says James Leisy, chairman of the Thomson-owned Wadsworth Incorporated, a San Francisco college-book publisher. "I was in London during the dispute at the *Times* and the *Sunday Times* when Kenneth took on the press in a question session. Gordon Brunton had said they would not be hearing from

Lord Thomson, but instead he got up and spoke with conviction and fervor."

While many tycoons pile up company directorships the way Kenneth collects Krieghoffs, Kenneth sits on only two outside boards of directors. One is the Toronto-Dominion Bank, which asked Kenneth to join in 1970, four years after it started doing business with Thomson Newspapers by lending money for the purchase of several U.S. papers. However, the present TD chairman, Richard Thomson (no relation to Kenneth's family), is on closer terms with John Tory, who sits on the board of the Thomson empire's other Canadian banker, the Royal Bank, than with Kenneth. Dick Thomson and John Tory met as teenagers at Toronto's exclusive Rosedale Golf Club and have remained best friends since then. Their families used to go on skiing vacations together when their children were younger. Now, the two men hold regular golf games in which the winner of the first nine holes buys hot dogs and a soft drink or hot chocolate and the loser of the next nine buys drinks at the end of the match.

The other board Kenneth sits on is that of Abitibi-Price. Abitibi's chairman, Robert Gimlin, lives a block from Kenneth, and his black poodle and Kenneth's terrier are romantically involved. However, the association with Abitibi dates back to when Abitibi gave Roy a helping hand in the early days of his business. Abitibi had held the only available radio license in the North Bay area, which it had originally obtained to provide a link to its lumber camps. When it switched to a telephone linkup, Abitibi no longer needed its radio license and gave it on loan to Roy Thomson for one dollar for a year's trial run until it determined if it needed it back. As it didn't, Roy got it for nothing under the terms of the agreement. In return, Roy later ordered his newsprint from Abitibi's northern mill rather than from Toronto. Subsequently, Abitibi invited Roy to sit on its board of directors, and Kenneth took over his seat in 1970. By coincidence, John Tory is also on Abitibi's board, having inherited the seat in 1965 after the death of his father.

The connection between Abitibi and the Thomson empire goes beyond the friendship of Gimlin and Kenneth and the board directorships to a business relationship. In 1981 Thomson Newspapers and Abitibi-Price agreed to joint ownership of Abitibi's newsprint mill in Augusta, Georgia. Such a venture is customary these days, and many other newspaper companies, such as Knight-Ridder and the *New York Times*, have similar arrangements. Gimlin says the joint venture provided an infusion of $50 million from Thomson Newspapers towards modernization and expansion of the plant at a time when it would have "decimated" Abitibi's Canadian capital due to a downturn in newsprint demand. Thomson Newspapers transferred some of its newsprint business from Abitibi's Canadian mills to the Georgia mill. "When you think of taking in a partner, chemistry and trust between the people are important," Gimlin says.

This goodwill obviously was an important factor because the joint venture came just months after Thomson Newspapers bid unsuccessfully to take over Abitibi-Price, losing out to Olympia and York Developments Limited of Toronto, the world's largest real estate developer. Ralph Reichmann, one of the three brothers running Olympia and York, is now the youngest Abitibi-Price board member, replacing John Tory in that category.

It was Tory who instigated the Abitibi-Price takeover bid as well as the bid two years earlier for the Hudson's Bay Company. Of the three key lieutenants in the Thomson empire today—Brunton in London, his deputy, Michael Brown, in New York, and Tory—Tory is the most powerful. His power does not simply derive from his office being located across the hall from Kenneth's. He is the only one of the trio to sit on the boards of the Thomson family's holding companies. He also is the only one to hold a senior position in both Thomson Newspapers and ITOL as the deputy chairman of each and to sit with Kenneth on the board of the Hudson's Bay Company. Furthermore, unlike the other two, Tory enjoys a personal friendship with Thomson. On Thomson's sixtieth birthday, Tory had a "dummy" front page put on Kenneth's copy of the *Globe and Mail*, the nature of which prompted Kenneth to worry, when he picked up the paper as usual from his front doorstep, as to whether all Toronto had got the same contents in their papers. It is inconceivable that Brunton or Brown would pull such a practical joke.

The distinction between the roles of Brunton, Brown and Tory is that Brunton and Brown are professional managers charged with operating and expanding the empire, while Tory is more of an aide-de-camp, screening telephone calls and ideas and deciding whether they are major enough to involve Kenneth. The three men complement one another ideally. Tory has the legal skills that helped Thomson Newspapers turn back courtroom and federal commission challenges to the simultaneous closing of its Ottawa paper and Southam's Winnipeg paper on the same day in 1980. Brunton is a fertile cauldron of ideas for new ventures, and Brown has the orderly mind required to impose a systematic overlay to glue together the rapid expansion in the U.S.

According to executives who have watched the Thomson-Tory combination in action, Kenneth is low key, almost humble despite his wealth and power, quiet, and concerned both "about doing the right thing and making money." He listens to all sides and then takes a position. By contrast, Tory, while pleasant and sociable, "gives the impression that he is operating under enormous pressure and carrying the weight of the world on his shoulders." He operates at a fast pace and likes to grasp the initiative in coming up with fresh ideas and solutions.

Nondescript in appearance, bespectacled, with a deep, resonant voice and a pleasant, although unrevealing, disposition, the fifty-one-year-old John Tory belongs to a family of high achievers. His father, John S. D. Tory, founded the Toronto law firm of Tory, Tory, Des Lauriers & Binnington, which has become one of the largest in Canada. J.S.D. wielded power in the grand manner. "He was strong-willed and ruled his law firm with an iron hand," recalls Ted Rogers, who articled at Tory, Tory before starting his Toronto-based broadcasting business, now known as Rogers Cablesystems. "His chauffeur would pick him up at 6:15 p.m. and take him to his estate in King, north of Toronto. The family also had a Maritimes cottage. If two of his clients got into an argument, he would call them in and adjudicate the situation." J.S.D. married twice, divorcing his first wife of thirty years in order to marry his second.

John Tory is an unidentical twin. Both he and his brother, James, had brilliant academic careers. They completed high school before they were sixteen and graduated, with A's, from the University of Toronto's Faculty of Law at the age of twenty-two. The twins were members of the Law Club, which conducts the business affairs and supervises athletic and social activities for the law students, and John was the club's vice-president in his second year. Both brothers played hockey and both told the *Torontonensis* 1952 yearbook that their future would be "practising law in Ontario."

While both were at the top of their class, the twins are otherwise unalike, according to Ted Rogers. "Jim is more easygoing and happy-go-lucky. He is not as well organized and never got his dockets all caught up. John is more low-keyed and looks like a university student or dean who has just come out of the library. Jim always looks a little disheveled and as if he has just left the student lounge." The twins live well, but not as luxuriously as their father. John's house has a swimming pool, and he also has an exercise bicycle in his bedroom on which he pedals for about twenty minutes daily, while watching television.

Both John and Jim joined their father's law firm, of which Roy Thomson was a client. About 25 percent of John's case load dealt with the Thomson companies. In 1973 John left Tory, Tory (although he remains a nominal partner) to join Kenneth as his top adviser. Thomson is not alone in placing such faith in Tory. Rogers also constantly consults Tory, who is on Rogers Cablesystems' board of directors. "I don't do anything of major significance unless John approves, because he is sensible without being stodgy," Rogers says. "He likes new ideas and examines them rather than rejecting them immediately as something that won't fly."

Rogers says Kenneth made the right choice in Tory's appointment because "John is terribly clever, always goes to the heart of the matter, is interested in other people, and is not arrogant." Roger's high opinion is echoed by Talcorp's Robert Smith, based on Tory also serving on Talcorp's board of directors. "His business ethics are so strong that everybody trusts him. He is very sound and practical. He works hard but is also a lot of fun, with his sense of humor helping to break up a tense business atmosphere."

Unlike the low profile of Marilyn and Kenneth Thomson, John Tory and his wife, Elizabeth, enjoy parties and are active in community service. In addition to being co-owner of a Toronto travel agency with Robert Smith, Mrs. Tory is a director both of the Shaw Festival and of the Toronto Symphony Orchestra. Her husband is on the board of Toronto's Clarke Institute of Psychiatry and is also honorary solicitor for the Canadian Mental Health Association.

John Tory's children are also big achievers. His eldest son, John, twenty-nine, is the principal assistant to Ontario Premier William Davis. John is following in his grandfather's footsteps; J.S.D. was a fund raiser for the federal Progressive Conservatives. Two other sons are in the investment business—Jeffrey is at Burns Fry Limited in Toronto and Michael is at S. G. Warburg & Company Limited, the London merchant bankers who are the Thomson empire's longtime financial advisers in the United Kingdom.

In addition to the abortive Abitibi takeover attempt, it was Tory who suggested the bid for the FP chain and the Hudson's Bay Company. In both cases, Thomson bought trouble. The FP takeover led to the eventual closing of the Ottawa paper, prompting a federal royal commission and the charge of conspiracy in conjunction with Southam. Although the *Globe and Mail*, the former flagship paper of the FP chain, gained 30,000 readers between 1980 and 1981, the first year under Thomson, it lost 40,000 in the next two years. The purchase of The Bay eventually forced the Thomsons to sell off shares in their two main holding companies—the Woodbridge Company and Thomson Equitable Corporation—to reduce the substantial debt arising from that takeover.

In 1983 the Thomsons reduced their holdings in ITOL from 82

percent down to 73 percent by selling close to 6.4 million of their shares in ITOL in the Canadian stock market. According to the holding companies' investment dealer, Wood Gundy Limited of Toronto, they made $76 million on the sale and still own 100 million shares worth a total of $1.2 billion. Wood Gundy chairman Ted Medland says about $20 million was earmarked for reducing debt incurred by buying control of The Bay, and the remainder is budgeted for acquisitions, mainly in the United States.

The decrease of the family's holdings in ITOL followed by a few months the sale of 10 percent of their interest in Thomson Newspapers, with that money also going to reduce the debt arising from The Bay purchase. Medland says the Thomsons waited for four years after acquiring The Bay to sell off some of their shares because previously they were undervalued. He says no further sell-offs are planned. "The family feels very comfortable with its remaining obligations because they can be easily serviced from cash flows."

Kenneth's pleasure in owning The Bay is underscored by his beginning the grooming of his son, David, as the third generation in the dynasty, at The Bay. David is described by family and business acquaintances as outgoing and intelligent, with lots of drive, and more akin in personality to Roy than Kenneth. Hudson's Bay executives organized a six-month "exposure program" for David, starting in 1982, moving him to different parts of the company, ranging from fur sales to general merchandise, for a week at a time. Subsequently, David said he would like to get some actual experience as a retailer and became assistant to the manager of a Toronto-area branch store and then manager of the city's west-end Cloverdale Mall store.

Roy Thomson had stipulated that the business would be run by Kenneth's branch of the family and by males only. So far, Peter is too young to be in the business, and David and Peter are the only boys among Roy's seven grandchildren. What will happen when Peter is old enough to join the company remains to be seen, as it would be the first time that two Thomson men around the same age would be in the business simultaneously. Peter is said to be greatly interested in computer technology. Only one other family member is involved with the business—Ronald Dawick, who is married to Kenneth's niece Linda. Dawick made a point of working elsewhere before joining the Thomson travel business in Canada.

Kenneth's daughter, Lynne, passed the Ontario securities course and worked for the retail side of McLeod Young Weir Limited, a major Toronto investment dealer. Attractive and stylish, she is now considering a fashion career. She accompanies Kenneth on business trips to parts of the empire, as does Marilyn Thomson, but only one female Thomson relative is in the business world's spotlight—thirty-six-year-old Sherry Brydson, the daughter of Kenneth's deceased sister, Irma. Sherry parlayed her $4.5-million inheritance from Roy Thomson into the development of the exclusive Elmwood Women's Club in Toronto, as well as interests in oil and gas, and Southeast Asian imports. Her business acumen is matched by a good sense of humor. When she married journalist Paul MacRae, their wedding announcement was in the form of a newspaper jokingly called the *Capitulator*.

When Kenneth was younger, his father said of him: "He's a fine boy but I'm just a little concerned that maybe he doesn't push enough." But that was years before Kenneth showed he was an acquisitor of big companies as well as of paintings. Although eight years have passed since Roy's death, during which the empire has moved into the U.S. in nonnewspaper businesses in a big way and acquired the FP chain and The Bay, Kenneth still regards this period of time as a transition stage. But while the empire may metamorphose more in the coming years, one thing is certain: it will continue to be run by a Thomson.

6

RUNNING THE EMPIRE

THE THOMSON EMPIRE TODAY is a mass of contradictions. On the one hand, decentralization and the entrepreneurial spirit are encouraged, but, conversely, executives are under the constraint of having to work out their budgets to four decimal points, a restraint that generates caution rather than risk taking. The North American newspapers' expenses are pared to the bone, but laying out millions for new acquisitions, be it newspapers or other businesses, is also encouraged. ITOL's and Thomson Newspapers' offices are splendidly furnished, while newspaper employees complain that they get scrap paper instead of notepads. The decentralization, about which Thomson executives speak enthusiastically and sincerely, is counterbalanced by the ultimate control being centralized in one man, Kenneth Thomson. Executives are well paid if they survive and equally well paid to leave quietly.

Although ITOL has its head office in Toronto in the Cadillac Fairview Building diagonally across the street from the Thomson Newspapers building, the most senior executive there is treasurer Alan Lewis. ITOL is actually run from London by Brunton, with its North American operations, including the Canadian book-publishing and oil and gas businesses, reporting to New York, which, in turn, reports to London. ITOL is run by a very small group of under a hundred people. "In terms of the ratio between sales and executives, International Thomson Organisation probably has the smallest corporate headquarters in the world," Brunton boasts.

The London office, called Thomson House, is far more elegant than the small, functional New York and Toronto quarters. A discreet gold nameplate at No. 4 Stratford Place, a short, quiet street off the bustle of the fashionable Oxford and Bond streets shopping district, is the low-key introduction to the heart of the ITOL network. No. 4 is not an impersonal office tower like the Cadillac Fairview Building or the Manufacturers Hanover Building on Broadway near 50th Street, where International Thomson Holdings Incorporated, the U.S. arm of the empire, has its headquarters. Instead, it is a charming, five-storey Regency-style house erected in 1790 for a member of Parliament, Sir George Yonge. Between 1848 and 1890, the London and Westminster Bank had its headquarters at No. 4 before moving to No. 1 Stratford Place. A company-owned, dark green, chauffeured Bentley sits polished and ready at the entrance.

Inside, a receptionist and security guard greet visitors in a sitting room to the right of the entrance. At the left is the aristocratic but not ostentatious combination boardroom/dining room, with a Regency-style mahogany table and thirty-four mulberry-colored Trafalgar leather armchairs, a Maria Theresa chandelier, a specially woven Royal Wilton rug designed to blend with the furniture, and a number of landscapes painted by eighteenth- and nineteenth-century British artists. "We're not extravagant but what we do, we do well," Brunton says. "It has to be elegant because sometimes the Prince of Wales, the prime minister, or other political leaders come, and style is important to the impression a company gives. We must have a superb dining room or otherwise we would have to eat at Claridge's." Considering Claridge's elitist reputation, dining there would be no hardship, and the hotel is within easy walking distance. However, more privacy is possible in the Thomson House dining room.

The formality of No. 4 is matched by the behavior of its occupants. A London book publisher, who was invited by Brunton to Thomson House some years ago to discuss a job opening, learned this the hard way. "I was met by a young executive who led me from the reception room to meet Brunton upstairs. I made a joke about it being similar to going through anteroom after anteroom during the reign of Louis XIV, and this executive stopped and gave me a warning. 'Take my advice,' he said. 'Don't make jokes like that to Mr. Brunton. We don't much like jokes at Thomson's.'"

Ownership of the empire's assets outside North America was shifted across the Atlantic in 1978 when ITOL was established to replace the Thomson Organisation, which had its head office in London. The reorganization, started in 1976, the year Roy Thomson died, merged the family's separately owned North Sea oil interest with the rest of their United Kingdom businesses. The family had originally regarded the North Sea as a high-risk venture, waiting until it was successful before incorporating it with its other businesses. Moving the ownership of the restructured company to Toronto had a more practical aspect than simply bringing it closer to the Canadian-based Kenneth Thomson. It also enabled investing abroad without being subject to the then stiff British exchange controls that could increase the cost of foreign investment by up to 50 percent. The company had decided international expansion, especially in the United States, was necessary because U.K. monopolies legislation placed constraints on further newspaper acquisitions, and Thomson already owned the largest newspaper group. Its only previous international investment had been small, amounting to about $100,000 in publications in South Africa.

About $20 million was paid to the United Kingdom under its exchange-control program to make the switch; then one year later the controls were eased, negating the purpose of the transaction. "It was for naught financially but there is always the worry that the regulations could be brought back," Lewis says. But the exercise was not really a wasted effort. It was a recognition that legally the power always resided in Canada because Roy Thomson and his Canadian heirs then owned 82 percent. In addition, it erased what would have been the unusual procedure of a Canadian-owned company investing in the United States through the medium of a London company.

The working apparatus, however, remains unchanged. The senior executives are still in London, and all the financial consolidation work is done there. Financial results of the Canadian-owned company are still reported in British pounds, but dividends to shareholders (27 percent of the company is now publicly owned) in Canada, the United Kingdom and the United States are paid in U.S. dollars, a custom among multinational firms.

Although ITOL's main emphasis is on the United States, it waited four years before finally setting up shop there under Brunton's next-in-command, Michael Brown. Until 1982 Brown was based in London, but that year he was transferred to New York and appointed executive vice-president and chief operating officer of a new North American division, International Thomson Holdings Incorporated, formed to encompass the rapidly growing U.S. operations. Brown has a nicely furnished office, dominated by maroon leather chairs, a conference table, and pictures of Thomson's North Sea oil rigs, but he rarely sees it. During his first year in the United States, he was in his office only twelve times. Other times, he was flying around the country shopping for acquisitions, with the largest letter of credit in his briefcase being $33 million for the purchase of Wadsworth. The heavy traveling schedule has taken its toll—the forty-nine-year-old reticent, but pleasant, Brown looks considerably older than his age.

Like Roy Thomson and Brunton, Brown's youth was one of hardship. At sixteen he left private school, to which he says his father, a manager at BICC (British Insulated Callender Cables), could no longer afford to send him and which young Michael "disliked." Brown then worked for a firm of accountants and took external college courses for his certification, which he got two years later. Brown next joined BICC, and by the age of twenty-eight was general manager of its underground cable division, which had 5,000 employees. But in 1969, despite a 20 percent drop in pay that took him three years to regain, Brown left BICC for the Thomson Organisation. "I didn't like the construction industry, especially as getting overseas contracts was not the most savory of activities in which to be involved."

Brown became the first nonnewspaper person to be appointed executive director of Times Newspapers. He made some dramatic changes with the result that losses of the *Times* fell by several million pounds. The changes included reducing production capacity by one-third while maintaining production levels, bringing in new management, raising the newsstand and overseas prices, and ending the practice of printing special editions on heavier paper for the Royal Family and prime minister. In 1972 he switched to the Thomson Organisation as financial controller and in 1974 became financial director.

For years Brown had been regarded as the heir apparent to Brunton, but with what Brown described as the "reasonable age gap" (of fourteen years) between him and Brunton, Brunton seemed in no immediate danger, especially as Brown described Brunton as his mentor. "We are close personal friends, see each other socially, and have holidayed together," Brown says. "I owe my career to Gordon, who gave me the opportunity and backing." At the end of 1984, in the natural line of succession, Brown will replace Brunton as president of ITOL, albeit earlier than might have been expected.

Brown receives high marks from Thomson executives and London investment analysts. "I consider him to be one of the shrewdest businessmen with whom I have dealt," Ed Monteith says. "He has a quick grasp of business concepts and figures. He sets very high standards of performance and stimulates management to achieve them." Adds Richard Groves: "Michael works at least a seventy-hour week. His memory recall is beyond belief. As a team, Gordon Brunton devises the overall strategy and provides the camaraderie and warmth, while Michael is more hard-nosed." Eric de Bellaigue, an analyst at the

London investment house of Grenfell and Colegrave, says Brown has "demonstrated financial skills, especially in the way Thomson got financing for its North Sea oil venture earlier than most people and kept to deadlines in development and production."

While Brown was the first to run the overall show for ITOL in North America, Alan Lewis in Toronto is at the center of ITOL's financial web. He joined ITOL in London in 1970 in the general accounts department and moved up to become chief accountant where he implemented the reporting systems that ITOL still uses today. "Before, it was a raggedy system, with which they could make do because ITOL was relatively small and had few interests outside the U.K.," he says. ITOL was still using a manual financial reporting system until the mid-1970s. Lewis brought in computers, which not only sped up the work load but also allowed speedier comparison of actual versus planned results. In 1978 Lewis was posted to New York to help Michael Brown set up ITOL's U.S. operations. Lewis wears several hats. In Canada, he deals with the press and investment analysts. He also chairs meetings of Thomson executives on Canadian international tax matters. He goes regularly to ITOL in New York, where he acts as a controller, and to the U.K. three times a year to work on shareholders' reports.

There is no direct cross-subsidization between Thomson Newspapers and ITOL, but the bulk of the dividends from both flow through to the Thomson family holding companies. Reliance on the newspapers to exploit opportunities in other fields was underlined in 1978 when the family hypothecated shares of Thomson Newspapers to obtain a loan from the Royal Bank of Canada to support exploration for oil in the North Sea. Another example is the family reducing its bank debt arising from the 1979 purchase of the Hudson's Bay Company through the sale in 1983 of some of its shares in its separate holding companies for ITOL (Thomson Equitable Corporation) and Thomson Newspapers (the Woodbridge Company).

ITOL is run on a loose, decentralized management system, allowing divisional executives extensive freedom. Each company retains its own name and board of directors. ITOL's United Kingdom office has only a staff of seventy, including cleaners, cooks and drivers. The Toronto office has just four employees, and New York, nine; in both cases, most of the employees are accountants. "The ultimate horror is the bureaucracy of modern industry," Brunton says. "We believe in short lines of communication and quick decisions based on carefully thought over homework in defining our objectives and plans."

The decentralization extends to the businesses not being located in one building, even when they are in the same city or put out the same product. For example, one U.K. company, Hamish Hamilton, is near Covent Garden, while Sphere's paperback division is several miles away in the banking and newspaper publishing district, and Thomas Nelson is located about one hour from London at Walton-on-Thames. Nelson's recently departed managing director, John Jermine, had made his office several miles away in Wokingham in the warehouse of Van Nostrand Reinhold Incorporated, which Nelson owns. He said he did this because he lived just four miles away, but his secretary said he decided to do so because it kept him "away from being bothered by trivia." Thomson North Sea Limited has its headquarters about two blocks from Thomson House.

The decentralization is even more extensive in North America. The headquarters of International Thomson Business Press (ITBP) are in a new, three-storey building with wrap-around views of the tree-lined grounds in Radnor, Pennsylvania, located just north of Philadelphia's monied Main Line residential district. ITBP is just one street from the headquarters of the Chilton Company, the publishing company where ITBP president Richard Groves worked previously. The North American book companies are in New York, Boston, Chicago and San Francisco. One of them, Warren, Gorham & Lamont, had its two-storey head office in the tower of the New York Sheraton Hotel until chairman Theodore Cross retired. Cross used to be general counsel for the Sheraton Corporation, with his office in the hotel, and chose to remain there. The U.S. oil and gas business, Thomson-Monteith Incorporated, is headquartered in Dallas, the home town of president Ed Monteith. The U.S. travel business is in Chicago on Upper Michigan Avenue, across the street from a local landmark, the Wrigley Building, and next door to the *Chicago Tribune*. In Canada, the travel business is headquartered near Pearson Airport (Toronto International Airport until 1983); the book companies—Thomas Nelson and Richard De Boo—in northeast Toronto; and the oil and gas business—Thomson-Jensen Limited—in Calgary.

The contrast in buildings extends to a contrast in personality, reflective of the national character. In the United Kingdom, management is urbanely forthright. In the United States, there is shirt-sleeved amiability. And in Canada, there is enthusiastic frankness at the travel company and uptight caginess at the publishing and oil and gas businesses.

The common characteristic among Thomson executives is their scant knowledge, if any, about the rest of the empire. A quarterly internal magazine, *ITO World*, was started in 1983 because of this ignorance. The glossy magazine, which runs as long as a hundred pages, is stuffed with news items and fact-filled, in-depth feature stories about ITOL, rather than the usual office party and marriage and birth notices found in most house organs. The professional approach reflects the background of the editor, Derek Jewell, formerly a music critic for the *Times*. Even so, executives in each country know little about what is going on in other Thomson businesses in their own country, let alone in other countries. In view of the bad reputation most Thomson newspapers have in North America, the lack of information may have a purpose.

The empire's decentralized style has flourished under Kenneth Thomson, who has encouraged it far more than his father did. "Roy Thomson built the business and knew it intimately, which was possible because while it was large, it was not that complicated, nor internationalized then," Michael Brown says. "He used to say, 'Don't forget that it's my money you're losing.' Kenneth is a very different person in a different time. The business is bigger, more complex, and more internationalized. We have gone into nonnewspaper businesses in the United States under Kenneth and now have big oil and gas, magazine and book-publishing, and travel ventures there. Kenneth is involved in every major decision but likes to delegate heavily. This makes it a lot of fun to work for him. At a certain executive level, you could make the same money at many firms. Self-esteem and the ability to enjoy yourself are just as important."

The delegation of authority is what also makes Brunton happy. "It's terribly important that you understand that the great ability I have here is that I can get on a plane, fly to San Francisco, agree to pay $33 million for Wadsworth, call Kenneth to see if he has any objections, and if not, tell the bank that I want the $33 million in twenty-four hours. Roy and Kenneth have both trusted me and this makes it possible to move speedily. I am sure I could not operate the same way with anybody else."

The loose control has attracted exceptional management, including the retention of former owners of their own companies. They are on a long leash, get high salaries, and have a liberal profit-sharing plan. Senior management is entertained generously at Christmas. There is a luncheon in London for the managers, at which they are presented with a watch or silver spoon or cigarette box from Asprey's on Bond Street. Kenneth Thomson often brings over maple leaf candy from Canada. At night, there is a dinner-dance for the managers and their wives.

There often is a dramatic change in each year's attendance because of the high firing rate at many Thomson companies, especially in the troubled book division. Very generous severance settlements stop fired employees from going to court and save the empire from bad publicity.

One ex-employee is said to have used his severance money to buy a summer home which he called "_____'s Settlement."

The firings or resignations make little impact on the running of the empire because it has a strong backup team trained in a battery of Thomson-devised management courses. Today's in-depth training is a far cry from the "seat of the pants" system the organization's first personnel director, Henry Hawker, found when he joined the company in 1969. Hawker, an ex-soldier and civil servant, instituted what he calls "a fairly sophisticated management personnel setup where none had existed," consisting of in-house training and sending managers to university business courses in London and at Harvard University.

When Hawker retired, he was replaced by Don Rose, whose background is unconventional for a personnel director. Rose originally was a parish priest in Wales before switching to industrial relations. He has developed a unique management-training system tailor-made to groom executives in strategic planning. Unlike regular management training in which executives attend lectures, the Thomson system is pegged to a one-on-one basis between an executive and a lecturer. If, for example, one of the company's rising stars has trouble in making verbal presentations, special tuition in public speaking is provided.

Rose has developed three programs, each geared to a different management level, in conjunction with London-area colleges. The lowest-level course covers general management for workers earmarked for the middle ranks. Each year, the company also selects from its operations around the world twenty-seven employees with the potential to be the manager of an operating division and sends them to Henley Management College in England where emphasis is placed on strategic planning. A further group of twelve people, all of whom are already operating managers within the empire who have been tagged for eventual promotion to the most-senior positions in the company, is sent to Oxford University's Centre for Management Studies. Again, stress is placed on strengthening skills on an individual basis. The participants also are sent to companies such as Shell Oil that have a good track record in long-term planning, to study their approach.

ITOL spends about $300,000 annually on the programs, considerably more than most British companies spend on management development. Selection of participants is based on an annual management audit introduced by Rose, so that the company will have successors ready in the event of promotion, resignation, firing or death. In addition, more management has been needed with the company's expansion internationally. Every person with a supervisory job is audited by his boss, and employees with special potential are singled out for the training programs. Senior management is also audited annually. Michael Brown's performance is evaluated by Brunton, who, in turn, is evaluated by the ITOL board.

The loose control of the Thomson empire, in which managers have tremendous latitude provided (and it is a big "provided"—they make a sizable profit), is a pleasant change for managers used to the reverse. "Thomson preaches and practises decentralization with close to religious fervor," says Robert Ewing, president of Van Nostrand Reinhold. VNR was acquired in 1981 by Thomson as part of its $63-million (U.S.) acquisition of Litton Industries. "VNR had been part of the Litton Educational Publishing Group, which was not a loose bunch of independent companies but a functional group that provided accounting, payroll and warehousing services. At Thomson, we are responsible for providing for ourselves all the services that Litton had at the group level. For example, Litton had an in-house lawyer, so one of my first questions to the Thomson people was about legal services. They told me that there is no Thomson lawyer for all their U.S. companies. 'It's up to you,' they said, which is a favorite expression of theirs. I asked if I should hire a lawyer on a retainer or fee basis and again they said I could make my own decision. I tried once more, facetiously asking if I could hire my neighbor's son who had just graduated from Columbia University and again they said it was up to me. The Thomson people are convinced that centralization breeds bureaucracy and inhibits the entrepreneurial management that they want."

The Thomson system is dramatically opposite to the heavily centralized, formalized, compartmentalized—and equally successful—methods of McGraw-Hill, the American publishing giant. "At McGraw-Hill, I had to get a replacement requisition for a clerk signed by the president," says Daniel McMillan, now head of International Thomson Technology Information (publications about computers, aerospace and electronics). "I left McGraw-Hill to build a business with somebody else's money. I talked with many firms in the United States and overseas and only Thomson had the resources, expertise, and management style I was seeking."

There are some deviations, however, from these glowing testimonials. One such case is Warren, Gorham & Lamont, a New York and Boston publisher of professional and college textbooks, newsletters and journals that Thomson bought in 1980 for $60 million (U.S.). The company was started in 1964 by three brothers: Theodore Cross, who became chairman; Warren, in charge of direct-mail marketing; and Gorham ("Gerry"), with responsibility for personnel and production. Since the firm was bought by ITOL, its sales have grown from $40 million to $60 million, but while the picture seems rosy, there have been some bumpy times. Cross says that Thomson gave "100 percent autonomy, just as they promised, and kept bureaucracy to a minimum."

However, he contradicts himself by saying that Thomson brought in new management in 1982 that diversified the firm "into areas where it didn't work out well." These included medical publishing and a series on Viet Nam, whereas Warren, Gorham traditionally published books on accounting and taxation. The firm also had a brief fling at publishing textbooks, on which profit margins are lower than on professional books because they cannot be sold by subscription like the professional books. Cross says the management professionals were imported because "the expectation normally is that the original entrepreneurs won't retain the same level of interest as when they owned it. My brothers and I assumed a less important role, and the thrust of the company's growth became the responsibility of the professionals." When the diversification cost the firm several million dollars, the Thomson organization shifted or fired the team it had parachuted into Warren, Gorham. Warren, Gorham returned to its original businesses but the Crosses did not regain their power. In 1984 Theodore Cross took early retirement at the age of sixty and his brother Gerry also left. Theodore Cross was replaced by ITOL's handpicked choice, Bob Jachino, who had been president since 1982 and is regarded as being strong in planning and controlling costs.

There is some mutuality of effort in there being one warehouse in the United Kingdom for all the U.K. publishers and another in the United States. However, the book firms are not bound to use a Thomson company for the foreign distribution of their books. VNR's books are sold in Canada through Macmillan of Canada rather than Thomas Nelson. Michael Joseph and Hamish Hamilton are represented in Canada by Collins Publishers, and in the summer of 1983 Sphere left Thomas Nelson in Australia and also moved to Collins. The reason behind not using Thomas Nelson is that it is an educational publisher and the other firms publish general titles. "Collins is the acknowledged leader in mass market paperbacks in Australia and the United Kingdom," says Jack Fleming, president of Thomas Nelson International.

The divisions' autonomy does not extend, however, to a laissez-faire head-office attitude about financial performance. "Head office doesn't make operating decisions, but I am not allowed to say I am just going to break even next year," VNR's Ewing says. Thomson has very high earnings goals. Profits are expected to double in noninflationary terms every five years. Operating profits, on average, are supposed to be equal to at least 20 percent of sales. Profit margins for each company are expected to be at the top end of their industry. The cost cutting done to achieve these profit margins even extended at one time to staff at Thomas Nelson Canada being asked to consider using both sides of the tape in their adding machines.

From the end of October until December 15, each company prepares its budget. Its executives then meet with the financial people responsible for that division and discuss their plans. New products are expected to take up to four years to be profitable and are segregated from established business to allow more exact performance measurement. After a company's plan is approved, it can spend up to $5 million on the unexpected before seeking the board's approval, which often can be obtained with a telephone call.

The divisions say Thomson's goals are realistic, but it is easier for some firms to achieve them than for others. At Warren, Gorham, for example, the target is realistic because Warren, Gorham sells by direct mail, eliminating the need for salesmen and making sales costs lower than if it sold through stores. One book alone can gross $2 million, based on the original book and four supplements a year. Production costs can, therefore, be spread over many books. Because 99 percent of the company's sales are by subscription, advertising is not a significant item as it is with companies selling through bookstores.

For Van Nostrand Reinhold, the task is more difficult. "Thomson gives enormous, exhilarating freedom to run a company but you better run it right," Ewing says. "Their operating profit goal is twice that of Litton. I'd be crazy to say that their goal isn't realistic, but VNR is a different type of operation. We deal in specialized trade books on cooking and crafts, which depend upon bookstores, rather than direct mail, for sales, and we're caught between a rock and a hard place. You have to give substantial discounts to get books into bookstores and all books are returnable. If you give discounts, you have to settle for smaller profit margins than if you're publishing books for professionals who buy through direct mail. To improve our profits we will have to lessen our dependence on bookstores and use mail order more. But we will not necessarily need fewer salesmen because we are marketing more books than we did before, since we are also handling books published by the Thomson-owned Jane's Publishing Company of England and CBI, a technical publisher which was transferred to us from Wadsworth."

The bottom-line philosophy that underlies ITOL dates back to the empire's origins, when it would have crashed without careful controls. As more newspapers were added to the Thomson group (the word "chain" was avoided because of the bad connotation it has with the public), Sidney Chapman developed a "down-to-earth budgeting and accounting system to get results quickly and make comparisons for good costing and budgeting." The system also was geared to omitting the expense of an army of head-office accountants. "We made sure each newspaper's general manager and accountant understood the system and they did the same with department heads. That way only abnormal variations had to be reported to senior management."

Work on budgets started in September, three months ahead of the new fiscal year. The system, which still is in effect, calls for each newspaper to submit a projected year-end report both on revenue and expenditures. The revenue side of the ledger includes: cash on hand; newsprint, ink, type metal, postage, office and janitorial supplies; subscriptions, and local, national, classified, and legal ads; and rent from tenants. The expenditures column, broken down by editorial, press room and composing room, includes property taxes (the Thomson papers generally own, rather than rent, their premises), the power bills, wages, maintenance staff, insurance, donations, production and delivery costs. Most Thomson newspapers, with the exception of its big city dailies, are delivered rather than bought at newsboxes. Editorial expenses are further split into wire service, reporters, photographers, and travel allowances.

Chapman devised further detailed instructions on expenditures reporting. For newsprint, these include the number of rolls inside the plant and in outside storage after the December 31 press run and the size and weight of the rolls; for newsprint ink, the amount remaining in the tanks; for type metal, the weight of each kind in storage; for mailroom supplies, the quantity of twine, baling wire, unopened paste barrels, paper by name of manufacturer, type, size and weight; for office supplies, not individual paper clips and elastics (as legend has it), but containers of pens and carbon paper; and for postage, by denomination in stamps and metered postage. Monthly statements are compared with the paper's forecast and its results a year earlier. Originally, each paper's report was submitted on big ledger sheets; now, it goes into a computer.

While Chapman's system is par for the course in most businesses, it shook the newspaper industry, especially recently purchased Thomson papers, which, under their former owners, generally had poor record-keeping and lurched from one financial crisis to another. Consequently, the system generated harsh criticism that Chapman and his successors regard as unfair. Keeping tab on supplies prevented pilferage of items for resale, Chapman says. "In the early days we had to be tightfisted to survive. Once we were on our feet, that couldn't be said about us. It's an injustice to say we count pencils—that's a myth from way back." However, it is neither myth nor ancient history, as the same practices continue today.

ITOL has financed most of its expansion from internal funding. Between the end of December and the beginning of May, when travel and book-publishing sales are traditionally slow, it gets bank loans if the need arises, although the company's debt-to-equity ratio is consistently kept at or below a low 1:1. The one instance when the company turns to the banks first is for financing its oil and gas ventures, because it prefers to place the risk involved with the banks rather than with itself. ITOL's main bankers are the Royal Bank and Toronto-Dominion in Canada. Out of sentiment, its United Kingdom banker for checking accounts is the Royal Bank of Scotland because it lent Roy Thomson £300,000 to buy the *Scotsman*. Since that bank is not involved in international banking, ITOL uses Barclays, National Westminster, and Lloyds for such deals.

One way the company could raise more money would be to make its various divisions publicly owned. So far that has been ruled out. "When outside interests are involved, there is less control and flexibility," Alan Lewis says. The empire has three investment dealers as advisers. Wood Gundy of Toronto is the financial adviser for Thomson Newspapers' Canadian and American operations. Their association dates back to the 1950s with then chairman Pete Scott ordering Ted Medland, the current chairman, to assist Roy Thomson in his 1953 election campaign for the House of Commons. Medland's job was to ring doorbells on Thomson's behalf. ITOL's financial adviser in North America is the New York firm of Brown Brothers Harriman. Its longtime United Kingdom adviser is S. G. Warburg.

Thomson Newspapers is traded on the Toronto Stock Exchange, and ITOL is traded on both the TSE and London Stock Exchange. Michael Brown says with ITOL now active in the United States, the logical step would be to list it on the New York Stock Exchange. However, this will not be done until at least 1986, after ITOL has settled into the U.S. scene.

In addition to pledging that a company will retain its autonomy, ITOL dangles another carrot before acquisition targets: they can pour more than the usual amount of money set aside by companies for research and development into generating new products. ITOL calls this its "accelerated-development fund" and defines its purpose in its annual report as "releasing any financial constraint on realizing the full, medium and long-term potential of the company." The bulk of the accelerated-development fund is being spent in the United States, ITOL's current base of expansion. From 1981 to 1983, it has doubled annually, from $5 million (U.S.) in 1981 to $11 million in 1982 and $20 million in 1983. In 1984 the expenditure was cut back to 1982 levels as ITOL digested its rapid U.S. growth, but Michael Brown says the company will be ready managerially and financially to resume a big push in 1985.

While many companies have such funds, ITOL is not as pressured for an immediate return because it has one large shareholder—Kenneth Thomson—who can afford to wait for the payoff. "Companies with greater public ownership are under more pressure regarding their bottom line, which can discourage their investing in the future," Alan Lewis says.

The divisions have embraced the concept enthusiastically. "It's exciting and unique for the publishing industry, an incredible opportunity to develop new programs without the normal constraints of having to produce profits, which is virtually impossible in new markets," VNR's Robert Ewing says. VNR's main accelerated-development project is the expansion of Compress, a small computer software programs firm that it inherited from Wadsworth in 1983. VNR plans to expand its product line and hire a full-time editor-in-chief and a marketing director. Although it is budgeted to lose about $250,000 in its initial stages, Compress's expansion has ITOL's full support because it wants to be part of the computer revolution.

Across the country in San Francisco, Wadsworth is also investing its accelerated-development money into new software programs. Wadsworth is ideally located to plug into the latest high-technology products because it is located in California's Silicon Valley, America's high-tech heartland. Wadsworth's chairman, James Leisy, soaks up further knowledge from his next-door neighbor, Gene Amdahl, the founder of Amdahl Incorporated, one of the most successful new challengers to IBM. Leisy says Wadsworth has already spent several million dollars over the last two years on new product development through its Wepco (Wadsworth Electronic Publishing Company) division. He is particularly enthused about "Statpro," which does the type of statistical and mathematical measurements on a microcomputer that used to be done on a big mainframe computer. He expects "Statpro," which sells for $2,000, to eventually make up to $15 million a year.

Wepco highlights the success of the accelerated-development fund and demonstrates the intracompany rivalries that can result. Leisy's goal is to separate Wepco from Wadsworth and make it a separate ITOL division, aiming to make it dominant in the higher-education field. As he envisions it, other ITOL firms producing software programs could co-publish or do joint marketing with Wepco, if they wished. This, however, would be a form of centralization, which ITOL seeks to avoid, and would tread on the ambitions of other software manufacturers. So whether Leisy's grand design emerges intact from boardroom debate remains to be seen.

Although ITOL managers have wide-ranging autonomy, the final decisions still are made by Kenneth Thomson. He may act as a benevolent landlord towards them, but he still is *the* landlord. As the landlord, he controls his empire through the four holding companies of Woodbridge (The Bay and Canadian newspapers), Thomson Equitable Corporation (ITOL), Standard St. Lawrence (Scottish and York Insurance) and Dominion-Consolidated Holdings (trucking). All four have the same executives—Kenneth is chairman; John Tory, president; James Melville, vice-president and secretary; Ian Croft, vice-president and treasurer; and Peter Mills, vice-president with responsibility for legal matters. They are all located on the twenty-fifth floor of the Thomson Building in Toronto.

Melville has been with the Thomsons the longest. Now sixty, he first met Roy Thomson and Sidney Chapman in 1950 when they bought the Fort William, Ontario, newspaper, where Melville worked in the accounting department. In 1960 Chapman asked him to develop an internal auditing division at Thomson Newspapers. He started as a one-person department. "I was involved in the closings of negotiations and the setting up of budgeting and accounting routines at every paper bought between 1960 and 1977 in North America," he says. In 1977 he was promoted to his present position.

Melville occupies the small office that was once Roy Thomson's. On one wall there hangs a pen-and-ink sketch of a broadly smiling Roy, done by a local artist when Roy was on a trip to Nigeria. The portrait was presented to Melville by Kenneth Thomson after his father's death. While some people remember Roy's legendary thriftiness, Melville remembers his thoughtfulness in bringing coins from China for Melville's young daughter after one of his many trips.

In addition to his business role at the holding companies, Melville also acts as a personal financial adviser to Kenneth and Marilyn Thomson and administers the trust funds of those of Roy Thomson's grandchildren who are still under thirty, the age at which Roy's will releases their inheritance to them. Melville helps Kenneth in his purchases of cars and paintings, although he says Kenneth is an expert on the price of works of art. Melville also guides Marilyn Thomson in her stock market investments. Only four of the grandchildren are still under thirty—Ken's three children, and Susan MacNamara, the married daughter of Ken's sister, Audrey. Although it is a formality, Melville approves the invoices for David's art purchases. Susan and her husband own a four hundred–acre horse farm at Cheltenham, Ontario, northwest of Toronto, where they buy and sell jumpers and host a major annual jumping competition.

Six years ago, the administration of the four holding companies was expanded by one person—Ian Croft, formerly the auditor of Thomson Newspapers at its Canadian accounting firm, Thorne Riddell. "We needed someone who was familiar with the company," Melville says. Peter Mills is John Tory's assistant. He has the asset of a legal background in a newspaper environment, having previously worked for FP Publications, and Tory was impressed by his ability during Thomson Newspapers' negotiations to buy FP. Croft and Mills sit in on meetings of the various Thomson companies in what is billed as an unofficial capacity; nevertheless, they obviously have an influential role.

Thus, while senior Thomson executives are sincere when they talk about their autonomy in the Thomson empire, the power really resides with one person—Kenneth Thomson.

Canapress Photo Service

The Thomson family crest, with a Canadian moose and beaver and the motto *Never a Backward Step*.

Author

The first step: a radio station above North Bay, Ontario's Capitol Theatre.
The *Timmins Daily Press*, first link in the newspaper chain.

Author

Canapress Photo Service

The Edinburgh home of *The Scotsman*, founded in 1817 and purchased by Thomson in 1953.

Roy Thomson outside his boyhood home in downtown Toronto.

Canapress Photo Service

Canapress Photo Service

Lord Thomson of Fleet, his daughter, Mrs. C.E. Campbell, and son Kenneth, with the regalia of a Knight Grand Cross of the Order of the British Empire.

Press nameplates decorated a wall in Thomson's Toronto headquarters.

Canapress Photo Service

Canapress Photo Service

Thomson with his grandchildren, including David
(front left) and Lynne (front right).

Ken Thomson with sons
Peter and David at the gala
opening of Toronto's Roy
Thomson Hall.

Canapress Photo Service

John Reeves

Ken Thomson in his office suite's Krieghoff Gallery.

Marilyn Thomson and daughter Lynne.

Canapress Photo Service

John Reeves

Chief lieutenants John Tory (above), Gordon Brunton (below left) and Michael Brown (below right).

Financial Post

Financial Post

Author

Bernard Suttil

Author

Sidney Chapman

Richard Groves

Author

James Evans

Author

James Coltart

John Reeves

Donald McGivern

John Reeves

Ken Thomson's Rosedale mansion in Toronto (above) and his London residence in Kensington Palace Gardens (below left). Thomson House, London (below right).

Author

Author

III

BATTLES WITHIN THE EMPIRE

7

THE BOOK WARS

ROBERT E. LEE and the Confederate Army had problems at Gettysburg during the U.S. Civil War, Napoleon made a disastrous mistake when he marched to Moscow, and the Thomson empire has had a wretched time with its United Kingdom book companies, where the power politics and financial problems have lasted longer than in any other Thomson division. There is a surface lull as the companies enter the mid-1980s, but it may be the lull before, rather than after, a storm.

Two decades after Roy Thomson diversified from newspaper into book publishing, most of the book division is finally profitable, although it is far from a major player in British book publishing. At most, Thomson is estimated to have 3 percent of the U.K. book market, and the division's leading publisher, Michael Joseph, ranks only twenty-seventh in sales among the U.K. book firms. The book companies' combined revenue and profit are well under 1 percent of what ITOL makes. Industry observers say the division is under the gun to shape up because Brunton's heir apparent, Michael Brown, lacks Brunton's publishing background and therefore would not be as inclined to retain borderline book firms.

The wonder of the book division is how so many bright, talented people could botch things up so much that financial losses, rather than profits, were the norm for years for many of the companies. Only an empire the size of Thomson's could have survived and endured such a deluge of red ink. The decentralization, of which the empire is very proud and which has worked well in other divisions and in the United States, was part of the problem, causing a lack of cohesiveness among the book companies and fierce cries of loss of independence when head office sought consolidation of warehousing to reduce expenses. In addition, personality conflicts raged within companies, between companies, and between the companies and head office. The financial losses and bickering led to corporate bloodletting, with heads rolling almost as fast as during the French Revolution. The worst blood bath was at Sphere, which had nine managing directors between 1974 and 1984.

Says one of the many former Thomson book executives, who now heads another major book firm: "It was a corporate jungle at Thomson's. There were too many highly paid people with not enough work to do and too much time for scheming. It was a highly political, very emotional atmosphere." Not surprisingly, Brunton prefers to view the revolving-door management changes more blandly. "You have to accept in life that sometimes you don't have the right management people in-house."

The upshot of the financial losses is that today many of the senior executives at the book companies are accountants, including the heads of Sphere and TBL Book Service Limited. The reasoning behind these appointments is understandable, but usually book companies are headed by people with strong marketing backgrounds.

The Thomson empire's U.K. book companies are Michael Joseph and Hamish Hamilton (both general trade publishers), Rainbird Publishing Group (illustrated books), Sphere (paperbacks) and Thomas Nelson (educational). Jane's, the world's leading publisher of military reference books, was acquired by ITOL in 1980. Of the older members of the Thomson book companies, only Michael Joseph has an unblemished record of steady profits. Thomas Nelson and Rainbird had losses during the 1970s, Hamish Hamilton is back in the black after several unprofitable years, and Sphere has had a dismal performance record, with constant losses from its inception in 1969 all the way through to 1981 when it finally turned a profit. TBL Book Service has had losses since its establishment in 1978.

Book publishing was the first stage in the empire's diversification program, launched in 1961, under the guidance of the newly hired Gordon Brunton, to reduce the empire's dependence on newspaper publishing. Brunton was concerned that revenue from the newspapers could be hurt by the decline in advertising caused by economic downturns and government legislation restricting acquisition of newspapers, and decided that the most clearly related areas for expansion were magazines and books. It was a logical decision, but neither field turned out to be as good as it looked in theory.

Thomson moved into both businesses in 1961 when it bought Illustrated London News, publisher of a magazine of that name as well as of *Tatler*, and owner of Michael Joseph.

Founded in 1935, Michael Joseph is a well-regarded middlebrow publisher. In what was an omen of the troubles ahead for Thomson in book publishing, the three senior executives of Michael Joseph resigned as soon as the acquisition was finalized. They did not believe a publishing company should be just one of many parts of an international conglomerate, and they also had a poor opinion of Roy Thomson's brashness. One of the directors, Peter Hebdon, however, rejoined the company as its managing director, largely due to the persuasion of Michael Joseph's widow, Anthea, who had become chairman on her husband's death. Hebdon ran the company until 1970 when he died at the Copenhagen airport on his way back from a gruelling business trip to Australia.

Michael Joseph is the only Thomson company on whose board Brunton still sits, which he says he does out of sentiment because the company did not collapse in the wake of the three executives' resignations. Rather, it became the crown jewel among the Thomson book firms, with such best-selling authors in its stable as mystery writer Dick Francis and veterinarian James Herriot. After Hebdon's death, Edmund Fisher, who had started his career at Rainbird's in 1963 at the age of twenty-two, was handpicked by Brunton to run Michael Joseph. "It was like taking care of a Swiss watch," Fisher says. "We had a superb list of authors, such as Francis and Herriot, who turned out a book a year and, as a result, running the company simply involved keeping things going nicely." In 1975 Fisher was transferred to Sphere, and Michael Joseph experienced its first management problems when Fisher's intended replacement dropped out at the last moment. Deputy managing director Victor Morrison was promoted but resigned in 1977 to do community service work.

The management problems, however, were masked because the company was lucky enough to publish a blockbuster bestseller, *The Country Diary of an Edwardian Lady*, during this period. "The clink of money made us forget about management problems," says a former Michael Joseph executive. The company's rebound was not due to its own inspiration; the book was brought to Michael Joseph by an ex-employee who had already been turned down by four other firms. The book was on the bestseller list for twenty-five months.

Michael Joseph's problem, however, was that it was too dependent on the *Country Diary* and James Herriot's annual books. The company derived close to half its revenue from these two sources, but the *Diary* was a one-time phenomenon and Herriot has not written a new book since 1981, forcing Michael Joseph to issue collections of his stories instead. Managing director Alan Brooke now faces the challenge of finding more mammoth bestsellers and lessening the firm's reliance on just a few authors.

While Michael Joseph treads the middle of the road, Hamish Hamilton is more of a highbrow publisher, although it also puts out Gothic romances and actors' memoirs. Its authors include Nancy Mitford, spy novelist Ken Follett, David Niven, Albert Camus and Jean-Paul Sartre. Other distinctions between the two firms are that Hamish Hamilton publishes children's books, more-serious fiction, and Africana, whereas Michael Joseph has no children's books, does more gardening, cooking and crafts titles, and puts out sports books under its Pelham imprint, which Hamish Hamilton does not.

Hamish Hamilton's two most prominent authors are Prince Charles and Prince Philip. Charles wrote a children's book, *Old Man of Lochnagar*, which sold 175,000 copies in 1982, one of the firm's all-time bestsellers. The illustrations were done by the president of the Royal Academy of Art, and the royalties went to charity. Hamish Hamilton staff never dealt directly with the prince during the editorial process, but worked through his private secretary. Prince Philip's book is a collection of his essays and speeches, and all royalties go to him.

The firm's leading woman author is Susan Howatch, whose Gothic romances consistently top the bestseller lists. She was signed by the firm as a gamble, with her first novel being read by an editor during a trip to the U.S. where the writer then lived. "The manuscript was so thick, the editor thought the small plane he was in would collapse," jokes Christopher Sinclair-Stevenson, Hamish Hamilton's current managing director. Tall, lean, and elegant in manner, he has been with the firm since 1961, starting as an editor.

Hamish Hamilton was founded in 1931 by Hamish "Jamie" Hamilton, a medical and then law student who opted for publishing. Now eighty-four, Hamilton retired in 1975 and lives in Italy (his second wife is an Italian countess), but he retains an association with the firm as its president. This title is rarely used in U.K. business, with the "managing director" label more usual, but ITOL suggested that Hamilton accept the title "as a special tribute to him," says Sinclair-Stevenson.

Hamish Hamilton is a phenomenon among the Thomson book firms because it alone has escaped management turmoil. "It was run by the founder for a long time and that imposes stability," Sinclair-Stevenson says. "The editorial, production and design staff has been basically the same since I started over twenty-three years ago. Although sales and promotion staff have a habit in this industry of moving around, we have had only three sales directors since 1961."

Since both Hamish Hamilton and Michael Joseph publish general trade books, ITOL has toyed with the idea of merging them, which would mean they would have the same sales representatives rather than separate teams. This would save money, since most of the 3,000 bookshops in England are individually owned, compared to the big chain operations in North America. "Bookshops are traditionally what people do in the U.K. when they retire, and the shops generally are not that efficient, nor do they sell many books," says Michael Geare, editor of the *Bookseller*, the industry's trade magazine.

The temptation, therefore, is for book publishers to send sales people out with several lists. A merger of Michael Joseph and Hamish Hamilton would make such consolidation possible, but neither firm wants an amalgamation. In 1980, the last time it was proposed by Thomson head office, the boards of both companies threatened to resign.

Sinclair-Stevenson remains adamantly opposed: "A merger would destroy our individuality, and individuality is of paramount importance in book publishing." Book industry analysts also say a merger would not necessarily be beneficial. "Very often it doesn't work when sales people represent several lists, because the law of diminishing interest on the part of the booksellers comes into effect as they go through list after list," says Michael Geare.

While Hamish Hamilton and Michael Joseph both retain ties with the founder, Rainbird Publishing Group has severed its connection with the founding family. Patriarch George Rainbird has no contact with present management and does not even receive complimentary copies of Rainbird's new books. His son, Michael, who became managing director in 1977, was forced to resign in 1980 by a decision to which his father was a party, causing a family rift. Michael Rainbird used his severance money to start a rival company, taking some of Rainbird's staff with him.

Self-taught, cultured, and a wine connoisseur, George Rainbird left school when he was fourteen. In 1951, with about £500, he started his publishing house, specializing in illustrated books. Rainbird is what is known in book publishing as a "packager"—he would sell the idea for a book to both domestic and foreign publishers, who would then distribute it. In the United Kingdom, Rainbird was the first international publisher to negotiate simultaneous domestic and foreign publication. One of his most successful books was *The Concise British Flora in Colour*, written by Keble Martin, a country minister, at the age of eighty-five. The book has sold more than one million copies, but it was initially a hard sell for Rainbird. It was also an unexpected windfall for Martin, whose work had previously been a labor of love but not of income.

"Martin was a botanist, horticulturist and artist who had the idea of painting more than 1,400 English species of flora on exactly one hundred pages," Rainbird says. "He went to seven publishers, all of whom were horrified at the expense of a hundred color plates. He was ready to give up, but he had a formidable daughter-in-law. Prince Philip had been sounding off on the importance of country holidays, and so she wrote him about the book and enclosed some sample plates. Philip sent it to another publisher who gave it to a friend of mine who gave it to me. I showed it to the head librarian of a natural history museum, who said it was one of the greatest things that had ever happened in botany. So I spoke to Peter Hebdon at Michael Joseph, who knew little about botany but agreed to print 50,000 copies. When I went to Martin to tell him the good news, he greeted me in his Sunday best and before I could talk, he immediately said he had no money and could put nothing into any publishing venture. I told him instead that we wanted to pay him a £2,500 advance."

There was a happy ending for everyone. Martin married his house-keeper and lived until he was ninety-one, with the royalties pouring in from his book, and Rainbird's persistence and faith provided his company with a nest egg—the book has never gone out of print and provides a steady, reliable flow of revenue.

In 1965, when Rainbird was sixty, he decided to sell his company to the Thomson Organisation "on condition that Roy Thomson—the big chief—promised I would be left alone to run the business as I always had. Roy said not to worry about that, but then he looked over his glasses and said in saltier language than I'm using, 'Of course, if you mess up, I'll have to step in,' but he never did."

In 1970 Rainbird was asked to join the board of Thomson Publications, the newly created group management superstructure for the book and magazine divisions. Rainbird's soon began a descent into a maelstrom of power politics and ill-fated new publishing lines that resulted in losses or, at best, razor-thin profits. His first successor, Edward Young, was formerly a production designer at Penguin paperbacks, where he is credited with designing that firm's well-known trademark of an overweight penguin. Highly regarded, Young retired in 1973 and the management shakeup began. He was replaced by David Herbert, formerly the editorial director. Herbert lasted until 1977 when he was sacked because of Rainbird's poor financial performance, including a 50 percent drop in revenue between 1975 and 1976. Herbert organized his farewell party and left to start his own publishing house.

The next managing director was Michael Rainbird, who had joined his father's business in 1972, at the age of thirty-two, after working at Viking Press. He pushed the company to its highest-ever revenues, but the success was short-lived because Rainbird's embarked on an ill-timed new venture of publishing cheaper books for the U.S. market. The suggestion for the new line of books came from Bryan Llewelyn, then head of Thomson Publications, as a counterblow to the just-started and already hugely successful Octopus Press, which was relying on sales in the U.S. for much of its business. The new line was called Albany Books because George Rainbird lives at Albany House near Piccadilly Circus, where Byron once had a flat. To cut production costs, the books were printed in Hong Kong. Initially, sales were strong, but they dried up when the advantageous exchange rate between the U.S. dollar and British pound ended. In one year alone, the project lost £300,000.

At the same time, Rainbird's was embroiled in staff battles, with sales directors and board members constantly changing. There was also a power struggle between Rainbird and Michael O'Mara, an American who was appointed editorial director at the suggestion of Robin Denniston, then in charge of the book division. Denniston says he "didn't realize when I hired O'Mara" that a clash would result but that "you can't have two people at the top." O'Mara won but left Rainbird's in 1983, just three years after Michael Rainbird was ousted.

The infighting at Rainbird's was a mere fistfight, though, compared with the wars at Sphere. The only U.K. book company in the empire that was created, rather than acquired, by Thomson's, Sphere was launched in 1966. It was a commonsense move in view of the large business in paperbacks done by the more than 15,000 confectionery, tobacco and news agencies in the U.K. Given this ready-made market, Sphere should have been a smash success. Instead, it just smashed. Every year there was a different managing director.

The players changed but the problems remained. "Thomson's thought if they put a lot of money into Sphere, they could buy their way into the market. But conversely, Sphere ate up cash, largely because it could not get the cooperation of its hardback sister companies to give it the paperback rights," says Desmond Clarke, who worked at Sphere and TBL in the 1970s before becoming head of the book-publishing industry's Book Marketing Council. Much of the trouble was due to Sphere's being a latecomer in paperback publishing. "By the time they entered, there were already several established firms that had most of the floor space and Sphere never really overcame this," Geare says.

Edmund Fisher, then safely ensconced in the security of the smoothly running, money-making Michael Joseph, was confident he could lick Sphere's problems, an accomplishment that would have made his already fast rise at Thomson's even speedier. While other Sphere managing directors wished they were any place else, Fisher asked for the job in 1975 when he was only thirty-two. He says he inherited a snakepit: "Sphere had never made a profit, it was demoralized, and it was riddled with debt. It had accumulated a debt of £2 million in just nine years in business and had losses of between £200,000 and £300,000 annually. A hardback publisher can make money from the publication of only ten books but a paperback publisher must have high volume and to have that he must have the big-selling writers."

Fisher was faced with the problem that Thomson's two biggest-selling authors—Dick Francis and James Herriot—were both published in paperback by Pan. He rammed through an edict that all Thomson hardback authors be published by Sphere, but Francis and Herriot preferred to stay with Pan, with its proven track record, even though Fisher offered them better royalty arrangements. Fisher was successful, however, in signing up two other bestselling authors: adventure writer Clive Cussler and romance writer Danielle Steel. He also got the paperback rights for *Star Wars* and *Majesty* (about the British Royal Family), both of which were big successes.

Fisher cracked down on Sphere's production and distribution divisions, eliminating about thirty jobs. He cut fat wherever possible, including pensioning one of the two head-office letter delivery men because he felt one was enough. He fired the editorial, sales and financial managers, too. Cleve Vine, formerly company secretary of the U.K. operations of Walter Kidde, an international conglomerate, was hired as the new financial controller to clean up Sphere's haphazard bookkeeping. "Previously, monthly results were often mixed together, making it impossible to determine if profits were being made," he says. Area sales managers were removed in places where Fisher believed sales representatives alone were sufficient. The amount of time between printing and distributing books was decreased to the point where studies showed Sphere no longer ranked fiftieth out of sixty hardcover and softcover firms in speed, but instead climbed to sixth. By 1980, Fisher says the surgery had resulted in Sphere's moving from below tenth place among the U.K.'s fifteen paperback firms up to number five.

While Fisher broadened Sphere's publishing list, its mainstay has always been a titillating series called the *Confessions of (a Window Cleaner, a Taxi Driver*, etc.), featuring a big-bosomed, nearly topless girl on the cover. Its continued publication is curious, especially as Fisher says that Roy Thomson did not want the publication "of dirty books or books about gambling and we respected that."

In view of Sphere's picking up during Fisher's tenure, the logical question is why he is no longer there or in a more senior position at Thomson's. There appear to be a number of factors. Fisher is bright and can be charming, but according to those who knew him at Sphere, he could also be "very abrasive, rude and profane." Certainly, his better side was not brought out by Bryan Llewelyn, who became managing director of Thomson Publications in 1977. They constantly clashed over Llewelyn's centralization plans for the book divisions, with the dispute reaching a head when Llewelyn took over Sphere's warehouse as the central warehouse for all the book companies, a move Fisher describes as "irrational rationalization." Sphere also had problems of overstocking, and although its revenue nearly tripled between 1975 and 1980, its losses in 1980 were the highest in six years.

In any event, Fisher was out in 1979, going to Robert Maxwell's British Printing & Communications Corporation to head its paperback division—Futura—and Francis Bennett was in. Bennett had just as suddenly left his position as managing director of the publishing house of W. H. Allen, which, like Sphere, had been losing money. It was only profitable in one year between 1976 and 1979. Bennett was managing director at Sphere for only half a year, stepping up to become Sphere's chairman and then head of all U.K. trade book divisions. His successor was then thirty-four-year-old Michael Goldsmith, an accountant with training in computers.

Even the venerable, 204-year-old educational publishing firm of Thomas Nelson & Sons, acquired in 1962, has had its share of fireworks. Its main problem was that, at Gordon Brunton's suggestion, it diversified away from school books, its traditional strength, and expanded its list of trade books, which entail greater marketing and distribution costs than educational books. It was a costly mistake, resulting in both substantial losses and quarrels between Nelson management, which had fought the change, and head office. But while Brunton made the error in judgment, it was the Nelson executives opposing him who ended up leaving.

Nelson's problems were Robin Denniston's top priority when he was made head of the book division in 1975. He selected two accountants as the repair team—Jack Fleming, president of Thomas Nelson Canada, and John Jermine, financial director of Nelson in the U.K. and formerly an accountant at several of the Thomson newspapers in the U.K. Denniston regarded Fleming as an ideal choice because he had just finished overhauling Nelson Canada. Fleming, now fifty-three, had chosen publishing, rather than accounting, as a career because he "realized I preferred people and things to numbers, which I found boring."

He became president of Nelson Canada in 1971 at a time when the company was overextended. "It had a cash problem from overspending on development, and the Thomson Organisation could not bail it out because it was then fully extended in terms of its own borrowings," he says. Fleming's solution was to sell Nelson's headquarters and then lease back the building. The surplus money, after rent, was used to pay off debts and for new products. In addition, Fleming hired a new financial director and expanded the editorial staff. By 1980 Nelson Canada had sufficiently recovered to build and own new quarters.

At Denniston's request, Fleming moved to the U.K. to steer Nelson U.K. back on course, saying he would stay three years, although he says no time limit had been placed for fixing the firm. The repair work was actually done in two years, but Fleming stayed for four, serving briefly as head of the whole book division, before returning to Toronto because his family was lonesome for Canada. He now runs Nelson's international operations from his Toronto office, reporting to Michael Brown in New York. Despite his youth, Jermine, who was twenty-eight in 1974, was made Fleming's assistant because of his background as a receivership manager at a major accounting firm and his management of his family's business.

The two men walked into a highly disrupted company. Most of the senior executives had left, the firm had lost £500,000 in its 1973–74 fiscal year, and money was being soaked up by the unprofitable trade division. Nelson was also paying rent for executive offices in London as well as for administrative and warehouse offices in Sunbury-on-Thames in Middlesex County, about fifteen miles west of London. Fleming's first step was to eliminate the extras. Sixty jobs were wiped out, the London office was closed, and its executives were transferred to Sunbury to an upper storey added in less than three months' time. The publishing line was pared back to educational books, and the trade books remaindered. The educational publishing program was carefully examined for winners and losers and then rejigged to concentrate on the high-growth subjects of mathematics, science and languages.

Before 1974 Nelson had no reading or math scheme in its primary

THE BOOK WARS 99

school list. In the secondary list, one or two books did well but the rest were peripheral titles that sold few copies. The company had eight divisions—primary, secondary, tests, Caribbean market, African market, English-language teaching, university and college—and the new management decided to concentrate on the most attractive, which were primary, secondary, and English-language teaching. While Nelson was not a pioneer in English-language teaching, the market has huge potential. At any one time, it has been estimated that 200 million people are starting to learn English as a second language. In China alone, 10 million people listen to a British Broadcasting Corporation program every week.

In 1975 Nelson introduced a five-year publishing program for each line. Its concept of forward planning was adopted by ITOL in 1980. In its primary list, Fleming and Jermine developed reading and mathematics schemes, and in the secondary list, they concentrated on those areas, such as English, French and physics, that had the largest number of pupils taking exams. Fleming and Jermine also decided that Nelson would only publish books that a whole class would use, instead of four-color library reference books and dictionaries, because these are individual, rather than classroom, purchases, making it hard to recoup their high cost of production.

The same thorough overhaul was done in the marketing division, with the U.K. sales team tripled in size to twenty-five people and an equal number hired to pursue overseas sales, which Fleming and Jermine had tabbed as a promising market. In the U.K., Nelson deliberately hired ex-teachers as sales people in the expectation that schools might buy more from them because of their background. To compete with other educational publishers, Nelson upgraded its production quality, hiring a graphic research firm to determine how many words there should be on a page, type size, and page size. An in-house photography studio was built and company photographers hired to build up a catalogue of pictures, rather than continue to use photo library resources.

In late 1983, with the overhaul of Nelson completed, Jermine left and was replaced by Timothy Sherwen, formerly the U.K. publishing director for the company. Sherwen is one of the more colorful people to head a Thomson book firm. His background includes the study of history and archaeology, a stint in the Royal Navy teaching English in France, selling agricultural and chemical products, freelance journalism, and ownership of a small educational publisher, his last stop before joining Nelson.

While Thomas Nelson's U.K. and Canadian operations have

dropped their general publishing program in favor of concentrating on educational books, the company's Australian division is a hybrid, with the result that managing director Barney Rivers is caught in a power struggle between the two sides on which he relies. That he is adept at walking this tightrope is evidenced by his now having held his position for over six years, a long time for a Thomson book company managing director.

Thomas Nelson Australia derives 65 percent of its revenue from trade books published by Hamish Hamilton, Michael Joseph and Sphere, yet Rivers reports to Jack Fleming and through him to Michael Brown, while Hamish Hamilton, Michael Joseph and Sphere managing directors report to Francis Bennett and through him to David Cole. But according to industry insiders, Cole and Brown do not get on well, and Cole had also wanted Gordon Brunton's position. Now that Brown has won, it remains to be seen whether Thomas Nelson Australia will be made into purely an educational publisher like its Canadian and U.K. sister companies.

The troubles at older Thomson book companies, such as Thomas Nelson, apparently did not provide the type of trial-and-error experience needed to avoid problems at the youngest in the family, TBL Book Service, the division's five-year-old centralized warehousing operation. TBL is a corporate version of the old movie musical comedies in which Judy Garland and Mickey Rooney played youngsters who decided on the spur of the moment to stage a show and the next day are in a Busby Berkeley extravaganza. Thomson executives similarly decided they wanted a centralized warehouse in existence almost overnight but instead of the instant, easy success that Judy and Mickey had, they found themselves in a classic case of Murphy's Law—everything that can go wrong, will. But, as in the movies, TBL's backstage problems were solved just before its opening and it was launched right on schedule.

The assignment to set up TBL Book Service was handed to Michael Goldsmith, then financial director at Hamish Hamilton. Goldsmith hired Desmond Clarke, who had submitted a paper on centralized distribution to the Thomson organization in 1977. "Other companies would have had a series of consultants' reports, two years planning, and three years setting it up, but Thomson's decided they wanted the whole thing done in eighteen months because the pace would be so fast the various book companies wouldn't have time to scream," Clarke says.

The book companies were likely to scream because the centralized system would strip them of their responsibilities for their own distribution, order processing, cash collection, statistical records, and reporting system. Each company made the most of its autonomy and performed these functions differently from its sister firms, a nightmare arrangement to systems analysts like Clarke and Goldsmith. "For example, Hamish Hamilton contracted out most of this work and had a small, inefficient warehouse in London, which hindered expansion," Goldsmith says. "Michael Joseph subcontracted both its computer and warehouse services, while Sphere did its own distribution. The purpose of TBL was to control our own destiny as publishers and establish a fast, efficient distribution system."

The only in-house warehouse that was large enough was Sphere's, located thirty-five miles from London in Camberley, down the road from Sandhurst Military Academy. The location had other advantages, too: the unions were not as belligerent as in London; there was good road transportation into London; and W. H. Smith, the U.K.'s largest bookstore chain, was located nearby.

Clarke and Goldsmith got off to an inauspicious start. "There were no offices, no computer operations, no staff, only a small filing cabinet, and a shell of a building," Clarke says. "Our first purchase was a kettle for making coffee." The two men found themselves drinking lots of coffee to keep awake during sixteen-hour days in order to meet an accelerated schedule. The original plan was to bring one company's books at a time into the warehouse, starting with Sphere's. But that was thrown out of whack when the warehouse that stored Michael Joseph's and Hamish Hamilton's books shut down, necessitating bringing in their books as well as Sphere's when the warehouse was still being reconstructed.

That was just the beginning of the difficulties. The temporary computer system wiped out a month's record of invoices; the computer and its programming were made obsolete by an increase in the volume of books; the warehouse manager and his deputy quit on the same day; and then a fire, set by an arsonist in the Sphere warehouse who pushed a burning rag under a door, destroyed close to seven million paperbacks (90 percent of the inventory). The fire presented TBL with the twofold problem of getting the books reprinted while not letting the bookstores know the extent of the damage, since that would result in the loss of shelf space in the stores. "Francis Bennett had just become head of Thomson Books and told employees what to say, warning that anybody who contravened this would be fired," Clarke says. "We kept the story out of the book trade press for a month, then downplayed it as a minor fire, and used a number of different printers to prevent rumors."

Despite the setbacks, Clarke and Goldsmith were still expected to meet TBL's start-up date. It was a cliffhanger, with Clarke saying "it wasn't until 1:00 a.m., June 30, that we knew we would be able to produce invoices by computer for the July 1 target date." Head office had placed Clarke and Goldsmith under intense pressure, but they were also well rewarded. Clarke, for instance, was given a week's holiday in Crete at a first-class hotel, as well as a Rover car.

The book wars not only rocked the various companies, but also the head office, with top management locked in ferocious combat. Instead of bringing cohesiveness to the book operations, Thomson Publications, the umbrella company, was the eye of the hurricane. Its first director, George Rainbird, was gifted in creating and selling ideas for books but not as interested in bookkeeping and administration. He ran the companies with a very loose hand—too loose, according to industry observers, because all the book companies encountered financial difficulties and huge turnovers in senior executives who lost out in the power struggles.

Rainbird's position was also weakened by his announcing and then withdrawing his resignation several times until his irreversible departure in 1974 at the age of sixty-nine. His previous reversals sparked derisive comment in the press. Typical of this was the *Spectator*'s "Bookbuyer's Bookend" column of 9 November 1974, just before Rainbird's final resignation:

> Bright men came and bright men went and Mr. Rainbird seemed to be going on forever. And then came last Thursday. While Fleet Street lunched itself, a press release of great moment arrived post-haste from Mr. Rainbird's office. The news was big, would obviously have wide repercussions, would tell the world that. . . . But no. Within four hours Mr. Rainbird's office was telephoning round to inform everyone that Mr. Rainbird had changed his mind, that the press release was inoperative, and that its content was not to be printed.

A week later, the press release was re-released, announcing that Rainbird would be succeeded by Robin Denniston, deputy chairman at Weidenfelds, another U.K. book publisher. "Life must have been pretty miserable at Weidenfelds," the "Bookend" column wrote about Denniston joining Thomson's, especially as trouble was brewing financially and managerially at all the Thomson book companies. Even Michael Joseph was becoming a problem child to head-office executives, who felt it had become far too independent-minded. "The company was being run by the UDI method—unilateral declaration of independence," Denniston says.

Denniston began whipping the book companies into shape but then encountered his own problems when the person to whom he reported, Geoffrey Parrack, was promoted and replaced by Bryan Llewelyn. Unlike Parrack, who had left the book managers pretty much alone, Llewelyn wanted to be directly involved, suggesting new lines of publishing such as Rainbird's ill-fated Albany series. He also felt it would be logical to split the magazines away from the books, as well as to make the Nelson school books a separate operation from the general trade book companies. This shrank Denniston's jurisdiction, leading to his resignation. "There was a certain logic in his decision, but I was hired to run all the book companies," Denniston says. He left and became academic and general publisher of Oxford University Press.

Today, the book wars have simmered down. However, Thomson Books is still regarded as being far from robust. Lack of cohesiveness and management strength continue to be singled out as the major problems. "They have trouble attracting top management and did not look at management development from within until recently," Desmond Clarke says. He feels they have few people of the calibre of the chairmen of the larger book companies. "Thomson book companies also need more marketing expertise, and they haven't put enough effort into creating the right image. Their key people have never been part of the literati or publishing establishments."

Adds the managing director of one of the largest U.K. publishers: "The Thomson operation is regarded as a conundrum because it has a policy of decentralization with the overall supremos such as Denniston and Bennett having little power, and yet the individual managers lack the fire to lead the companies. Distribution has been centralized, but there has been no parallel attempt to rationalize what the various companies are doing."

It is Bennett's job to ensure that the critics' prophecy of Thomson Books having to make it or else face the last rites does not become self-fulfilling, and he presents an upbeat, expansionary outlook. While letting each house retain its individuality in its publishing list, he is imposing cost-management guidelines and standardized administration to improve the bottom line. Bennett, who has a predilection for flip charts with flow patterns of management organization, says a common mistake of publishers is to expand their publishing list of a line of books, even though only one of those books sold well the previous year. His aim is to change that type of thinking at Thomson's.

"For example, Hamish Hamilton is one company with three lists— general trade for adults, a small lineup of children's books, and Elm Tree, a separate children's division. In 1982 Hamish Hamilton's children's list had a bigger profit margin than Elm Tree's on the strength of one book which was a huge success. The growth principle would therefore seem to call for Hamilton's children's list to grow in 1983, whereas in actuality it would need another major seller to do this. The moment a firm expands its list based merely on last year's results, it goes downward."

Bennett instead advocates keeping the physical size of the total publishing list unchanged by boosting the quantity of books that advance marketing shows will be blockbusters and shrinking the number of weaker books. "We x-ray the market eighteen months from now, so we knew in 1981 that Hamilton's children's list would not make as much money in 1983 as in 1982. As a result, Elm Tree carried the load in 1983. If you are going to work for books, your books should work for you."

At the same time that he is laying down the law on reckless expansion, Bennett is imposing administrative commonalities to reduce costs. The publishers are now buying paper as a group, resulting in discounts for their bulk purchases, and the physical size of books has been pared to fewer formats, thereby reducing the number—and cost—of printing-plate sizes. As of January 1982, TBL began charging each firm for storage pallets, distribution costs, and rush orders rather than absorbing these costs. Bennett says this has provided an incentive to keep inventories slim. As of March 1983, the companies began reporting their results in standardized reports, allowing easier forecasts and comparisons than when each used separate procedures. In July 1983 the export operations of Michael Joseph and Hamish Hamilton were merged, and they now also share the same overseas agencies.

No changes have been made in the type of publishing program at Michael Joseph, Rainbird's, or Hamish Hamilton, but Sphere and Nelson's are both broadening their publishing profiles. Sphere's dormant Abacus imprint has been revitalized as a paperback publisher of high-quality fiction and nonfiction. While such books do not sell in the same quantity as mass market paperbacks, they yield fatter profits because they are priced higher. Sphere also is increasing its output of "instant" books geared to special events. One such book, a spoof of the marriage of Prince Charles and Princess Diana, *Not the Royal Wedding*, sold 550,000 copies in two and a half months.

With industry-wide sales at confectionery, tobacco and news agencies leveling off, Sphere is concentrating increasingly on bookstore sales, at which its Abacus line is targeted, and has enlarged the size of its sales force to the retailers. The old problem of Sphere not getting the paperback rights for Michael Joseph and Hamish Hamilton books is being eliminated by stipulating in contracts with newly signed authors, including established writers like Irving Wallace, that Sphere has first option on its sister firms' hardcover books.

Thomas Nelson, meanwhile, is widening its market by branching into video and computer programming. Its video company, Nelson Filmscan, is the result of a Nelson executive's trip to Japan, where he became aware of the large sales of Japanese video equipment to Europe. He suggested that video could be used to teach English as a second language and that Nelson could make instructional films as tie-ins with its books on that subject. The films' main buyers are Japan, Arabic countries, and Europe. The move into developing computer programs to be used in educating students from primary levels through university followed the British government's decision to provide funds to schools to buy computers. So far, Nelson has spent £500,000 on development of the programs but has yet to make a profit.

TBL is also running more smoothly. To the surprise of many, Cleve Vine, who had been acting managing director at Sphere in between Fisher and Bennett, was appointed managing director of TBL in 1979, while Goldsmith, seemingly the more natural choice in view of his work at TBL in its early days, became the head of Sphere. Vine has concentrated on speeding up every facet of TBL, ranging from distribution to collection of payments and handling of orders.

Distribution time has been sliced from several weeks to several days by switching the transport of books from a publishers' distribution service to a courier company, which Vine found cheaper than if TBL had its own trucks. An improved data-retrieval system has reduced the number of unpaid bills on the due date from 40 percent to 5 percent. In 1983 TBL geared up a telephone ordering system, in which bookstores are linked to TBL's computer terminals and use international book classification numbers to place their order. The improvements have given TBL's order department the capacity to handle up to 600 orders a day. As of summer 1983, bulk palletized stock was consolidated from five warehouses into one, near the main Camberley warehouse.

While the empire's book publishing in the U.K. was founded on acquisitions, Bennett says future growth will be internally generated rather than through purchases. With Thomson Books' profit up almost eightfold in 1983 over 1982, Bennett has bought the division and himself some breathing space. "Thomson's allows people to get on with it, without interference, and has great patience. But it's not soft," he says. Whether the Thomson book wars are over or simply on hold remains to be seen.

CHAPTER

8

THE TRAVEL WARS

WHEN JULIUS CAESAR captured Gaul, it was hailed as a brilliant success, but it took him nearly ten years to achieve victory. It took Thomson Travel almost as long—nine years—before it was securely established. In those years it survived pitched boardroom battles that resulted in its founders being fired or kicked out to pasture, as well as the most brutal price war the United Kingdom's travel industry has ever experienced.

The patience in waiting for Thomson Travel to thrive has paid off; today, it is the U.K.'s largest tour operator, with triple the revenue of its closest competitor. It owns the U.K.'s largest charter airline, with thirty-three planes flying four million passengers a year to fifty destinations, and boasts the latest in computer technology for reservations and travel trends. It has twice as high profits on the same amount of revenue as Thomson's U.K. newspaper, magazine and book-publishing businesses. Its success in the U.K. gave it the funds to enter the U.S. travel market, where, after just four years, it has become one of the top three tour operators.

Twenty years ago, however, the outlook was not rosy for Thomson Travel. The empire's approach was as ad hoc as it had been with its book business, albeit with better results. In both cases, Thomson decided it wanted to be in books and travel and for instant entry it would buy a company—any company—regardless of its stability. It would then play Pygmalion, reconstructing the firm rather than scouting for months for the perfect match. The approach was akin to a person shopping for a car and rather than comparing engine size and miles per gallon, expressing a preference for something blue. In the case of the travel business, Thomson's choice was more limited than with books because there were very few firms available for purchase.

Thomson's elected to diversify into travel because the development costs were low and because travel, like publishing, calls for marketing that is consumer oriented. In addition, the travel industry did not require much technical know-how and operated on a different high-low money-making cycle than newspapers. One of the travel industry's peak periods is the early part of the year when newspaper advertising revenue slumps. Also, the field was open in the 1960s in the U.K., as there were few package tour operators just at a time when more people could afford to travel. England's damp weather was also helpful, Brunton says. "The British climate has always been unpredictable and if the opportunity was available to holiday in the sun in Spain at less cost than watching the rain from a Blackpool boardinghouse, then it seemed a reasonable choice that many people were likely to take."

When Brunton was given the go-ahead for his travel business proposal by Roy Thomson in 1964, he made a beeline for a college chum, Vladimir Raitz, who had founded Horizon Travel in 1949, the U.K.'s first major package tour company. Raitz and Brunton had known each other since they were seventeen; they had attended the London School of Economics together and had lived in the same building. After graduating, they met frequently for lunch and co-owned a not-too-successful racehorse. By 1964 Raitz had built Horizon into one of the U.K.'s largest tour operations, pioneering trips to many European destinations. Horizon's success prompted Brunton to offer to buy it, but Raitz rejected a deal. However, Raitz said he would act as a marriage broker, for a fee he will not disclose, and help Brunton acquire some travel firms.

He lined up two prospects in case one fell through. The first was Skytours, which was about the same size as Horizon, then doing £10 million of business annually. The fallback candidate, if the Skytours deal collapsed, was the much smaller Riviera Travel, which did about £2 to £3 million annually. As it happened, both firms were willing to sell, and both deals were signed on 30 April 1965. "The Skytours negotiations culminated in a meeting with its founder, Ted Langton, Thomson's accountants, Price Waterhouse & Company, and Roy Thomson, who asserted his personality immediately," Raitz recalls. "He told Price Waterhouse's senior partner he didn't know what he was talking about regarding the accounts. Roy believed that. Shortly after

Skytours and Riviera were bought, a third firm, Gaytours of Manchester and Liverpool, owned by Norman Corkhill, was purchased. The combined price for all three came to under £1 million.

Skytours and Riviera, particularly, had colorful founders. Skytours' Langton, now dead, was a self-styled "Captain" and was in his sixties when he sold to Thomson's. He also owned a nightclub called the Blue Angel, where female impersonator Danny La Rue got his start. Langton would come into his office six days a week at 10:30 a.m. and head off to his club around 8:00 p.m. Both his appearance and his personal life, crowded with a wife and a young girl friend, were in disarray. "Cigarette ash dripped over his suit and he was always complaining about his health," Raitz says. "He would get drunk from time to time and have serious rows with his girl friend."

Langton's eccentric private life was matched by equal daring in developing Skytours, where he was in charge of everything, from designing brochures to setting prices. He is credited with developing the U.K. package tour industry as a mass market operation by being the first to prebook and prepurchase hotel accommodation. Skytours' five to ten year contracts, usually with small, new hotels, provided financing for the hotelier, who, in return for the block bookings, was willing to guarantee lower room rates. Langton also introduced the concept of tour operators controlling the prices of their vacations through owning their own airline. He developed this idea because British Airways had nine long-range turbo aircraft mothballed since the airline had switched to 707 jets. Consequently, British Airways was only too pleased to sell five of the turbo planes to Langton at a low price to get rid of them. Having its own charter airline, called Britannia Airways, propelled Skytours into the forefront of the U.K. travel business, with the number of customers quintupling in two years.

Riviera's co-partners were Aubrey Morris, a former taxi driver, and Joe Morrison, an accountant, who according to Raitz were always arguing. (Morrison took his money and departed from Riviera after the Thomson takeover.) While Skytours operated out of London, Manchester and Glasgow, Riviera's business primarily came from the southeast side of London.

The honeymoon was brief between the old and new owners. Within a year, Langton, Morris and Corkhill all briefly held the managing directorship of Thomson Travel and then were booted out. They could not change from being entrepreneurial loners into organization men, running things by computer studies rather than by intuition.

Langton was the first to go, embittered by the realization that he had sold Skytours for too little money. Thomson's had paid him a reputed

£775,000, which he regarded as an enormous sum at the time. But Langton, who used to do his financial figuring on the backs of cigarette packages, had been so flattered by the size of the offer, according to those familiar with the sale, that he did not calculate the value of the assets and goodwill of his company properly. He was extremely upset when Thomson's brought out the first year's results for their new travel business and he realized that the profit generated by his old firm was greater than his sale price.

Langton's fury at Thomson's was matched by Thomson executives' dislike of him. "He was very difficult to deal with because he was autocratic in the way he ran his business and about reporting and budgeting," says Robert Smith, who was then Brunton's executive assistant. Smith has been described as Brunton's "hatchet man" by ex-Thomson travel employees, but he says that while he was involved in the firings of some people, Brunton made the final decisions. Langton was among those who were fired, and his departure was brutally engineered—like something that happens "in a bad novel," according to those who witnessed the action. As they tell it, one Friday night the carpenters removed Langton's files and put new locks on his filing cabinet and door.

Morris was next on the chopping block. His bad fortune was that his inexperience in running a big company was showcased, even more than it might have been normally, by a collapse in the travel market. Prime Minister Harold Wilson had devalued the pound and restricted the amount of money travelers could take abroad. The timing of these restrictions was ghastly for Thomson's because it had just printed its travel brochures and therefore could not adjust its prices. Morris found himself with a disaster on his hands because travelers canceled their trips, leaving Thomson's stuck with expensive long-term hotel commitments and too much airline capacity. At the same time, the Riviera and Skytours factions were warring, each trying to protect themselves, with Morris naturally tilting towards Riviera.

The luckless Morris could not cope with all these difficulties. Unlike Langton, though, he was not fired. Instead, he was reassigned to the Thomson Organisation's long-range planning department, the equivalent of being exiled to Siberia. He was soon joined there by Norman Corkhill, who had lasted as Thomson Travel's managing director for only nine days. Corkhill was later named to the post of chairman of Thomson Travel and, as such, he traveled around the world as the firm's goodwill ambassador until 1979. When Roger Davies became the division's new managing director, Corkhill retired to Majorca.

After Morris and Corkhill passed from the scene, the atmosphere at Thomson Travel became even more turbulent, with the power struggles intensifying and employees not knowing from one day to the next who was in charge, who would be replaced, or if their own jobs were in jeopardy. Corkhill's replacement, for a blink of an eye, was Hilary Scott, an accountant with no experience in travel. According to former Thomson Travel executives, Scott had somewhat less than lukewarm support from Key Thomson Organisation powers, particularly Robert Smith, who although he had no formal position in the travel division, wielded influence because he was Brunton's assistant, and Alan Todd, a former Thomson publishing executive. Whether it was his unfamiliarity with the travel business or the power politics, Scott soon was moved out to long-range planning, joining his banished predecessors, Morris and Corkhill, in what was fast becoming the graveyard of Thomson Travel managing directors.

Scott was replaced by Alan Todd, who did not last long either. His fatal mistake, according to employees of the period, was to produce marketing forecasts that were blacker than the reality so that he could say a year later how well he had made things turn out. "Brunton tore the reports in half and said they were of no use to him," says a witness to that scene. Shortly afterwards, Todd vanished from Thomson Travel's executive ranks, resurfacing as the head of the South African operations of the British conglomerate Slater Walker. In 1970 Smith became head of Slater Walker's Canadian operations (Slater Walker pulled out in 1974 as the controlling shareholder, and the firm was renamed Talcorp in 1976).

By 1970 Thomson Travel was known in the industry more for its whirling turnstile in the executive suite—five managing directors in five years—than for any accomplishments in the industry itself. The one smart decision during this time of chaos was the switch from turbo prop planes to 737 jets, putting Thomson's ahead of its competitors in high-speed aircraft. Then in 1970 the situation began to improve with the appointment of Bryan Llewelyn to the managing directorship. He not only survived in the position but resolved the division's traumas, made it the victor in a bruising price war, and then piloted it to the number one spot in the industry.

Llewelyn's success was due to his merging the package tour and airline sides of the travel business, allowing for a vertical integration by which each fed business into the other. He also applied his experience as marketing director of the Thomson U.K. newspapers to his new job. Just as today's newspaper is dead tomorrow, Llewelyn treated empty airline seats as dead because no money was made from them. He therefore went after volume through low prices and was still able to make money since the overhead costs were the same whether a plane was filled or not. Once the overhead was covered with more passengers, everything surplus was profit. If Thomson's could not fill its aircraft with its own clients, it would charter its aircraft to other airlines.

This vertical integration gave Llewelyn the financial clout to clobber Thomson's major rival, Clarkson's, in a price war lasting from 1970 until 1974, when Clarkson's, and many others, collapsed in the biggest bankruptcy to that date in British history. Bathed in the glory of his turnaround of Thomson Travel, Llewelyn moved on to his downfall at Thomson Publications, having first promoted his handpicked successor in travel, Roger Davies. The package tour business of the company has continued to flourish under Davies, but he also diversified it into direct selling of holidays through two retail chains, which angered travel agents, infuriated at competition from a wholesaler who is the major supplier of package holidays. Thomson's survived the fury because its number one position forces agents to deal with it, but the move may not have been worthwhile, since the results of both retailers are slim.

Davies personifies today's cut-and-dried travel executive who is guided by computer studies on travel trends; he provides a sharp contrast to flamboyant figures like Langton who carried their files in their heads and would have their customers walking in the front door of a hotel as the just-finished carpenters departed through the back.

Short and boyish-looking with a puckish sense of humor, the thirty-nine-year-old Davies is praised by competitors for his shrewdness. At ease in the maneuverings of a big corporation, his career has been one of uninterrupted success and rapid promotion.

After graduating from Exeter University in history, Davies joined the marketing department of J. Lyons & Company, a leading U.K. food manufacturer known especially for its teas and cakes. When Llewelyn hired Lyons's marketing manager, he brought Davies with him. Davies's first job was to produce travel brochures, but eventually he became Llewelyn's assistant. He met his wife, Adele Biss, at Thomson's, where she was a trainee in the travel division. She now owns Biss-Lancaster, a public relations firm whose clients include the Association of British Travel Agents.

Davies launched Thomson Travel's retail business, called Portland Holidays, in 1979, with the first travel departures in 1980. The venture was designed to reduce the company's heavy dependence on independent retailers and compete against a number of Scandinavian direct-sell companies that had entered the U.K. market in 1977, as well as against Martin Rooks, a direct-sell firm bought in 1977 by British Airways. "These firms' business was growing fast, and as the brand leader in the travel industry, we were nervous that this method of distribution would develop to the point where our traditional market was threatened," Davies says.

Direct sell now accounts for 15 percent of package tour sales, and Davies says Portland, with about a 4 percent share, ranks second after Martin Rooks. Nevertheless, he says Portland is unlikely to ever exceed 20 percent of Thomson Travel's business, or 200,000 out of the 1 million holidays sold annually by the parent company, even though customers going to Portland avoid paying the usual 10 percent agent's commission. Portland is still short of that target of 200,000, its 1983 sales totalling 160,000.

Davies says Portland will be unable to enlarge its market share because it offers only a limited choice of holidays compared with the smorgasbord available through mass market retail agents. In addition, about two-thirds of the travel agents who sell Thomson holidays now have access to Thomson's videotext reservation system, making it possible to do more bookings. Travel agents' anger over Portland has not affected business, with Thomson Travel racking up record years since Portland's launch and, with the exception of one year, being annually voted tour operator of the year by the agents. In 1982 Portland started a camping division, offering self-drive holidays to popular campsites in France, where it provides frame tents with a kitchen and three double bedrooms. Incentives are offered to earlybird bookers, with the 1983 premium being a free road atlas of France and six bottles of wine. The concept was a big success, reeling in about one-third of Portland Camping's customers.

It took only one year for Portland to turn a profit, but as its aftertax profits are well below $500,000 (Canadian), travel industry observers say that it is being subsidized by ITOL. "Portland is not selling enough holidays to justify the millions of dollars that have been spent to publicize it in order to build up its mailing list," says BBC travel commentator John Carter.

While Portland caters to consumers, a second Thomson retail travel agency, Lunn Poly, strictly goes after business travelers. For that reason, even though its sales are three and a half times those of Portland, it is not well known by the public. Lunn Poly is the result of a merger between Sir Henry Lunn, a rival to travel mogul Thomas Cook, and the Polytechnic Touring Company. It was acquired in 1972 from the Cunard Group by Thomson Travel. Following its 1984 acquisition of two other U.K. travel agencies, Lunn Poly jumped from fourth to second place in market share. But Davies is quick to admit that it still has under a 5 percent share of the retail travel trade. Its customers include Shell Oil and Barclays Bank.

Davies's pride and joy is Thomson Travel's videotext system, which went into nationwide operation in 1983 after a one-year trial run in the London area. Called TOP (for Thomson Open-line Programme), it cost between £500,000 and £1 million to develop, and Davies boasts that no other U.K. tour operator has as sophisticated a system. TOP has a capacity for booking 1.3 million holidays and offers several alternatives, such as a different hotel or different travel date, if a tour is sold out. Davies says TOP enables handling peak-season bookings in January and February as well as high-volume lunch-hour traffic without hiring extra staff.

Aggressive marketing moves like TOP have become high priority at Thomson Travel, as it is facing increased competition from its rivals, culminating in a Christmas-brochure price war in 1982. The Christmas dogfight was prompted by Davies's recognition that while Thomson Travel is far and away the leader in the U.K. travel industry, it has been losing market share to its lower-priced competitors. Between 1979 and 1982, according to industry surveys, Thomson's sales rose an average of 33 percent, well behind the gain of 50 percent plus by its two closest rivals, Horizon and Intasun. These inroads prompted Thomson Travel to end its twelve-year association with the Leo Burnett advertising agency in 1981 and move its £1.5-million account to J. Walter Thompson.

Despite its revenue being one-seventh that of Thomson Travel, Intasun in particular has been whittling away at the larger firm primarily because Thomson's suffered from what Roy Thomson once described as the Heinz beans problem. According to him, once a product is in the Heinz beans position of market leadership, competitors' main way of wrestling away market share is through lower prices. That is what happened in the U.K. travel industry. Prior to 1982, Thomson's and Horizon would issue their summer brochures first; a few weeks later, the brochures of Intasun and other companies with lower prices would be published. Thomson's likes to get its brochures out in September to get first crack at the up to 50 percent of the traveling public who book early.

In 1981 this custom hurt Thomson's because instead of the usual minor price differences, Intasun brought out brochures with considerably lower prices. Forewarned, as the expression goes, is forearmed, and Thomson's September 1982 printing of its summer 1983 brochures was only one-third the normal quantity. Sure enough, a few weeks later, Intasun brought out its brochure, this time with an even bigger price gap between itself and Thomson's. With Intasun offering prices of up to £30 less (or 7 percent off the regular price), Thomson's was faced with the potential defection of much business, a threat at any time, but especially in 1982 when the travel industry was in a slump.

But Davies says that because it had anticipated this trouble, Thomson's was able to react quickly by getting the remaining two-thirds of its brochures printed, with its prices slashed to meet Intasun's, within two weeks. Rivals, however, paint a less rosy picture. Whereas Davies claims the revised print run cost £300,000, competitors say the real cost was many times higher, including what Thomson's lost by undercutting its original prices, although extra bookings resulting from the lower prices helped it recoup this money. "Their muscle is such that they got a lot of TV coverage making them look bold and dramatic. And their timing just before Christmas was impeccable," the managing director of one rival firm says.

Printing new brochures once is not nearly as expensive as running hotels, and therefore Thomson Travel has dropped all but one of its hotels, a feature of its business since it entered the field in 1965 and acquired Langton's hotels. As of 1983, Thomson Travel owned only one hotel, located in Malta, and leased one in Sicily. It used to own or lease hotels in Spain. Davies says he is pulling out because hotels are too chancy. "A lot of money is tied up in a resort and no resort is popular forever," Davies says. "The hotels we had were inherited from Skytours and were a mixed group, rather than identical in concept. Also, because we offer all price ranges in hotels, our tour business doesn't lend itself to hotels." With the expiration in 1983 of the lease for the Sicilian hotel, the lone survivor is the Maltese hotel, which will remain as a symbol of the old days because it has one nice redeeming feature— it is profitable.

In 1979, as part of the Thomson empire's thrust into the United States, Thomson Travel opened a U.S. branch in Chicago, called Thomson Vacations. It operates independently of the U.K. company, reporting instead to Michael Brown. Like most of the Thomson empire's senior executives, Thomson Vacations' president, Richard Roberts-Miller, is young. The forty-year-old Roberts-Miller, a bespectacled chain-smoker, looks as if the most exciting thing he has ever done is take the Chicago subway. But in reality he is a marketing whiz, credited with introducing Thomson's package tours to Timbuktu, Peking and—his most bizarre idea—Siberia in the winter, basing his suggestions on statistical reports, studies, computer printouts, and questionnaires.

Roberts-Miller began his career at Thomson's doing marketing research for its U.K. newspapers. Next, he was made manager of Thomson's nine-person U.K. head-office research department, covering publishing and travel. As the travel side's work expanded, it was decided in 1973 to set up separate publishing and travel research offices, and Roberts-Miller was placed in charge of the travel section's research. He peppered Thomson tour customers with in-flight questionnaires to measure their reaction to what Thomson's was offering. The company's number of departure points was enlarged to include cities whose runways, while shorter than at Heathrow, were long enough for some Boeing 737 jets.

He also developed programs to increase winter travel, traditionally a slow season in the United Kingdom in contrast to North America. "Rather than wait for the market to move in the direction of winter holidays, we took the lead by switching our destinations to places that are hot in the winter, such as the Canary Islands, and filled up more of our airline seats," he says. Whereas winter traffic to the usual places of Spain and the Mediterranean had totaled 275,000 persons, Roberts-Miller says the added destinations boosted the volume to 350,000 by 1978, the year he was named to head the U.S. operations. The Siberian tour was part of a public relations program to obtain a high profile in the winter by offering an unusual destination each year. When interest in Siberia ebbed (and it was never high), Roberts-Miller substituted a tour to Mongolia.

Not many people really wanted to go to Mongolia in the winter either, but a drive to increase Thomson Travel's ski vacations did much better. Using his questionnaire routine, Roberts-Miller was able to determine what type of resorts skiers liked most. Then, he went after the U.K.'s number one ski tour operator, Ingram's, which specialized in luxury tours for avid skiers. Thomson Travel cut heavily into Ingram's market by charging less for high-class resorts and making up for the low profit margins by high-volume business.

The travel research department also revamped Thomson Travel's summer program, with the changes covering the structure of holiday plans rather than new destinations, as with the winter campaign. Increased emphasis was placed on budget vacations, through offering only some meals or self-catering rather than full board, and on ten-day trips rather than the traditional two-week ones. Roberts-Miller was not just thinking of clients' pocketbooks with these alterations. The adjustments also helped Thomson Travel sign up more people during the summer months than previously, and more people naturally bring in more money.

Thomson's entry into the U.S. travel market in 1979 was its second landing in America, having stubbed its toes in its first attempt in the mid-1970s. At that time, it opened a New York office and sold package tours that fed into the U.K. programs. "It didn't work because destinations that are ideally suited for British clients do not necessarily appeal to Americans," Roberts-Miller says. Nevertheless, with Thomson's market share leveling off in the United Kingdom and high unemployment dampening travel plans, the American market became even more attractive despite Thomson's initial failure there. Europe had also been considered but was ruled out in favor of what was regarded as the more economically and politically stable U.S.

In its second try, Thomson's chose Chicago as the base for its U.S. operations primarily because of two famous trademarks: O'Hare Airport, the busiest in the United States, and the city's windy, harsh winters. "The rotten weather stimulates people to want to go to resorts to which there are lots of scheduled flights," Roberts-Miller says. In addition, Chicago had the requisite economic climate. "It is undersupplied with tour operators, in contrast to New York, and until 1979 had been relatively recession-proof because of its diverse business base."

Its second arrival in the U.S. was inauspicious for Thomson's because it coincided with the onset of the worst recession in decades in the U.S., and the Midwest was harder hit than the rest of the country. In addition, tried-and-true U.K. methods could not be transplanted across the ocean; instead, Thomson's had to adopt American sales techniques to survive. "Travel agents in the U.S. are even more opposed to direct sell by wholesalers, so we are only using travel agents here," Roberts-Miller says. "Americans like more-upscale hotels than Britishers; they don't want meals included, because they like to sample local restaurants; and there are not many charter airline operators, and of those that do exist, many are unreliable or lack financial backing." Instead of starting an American version of Britannia Airways, which would be very costly, Thomson Vacations uses three different airlines.

Thomson's also faced another obstacle that it had not taken into account in its scouting of the U.S. market—deregulation of air fares, which occurred just as Thomson Vacations opened in Chicago. Even though Thomson's is a low-margin, high-volume operator, it was hard for it to compete at the height of the airlines' discount war, in which up to 70 percent of their sales were at bargain prices, resulting from deregulation. To avoid being driven out of a market on which it counts for much of its future, Thomson's shaved its profit margins below their usual levels for its first three years in the U.S. This had two unwelcome results; it aggravated travel agents and kept the company unprofitable until 1984. "They put agents in a peculiar situation by offering last-minute bargains," says an executive at a major Chicago travel agency. "Agents were caught in the middle because they had booked their clients at the full rate, and then, when the clients talked to their friends who booked later, they found they were paying less. This created ill will between the travel agents and Thomson's."

If the aggravation this aroused had resulted in bonanza sales, it might have been worth it for Thomson's, but the expected sales rush did not materialize. The recession plus the price war also held back Thomson Vacations from the sales gains it had projected in its optimism before entering the U.S. market. Although sales did increase substantially, they were disappointing in light of the forecasts. Its first-year sales of 25,000 were 10,000 fewer than predicted; 1981 sales were up 42 percent over 1980, but the target had been 60 percent; and 1982 was up 44 percent compared with a 50 percent goal.

However, 1983 justified Thomson's faith in the U.S. market, with its sales of 120,000 up 100 percent over 1982. Roberts-Miller says that Thomson Vacations has become the largest U.S. client of Holiday Inns and books the most package tour vacationers into Mexico and Jamaica. Its growth in staff reflects this, increasing from 36 in September 1979 to 190 in 1984, including 60 representatives at resorts. A branch network is planned, starting with a Los Angeles office, opened in October 1983, to cover both Los Angeles and San Francisco.

Thomson's original U.S. strategy called for it to grow through acquisitions as well, but two painful purchases convinced the company to rely on internally generated expansion. One of the acquisitions, Arthurs Travel, a Philadelphia agency specializing in incentive and business travel, was to be an American version of Lunn Poly but has been an unprofitable disappointment. Its days, therefore, appear to be numbered. The other, Unitours of Los Angeles, has been split into retail (Unitours) and wholesale (Club Universe) divisions to provide a more rational structure. Nevertheless, it continues to be a problem because its businesses go off on wildly separate tangents. Unitours specializes in beach vacations, and Club Universe in long-distance tours to such places as China, thus precluding any joint operation and consequent lower operating costs.

Even though Thomson Vacations got off to a slower than expected start in the U.S., it moved into Canada in September 1982. Thomson's was obviously confident in the Canadian market because it set up shop when the travel industry was undergoing great uncertainty. Sunflight-Skylark, Canada's largest package tour operator, had collapsed just four months earlier, and on top of that, the recession, which was then lifting in the U.S., was still severe in Canada, resulting in a decline in travel. Thomson Vacations' general manager in Canada, Ronald Dawick, says that despite the inhospitable climate, it was decided to proceed because Thomson's could capitalize on its "stable reputation and having been in business for twenty-seven years."

Although Canadians are even more package tour inclined than Americans, especially for winter sunshine escapes that Americans living in the South do not need, Thomson's had deliberately deferred moving into the Canadian travel scene. "In the 1970s when Thomson Travel began to develop plans to insulate itself from declines in the U.K. economic climate, it sent an investigative team to Canada and the U.S.," Dawick says. "It found that the package tour industry was more mature in Canada, whereas the U.S. market would be easier to enter because it lacked large tour operators."

Outside of Kenneth and David Thomson, Dawick, who is related by marriage to Kenneth's niece Linda, is the only member of the family working at the Thomson empire. He joined Thomson Travel in the U.K. in 1970, immediately after university, and stayed there until 1974 when he and his wife decided to return to Toronto. To prove that he could succeed on ability and not on connections, Dawick left the family business and joined Wardair for six years, setting up the charter airline's package holiday business and becoming sales director in charge of dealing with both tour operators and retail travel agents. Subsequently, he opened a management consultant business specializing in travel, then rejoined Thomson's when it opened its Canadian travel business. Friendly, intelligent, and prematurely gray, Dawick says his "working in senior positions outside the Thomson organization" has prevented any awkwardness stemming from his being chosen to head the Canadian travel operations.

Thomson Vacations has started on a modest scale in Canada, keeping down its costs by tying in with its U.S. parent. Even so, Dawick says the first-year start-up budget exceeded $1 million. Although customers fly nonstop from Toronto, the same resorts are offered to Canadian travelers as to American, which means Thomson's can get better prices from resort operators because it is funneling more people to them. In addition, the Canadian company does not have to hire separate resort representatives as it would have to if it used different hotels. The Chicago office prepares the Canadian brochures, using the same pictures and descriptions as in the American ones, and then sends them to Canada for printing.

Tickets and invoices are prepared in Toronto, but the Chicago accounting staff pays the resorts for both the American and Canadian travel companies. In its first year, the Canadian office, located in Toronto near the airport, did not have reservations clerks. Instead, customers phoning the Thomson Vacations number in the telephone book would actually be dialing the Chicago office. However, Dawick admits that while the cost savings justified this system, it also caused irritation in the early days when Thomson's was particularly anxious to make friends. "Nationalistic Canadian travel agents resented calling the U.S., and if the telephone transmission was bad or the line was busy, they would blame it on having to call Chicago."

In addition to cost sharing, Dawick has kept the company from overextending itself, which has been the downfall of the several Canadian tour operators who have gone bankrupt in recent years. Toronto is the only place where Thomson Vacations has a Canadian office, and so far the company is only going after business in Ontario, with plans to go national on the back burner until Thomson's is well established in the Toronto and other Ontario markets.

Although the Chicago and Toronto divisions share production expenses, they realize that despite the many similarities between Canadians and Americans in their leisure tastes, when it comes to travel, there are profound differences. "It's very difficult trying to sell summer destinations in Canada; instead, Europe or domestic vacations are more popular," Dawick says. "But in Chicago, people are oriented to summer holidays in places like Mexico. The competition is also stiffer in Toronto, where we have a dozen major rivals. Thus, in Chicago we can insist that confirmation be given immediately or we won't book the destination, but in Toronto we have to give a twenty-four-hour option. Even in the U.K., where the market is extremely competitive, tour operators can dictate terms to the retail agents."

Thomson's had an unpleasant surprise when it found out too late that the all-inclusive pricing system it used in the U.K. and the U.S. did not work in Canada. Its all-inclusive prices included taxes, service charges, and gratuities, whereas Canadian tour operators often exclude some or all of these, saying only in fine print that they cost extra. Thus, Thomson's was perceived to be more expensive than its rivals even though it was usually the same and sometimes less.

"For example, in January 1984 we charged $729 to Ross Hall Resort in Jamaica plus $60 service taxes, whereas CP Air charged $699 plus

$97 tax," Dawick says. "Our total of $789 was slightly less than theirs of $796, but their quotation seemed less at first glance. As a result, we're succumbing to the Canadian way of pricing because doing it our usual, all-inclusive way is like pushing water up a hill." Because it found that Canadian travelers' main concern is price, Thomson's has altered its advertising to emphasize price, whereas in its first year, in the wake of the collapse of Sunflight-Skylark, it stressed that it was a stable firm.

In Canada, Thomson Vacations faces a unique situation that its U.S. and U.K. relatives do not encounter: the Hudson's Bay Company and Simpsons Limited, which are also part of the Thomson empire, both have travel agencies in their department stores. "Because we are all ultimately owned by Kenneth Thomson, we were concerned there might be some backlash among other travel agents, so we have gone out of our way to keep our distance from The Bay and Simpsons. We are concentrating instead on the more than one thousand individual travel agents in Ontario," Dawick says.

The competition and the slow travel market limited Thomson's to reaching only two-thirds of the 15,000 sales it had targeted in its first year in Canada. But it was not caught having to pay airlines for empty seats because it was able to sell them to other tour operators. In the 1983–84 season, Dawick expects sales to reach 15,000; nonetheless, he realistically says that in Canada's competitive market the most Thomson's can expect is 20 percent of the package tour business. With about 5 percent now, it has a long way to go to reach that mark.

As it heads into its twentieth year, the Thomson travel business is no longer wracked by the executive warfare of its early years. However, it has another just as potent enemy—cutthroat competition—and it will have to work hard not to lose ground.

IV

THE MEDIA DOMAIN

9

THE NORTH AMERICAN NEWSPAPERS

THE GOOSE THAT LAID the golden egg for the Thomson empire has often been tarred and feathered—but it has never been plucked. Instead, the "goose"—the chain of fifty-two Thomson-owned papers in Canada and eighty-eight in the United States—has become fatter despite withering criticism directed at most of the papers for poor editorial quality, leveled both by the journalism profession and investigative commissions set up by the Canadian government.

Indeed, although it is smarting from receiving the most severe roasting among the chains for poor quality by the 1980–81 Canadian Royal Commission on Newspapers, the Thomson chain is at its most powerful. The $3-million commission lambasted chain ownership, but none of its recommendations, including one calling for the breakup of the Thomson chain, have been implemented. Its proposal for a federal newspaper act limiting the growth of the Thomson and the rival Southam Incorporated chains was first accepted and then killed off by the Trudeau government. The final challenge to the power of the Thomson and other Canadian newspaper chains was broken in late 1983 when Thomson and Southam were acquitted of conspiracy and merger charges laid in connection with their putting an end to competition between them in several cities by closing papers.

Not only are the challenges to its size crushed, but the Thomson chain is financially blue chip and recession-proof. Through fair and foul economic weather, it consistently rings up the highest profit margins among North American newspaper and magazine chains, ranging from 25 percent in boom economic times to 14 percent during the recent recession. Its low point is equal to the highs reached by most other Canadian and U.S. newspaper organizations. Its profit margins surpass those of both Southam, Canada's largest newspaper chain in terms of circulation, and the Gannett chain, the largest in the U.S.

Thomson Newspapers has become big by acting small. It has achieved its record results even though the combined 2.5 million circulation of its 140 North American papers just slightly exceeds the 2 million circulation of the *Wall Street Journal* alone and is half that of *Time* magazine. Moreover, in Canada only twelve of its papers have more than a 20,000 circulation, and in the U.S. only seventeen do. To Thomson executives, small is beautiful. Although most of their papers have small readerships, they are usually the only paper in town, giving them a monopoly on local print advertising. Small also enables them to almost always keep out newspaper unions and thus maintain wages below union levels. The company is not good at handling unions. Only a handful of its North American papers are unionized, and of these the majority have experienced strikes over low wages.

In North America, Thomson looks to the U.S. for its future growth because most of the papers in Canada are already chain-owned. The U.S., however, is more open than the Klondike during the gold rush: out of 9,396 weeklies and dailies, only 3,422 are part of a group. Until 1983, when the *Toronto Sun* (owned by Toronto-based Maclean-Hunter Limited, a magazine and newspaper publisher as well as a cable television operator) bought the *Houston Post*, Thomson was the only Canadian newspaper publisher to have entered the U.S. market. It made an early entry in the 1960s and maintained a very low profile as it snapped up paper after paper. The company's first U.S. manager, Ed Mannion, even made a point of not correcting people who thought he had a Virginian accent in order to allay their fears of a Canadian takeover.

The success of the Thomson North American papers is in stark contrast to the shaky financial status of its United Kingdom newspapers, battered by the recession that triggered a drastic decline in classified advertising—their financial backbone.

While Thomson no longer owns a national paper in the U.K., in Canada it has poured millions of dollars into developing the prestigious *Globe and Mail* of Toronto into a national newspaper. Since 1980, when the national edition was launched, shortly after the Thomson purchase, more than $5 million has been invested in electronic equipment in order to move to satellite printing, and over $20 million a year is now being spent on printing and distributing the national edition, even though circulation is only about 90,000.*

Obviously, expenditures still far outpace revenue from the *Globe*'s national edition, and Thomson's continued backing of it highlights the curiously schizophrenic nature of the Thomson newspapers. It is a wealthy chain with a poor reputation, despite exceptions like the *Globe and Mail*. But when either Roy or Ken bought a well-regarded paper, such as the *Times* or the *Globe*, they put their money into preserving the paper's quality. Such papers are the exception rather than the rule in the Thomson empire, however, and it is this dichotomy that has given the chain a black eye throughout the years.

The empire has not seemed to care about its bad image. The problem stems from the Thomson empire regarding its newspapers as a business like any other, in which financial rules must be followed and a profit made, whereas journalists like to feel that their profession is a lofty calling and not just another enterprise. "Thomson Newspapers is run like most manufacturers run a shoe factory, and the average writer, with no clue about how a newspaper operates financially, regards Thomson's tight operating budget as penny-pinching," says a senior executive at a rival Canadian newspaper company. "The average writer forgets that if there is no profit, they don't get their salary. Part of the Thomson Newspapers' problem is that Kenneth Thomson won't recognize what poor employee and public relations his papers have as a result of their getting a higher public profile and, therefore, becoming more of a target."

Thomson executives are not immune to the criticism, but at the same time, they see no need to change the thrust of their papers. As Thomson Newspapers executive vice-president Brian Slaight puts it: "We like to think all our papers are fine papers. There has been a tendency for some criticism of our papers simply because they are smaller papers and people in metropolitan areas may not understand the different functions of small town and metropolitan newspapers. The economics don't exist in a small town to produce the *New York Times*." Although most small town Thomson newspapers are unremarkable, one of its U.S. papers, the *Daily Gazette* of Xenia, Ohio, won a Pulitzer Prize for its 1974 coverage of a devastating tornado that hit that city.

While Kenneth is chairman and president and John Tory is deputy chairman of Thomson Newspapers, the lesser-known fifty-year-old

---

*In June 1984, the paper also launched an afternoon edition.

Slaight runs the chain on a daily basis. He tactfully says that Thomson and Tory are "intently involved" but contradicts this somewhat by saying in the next breath that "they are involved but have other time pressures, although they are always available for consultation."

Slaight is the second generation of his family to work for Thomson Newspapers. His father, Jack, was publisher of the Thomson-owned *Moose Jaw Times-Herald*, and later corporate director of circulation. Brian's wife, Annabel, is co-founder of the well-regarded *Owl* magazine for children. His brother, John Allan, a former radio announcer, heads several Ontario radio broadcasting companies.

Brian started working for the Moose Jaw paper as a youngster. His part-time job was as a "fly boy"—taking papers off the press and putting them on a nearby cart or table. He studied journalism at Toronto's Ryerson Institute of Technology and then worked as a reporter, news editor, and advertising salesman for various Thomson outlets before joining management as publisher of a number of papers, then as an assistant general manager at head office, general manager for Canada, general manager for North America, and, finally, his present position.

The chain has not had problems acquiring papers because, while it holds the line on salaries, it willingly pays top dollar for the papers themselves. It has rarely been rejected, although one standout exception occurred in 1977 when Speidel Newspapers, which owned eighteen papers in nine states, sold to the Gannett Company rather than remain vulnerable to a takeover by Thomson, then its largest shareholder.

The independently owned Speidel chain was a valuable prize because it had the only daily and the only Sunday paper where it published, and made substantial profits. In 1972 Speidel's founder died, and to the irritation of Speidel executives, the estate's trustee, unbeknownst to the executives, sold 6.9 percent of the shares to Thomson Newspapers. The trustee, Irving Trust Company of New York City, liquidated the shares in order to reinvest the money at higher interest rates. As the major shareholder, Thomson requested a seat on the board of directors and was rebuffed. Similarly, it was turned down by Speidel president Rollan Melton when it sought to buy the rest of the company. Discouraged by Melton's refusal to negotiate, Thomson Newspapers swapped its Speidel shares with the Gannett Company in return for Gannett's Newburgh, New York, *Evening News*.

When asked whether Thomson's legendary penny-pinching reputation affected his decision, Melton laughed and said, "Don't be Little

Miss Innocent. I'm not denigrating Thomson, but Gannett has a premier name and reputation. Gannett has allotted a greater proportion of its money to news budgets than we did for our papers. It also has enriched the retirement-income program." Gannett had another unbeatable advantage over Thomson: it is traded on the New York Stock Exchange, whereas Thomson Newspapers is only traded on the Toronto Stock Exchange. Because Speidel executives owned much of their company's stock, they did very well when they sold to Gannett, since Gannett's stock has appreciated handsomely in recent years and pays higher dividends than Speidel did.

While there was never high regard for the Thomson newspapers, they also never got much attention as long as they were confined to relatively small communities where monopoly was unavoidable. That situation changed abruptly early in 1980 when Thomson Newspapers acquired FP Publications, which owned papers in most of Canada's largest cities, where Thomson hitherto had owned no papers. The $164.7-million purchase included the *Globe and Mail, Winnipeg Free Press, Lethbridge* (Alberta) *Herald, Victoria Times* and *Victoria Daily Colonist, Vancouver Sun, Ottawa Journal* and *Calgary Albertan* (which was later sold).

Growing worry about the increasing concentration of newspaper ownership in Canada, as highlighted by the FP purchase, erupted on 27 August 1980 when, within hours of each other and with no advance notice to employees, Thomson Newspapers closed the *Ottawa Journal*, putting 375 people out of work, and Southam shut down its *Winnipeg Tribune*, leaving 370 people jobless. Both papers had been bleeding red ink for years and trailing their rivals—owned by Thomson in Winnipeg and Southam in Ottawa—in circulation, even though each had been gaining in circulation prior to their demise. On the same day the closures were announced, Thomson sold to Southam its interest in two other major newspaper operations—Gazette Montreal Limited, publisher of the *Montreal Gazette*, and the Pacific Press Limited, publisher of the *Vancouver Sun* and the *Vancouver Province*. Two days later, Thomson terminated the respected FP News Service, which primarily provided coverage of Parliament and the federal government.

Kenneth Thomson said the decision to close the *Journal* was entirely economic. Paraphrasing his father's famous statement about his ownership of Scottish Television, Kenneth said ownership of the *Journal* was "a license to lose money." The paper had not made a profit for five years and was projected to lose $5 million in 1980 on top of a $7-million loss in 1979. Although Thomson and Southam insisted their decisions were reached independently, in appearance it looked as if the two giant chains were carving up the country between them.*

Within six days of the *Journal* and the *Tribune* going out of business, the Trudeau government established the Royal Commission on Newspapers. Its mandate was broad: to examine not just the closing of the two papers, but also the growing concentration of newspaper ownership in Canada. One of its concerns was that Thomson might buy Southam, which is vulnerable to a takeover because of its wide public ownership. The federal government also started legal proceedings, charging Thomson and Southam with illegally conspiring to close the two papers.

The commission was dubbed the Kent Commission after its then fifty-eight-year-old chairman, Thomas Kent, whose background is as imposing as his six-foot, three-inch height. He was a former deputy minister for manpower and immigration and regional and economic expansion under prime ministers Lester Pearson and Pierre Trudeau; president of two major Maritime companies, Cape Breton Development Corporation and Sydney Steel; and a former newspaperman. Born in England, he was an editorial writer for the *Manchester Guardian* before coming to Canada as editor of the *Winnipeg Free Press*. He remembers with pleasure the tough deal he insisted on with the Siftons, the paper's owners: "I had autonomy even though the owner was often unhappy over what I did with his newspaper, and I said I wanted a percentage of the profits subject to a guarantee that the amount would not be less than the salary of a senior deputy minister in Ottawa."

In light of his distinguished career and background of independence while working for highly respected papers, Kent had a low tolerance for poor-quality papers. Unlike many commissions that pussyfoot around, carefully avoiding antagonizing either side, the Kent Commission was very outspoken. Its most scathing remarks were directed at the Thomson papers. The commission was not only distressed over the low quality of the Thomson small town papers but also over the papers being part of a conglomerate the commission regarded as being built on the cash generated by the newspapers. It would have preferred the money being spent instead on improving the papers. In its report, the commission wrote:

---

*Southam has about 27.6 percent of national circulation, and Thomson, 21 percent.

For conglomeracy, almost nothing can be said. Industrial conglomerates produce poor newspapers; it is a law of general application. Thomson Newspapers, though very big in Canada, is a minute part of an international conglomerate and exhibits the characteristics of the breed. Its small town monopoly papers are, almost without exception, a lacklustre aggregation of cash boxes.... The proprietors (of chain newspapers) from Southam to Thomson to Irving [a family-owned New Brunswick chain] strenuously assert that they leave complete discretion over news and editorial judgments to their individual publishers and editors.

To the extent that this is true, and even if it is a virtue, it leaves no role for the owners except that of running a business and cultivating the bottom line.... Relinquishing policy control to the managers of the local paper, it is argued, ensures the paper's position as the authentic voice of the community. But can that be true in any real sense when those local managers are, as typically happens, parachuted into the community from somewhere else in the chain? Management exerts control in two effective ways: by appointing executives and by setting or approving budgets. Both these decisive functions are performed in the head offices of the chains. Beyond any question, they thus determine the character and orientation of the branch plants.

With its opposition to conglomerates owning newspapers, the Kent Commission was inevitably hardest on the Thomson newspapers, as they alone, among Canadian newspaper chains, are part of a multinational mixed conglomerate. By contrast, Southam was treated gently. It had several advantages over Thomson. While it is a chain, its papers are in the big cities and, therefore, generally provide more extensive coverage than the small town Thomson papers. There are weaker Southam papers, most noticeably the *Ottawa Citizen*, which is constantly criticized by journalism professors, but Kent is ready to excuse it, saying it has improved in quality since his commission was formed. He has no similar compliments for the Thomson papers.

Southam, like Thomson, is more than a newspaper empire, but its empire is in communications—magazines, the Coles bookstore chain, and cable television. One of the contradictions of the Kent Commission is that it was less concerned about this concentration of power in Canada's communications industry than about the diversified Thomson empire. The contradiction is traceable to Kent's belief that "the steel industry should be run by steel experts and newspapers by newspaper experts." The commission was convinced that because

Southam's return on net assets was declining while Thomson's was increasing,

> the Southam approach is not single-minded. It is not solely profit maximization. . . . (But) in a mixed conglomerate, such as Thomson, the only obvious measure of success is a quantitative measure, that is, Return on Investment. The newspaper is a cash cow whose revenues can be milked not only to buy other papers, but also to finance expansion into other ventures.

Southam executives have also won friends among media critics through their skill in going beyond mere lip service in showing journalistic conscience. The company provides more in-depth professional development training than Thomson, and while Thomson concentrates on such matters as typography, circulation and advertising, Southam places more emphasis on management development. Throughout the 1970s, Thomson did hire a series of editorial consultants to improve its newspapers but none lasted long; they quit in frustration, since their efforts got lost in the company's efforts to squeeze more profit out of the newspapers.

A survey by the Kent Commission, covering 1978 through 1980, found that only eight of the Thomson papers spent more than the average ratio of editorial expenses to revenue for Canadian newspapers with circulation of over 25,000, while twenty-nine of its papers spent below average. Of the eight big spenders, three were FP papers in the first two years studied. By contrast, eleven of the fourteen Southam papers were above average and three were below.

Since 1962, Southam has also annually awarded more than $100,000 in university fellowships to journalists. Southam's president, Gordon Fisher, the great grandson of the company's founder, would never be caught making the blunt statements that Roy and Kenneth Thomson have about the importance of newspapers being profitable. Instead, Fisher likes to depict Southam as a family business and talks a lot about the importance of newspapers to Canada's social fabric. As a result, even though Southam did the very same as Thomson on the fateful 27 August 1980, the commission did not skewer Southam the way it did Thomson Newspapers. If Thomson was the bad guy of Canadian journalism, Southam was the good guy in the commission's view. Kent still feels that way: "In a world which contains the Thomson chain, Southam looks pretty good."

The commission called for sweeping changes to reduce the concentration of newspaper ownership in Canada, including a newspaper act to regulate mergers in the industry. Striking at the Thomson chain, the recommendation proposed that it sell either the *Globe and Mail* or the rest of its chain. Since it is Canada's only national paper, the commission regarded the *Globe*'s monopoly as putting too much power in the hands of Thomson Newspapers, especially as Thomson already owned one-third of Canada's other dailies. The commission said that Thomson should not sell to another conglomerate unless there was no alternative.

In retrospect, Kent says he envisioned such a sale being made to a group of investors who would place their ownership in trusteeship and take no active role, along the lines of the way the *Manchester Guardian,* his old employer, is run. At the *Guardian,* any surplus money left after the shareholders take their percentage is ploughed back into the paper and the editor is hired under a fixed-term contract. Only one Canadian paper, the independently owned *Le Devoir* of Montreal, operates under a similar system. The publisher is appointed for life and controls the majority of the shares. Consequently, he is not subject to the dictates of the board of directors and can appoint or dismiss its members at will.

The Kent Commission's report caused Canadian newspaper publishers to go into a paroxysm of fury when it was released in August 1981. Only the Halifax *Chronicle-Herald* found something nice to say about Kent, and that was that he was a good Nova Scotian (Kent has been dean of the Faculty of Administrative Studies at Halifax's Dalhousie University since 1980). But three years later, the sound and fury has died down and with just cause, as none of the report's recommendations have been put into legislation.

The court case launched by the government was doomed from the start, as there has never been a monopoly conviction under the Combines Investigation Act under which Thomson and Southam were charged. The act has proved ineffectual against business mergers, takeovers, and agreements to limit competition because the prosecution must prove all the components of an offense beyond a reasonable doubt. In the case of the twin closure of the *Winnipeg Tribune* and *Ottawa Journal*, the court ruled that the decisions were logical in view of their enormous losses and that the transactions were conducted "in entirely open fashion."

A few weeks after the court ruling, Tom Kent, puffing quietly on his pipe, assessed the events of the three and a half years between the start of the commission's hearings and the court's ruling. No, he was not surprised at the ruling, and no, he did not expect the federal government to tighten up its anticombines laws very much. "The court's decision once again confirmed that Canada's anticombines legislation is irrelevant to all real issues and business economics today. There isn't much that can be done to toughen up the legislation because Canada has a relatively small economy and the scope for competition is limited. Newspapers are an extreme example of that. Very few communities in Canada can support two competitive dailies. Although Toronto has three, in most Canadian communities one of the rival papers will lose money and go under."

His voice free of bitterness, Kent went on to say that he "felt cheated in a sense" by the court's decision in view of its striking at his commission's *raison d'être*. Nor had he modified his strong opinions about either Thomson newspapers or papers being owned by conglomerates. "Nobody at Thomson cares about newspapers—they're run by accountants whose common criterion is the bottom line and the papers are used as a cash cow to build up the rest of the empire. There should have been a newspaper act, similar to the Bank Act, preventing newspapers from being owned by persons or companies whose other businesses are larger than their newspaper business."

Although Kent realistically admits that the court's decision in large measure nullified his report, time, he says, is on his side in forcing newspapers to improve. "If they perform their role badly, they will be replaced by magazines and the electronic media. Even Thomson, which milks its small town papers, faces competition from weeklies and the coming advertising of jobs and shopping for groceries via the television screen. As of now, small town monopoly papers supply far less content than they could afford to provide. What they take out of small communities is shocking in terms of the large profits they make through producing poor papers. Now, they have the money to produce better papers, but if growing competition results in their making less money, the result will be shoddy newspapers. In the short run, the papers may have won as a result of the court's decision, but in the long run, they may have ensured their own demise because of their delusions of grandeur and power."

Nineteen eighty-three was both a good and a bad year for Thomson Newspapers. The good news was the court's decision and the federal government's pullback from a newspaper act. The bad news was the national attention focused by the Thomson-owned *Globe and Mail* on disputes at two other Thomson newspapers over what the reporters involved described as threats to their journalistic integrity. For their part, Thomson executives felt many papers and magazines covering the disagreements provided inaccurate and slanted coverage because of the long-running hostility in Canada towards the Thomson papers.

The first dispute concerned community protests in Lethbridge, Alberta (population 56,500), over changes in the city's paper, the *Leth-bridge Herald*, following its purchase in 1981 by Thomson as part of its acquisition of the FP chain and Thomson bringing in a new managing editor. So concerned were some Lethbridge residents over what they regarded as trivialization of the paper, as well as the firing of experienced staff and the closing of the paper's provincial legislature bureau, that they formed the "Committee for Quality Journalism" to seek improvement of the paper.

The committee and ex-reporters charged that the new management had eliminated in-depth reports on major local issues in favor of front-page fluff stories on such subjects as a new restaurant and a three-legged dog. A four-year reporter was fired because he refused an editor's request that he make a fourth attempt to interview the grieving family of a teenage accident victim. Photographers said they were given inconsistent instructions, first to shoot posed pictures, then to take pictures candidly. Management also had cause for unhappiness—vandals sprayed obscene slogans referring to the Mormon religion of the new managing editor, John Farrington, on the exterior of the paper's office.

The dispute led to a unique public hearing in the fall of 1983 before the Alberta Press Council, which apportioned blame to both sides. It said the paper should have continued to publish protest letters about its content for longer than the one month it did. But it also said the committee was at fault for "its strident tone" and for not meeting with *Herald* management when finally offered the opportunity.

Brian Slaight has this to say about the dispute: "Perhaps the editor made some changes faster than he should have, but they were changes he felt necessary to improve the paper. The protest was by a smallish group and while the council said the paper should have printed more of the complaints about the charges, after a while complaint letters, be it about the local hospital or the local paper, become repetitive. There was so much distortion in the coverage of the dispute. For example, *Maclean's* magazine said the death of Soviet Union leader Leonid Brezhnev was reported inside the paper, when actually it was on page one. In increasing local coverage, the paper was carrying out what the Kent Commission said about the distinct responsibility of local coverage." According to Slaight, the coverage of the teenager's accident was prompted by the unusual circumstances of his death. The boy disappeared while surfing in Hawaii. The reporter who was fired had not refused to make an initial phone call to the youth's family. Moreover, Slaight says, the reporter was fired by an editor who had been appointed to his job by Farrington's predecessor. "The dilemma between covering a news story and invasion of a bereaved family's privacy is one of those troublesome areas in news coverage for which there is no clear-cut answer, and Thomson Newspapers has no policy for handling such matters. The decision is up to the local editor, reflecting our autonomous approach."

At the same time as the Lethbridge dispute, Thomson Newspapers was receiving further unwelcome publicity over its firing of the managing editor and his reporter wife from the *Daily Times* of Brampton, located about twenty-five miles west of Toronto, and the home of Ontario Premier William Davis. The reporter, Judi McLeod, and her husband, John, maintained they were fired because the paper caved in to pressure from local and provincial politicians over both her stories critical of city council and local members of Davis's Progressive Conservative party and an editorial John wrote asking Davis to stop party members from "meddling" in local politics. Her biggest scoop was about a secret council session at which members voted themselves a 47 percent wage increase. Thomson executives maintain that any pressure the McLeods say came from politicians opposed to their coverage was counterbalanced by support from other local politicians. They maintain the firings stemmed from Judi's stories not being objective and from her husband defying the publisher's order that she be reassigned by reinstating her instead. A reading of her stories does reveal that they lacked a substantial number of corroborating sources. One story referring to a "public outcry" quoted the opponent of a politician and two anonymous local residents.

The McLeods were not dewy-eyed novices to the Thomson organization. John McLeod had joined Thomson Newspapers back in 1973 and had worked for the *Ottawa Journal*, serving on its editorial board. He also had been managing editor of the *Oshawa Times*, where he met Judi, and for two years he ran head office's news management training program. His first move at the *Daily Times* was to upgrade salaries. "When I joined the paper, the highest-paid reporter, who had had five years' experience, was making $265 a week, about half what big city papers pay. I increased the salary to $450."

In 1981, however, the paper got a new publisher, Victor Mlodecki, an accountant who had previously been publisher of Thomson's Kirkland Lake, Ontario, newspaper. McLeod says Mlodecki introduced a sweeping cost-cutting program. "He replaced toilet paper rolls with lower-grade sheets of paper, and people had to sign for nineteen-cent pens and for notebooks," McLeod says. "Every type of form was examined to determine whether it could be printed on newsprint rather than bond paper to save money. Customarily, newspapers provide free copies of the paper each day to their newsrooms when they come off the presses. We had twelve people in our newsroom and originally received ten copies, some of which had to be clipped and filed. Then the number given to the newsroom was cut in half to save money, even though the production cost per paper was only three and a half cents. If photographers needed batteries for their cameras, they bought their own or charged their cost up as mileage. Reporters who took sources for lunch were not allowed to charge this up on an expense account, as is usual in the newspaper industry. Since the only expense staff were allowed was for car mileage, some would charge up some lunches as mileage.

"Our paper was not unusual in its tightfistedness. At another Thomson paper that I toured in 1974 when I was serving as the company's news consultant, I found the city hall reporter sitting in his coat typing a story because the publisher had the heat turned down every night. In the summer, production workers in the hot-metal-type shop propped up the water fountain handle to keep the water running to get some cool air because there was no air conditioning. The publisher ordered the advertising manager to go into the composing room every fifteen minutes to check that this practice had stopped."

Nevertheless, despite his criticism of the cost cutting, McLeod stayed with the Thomson organization. In addition, Thomson head office raised no objections when a few months after he was hired by the *Daily Times*, John parachuted his wife into the plum job of city hall reporter. Judi, then thirty-five, had been a reporter since she was eighteen and had been the education reporter and lifestyle editor at the *Oshawa Times*.

Although there was friction between the McLeods and the publisher over their stories, the final blowup occurred following an article Judi had *not* written. That story, written in November 1982 just days before the municipal election, reported that the two members of council who had missed more meetings than any other members were the mayoralty candidate, whom John's election editorial subsequently opposed, and the council member about whom Judi had written critical stories the most frequently. There were several repercussions. The mayoralty candidate lost the election, and the councillor issued libel notices against the paper. He chose as his attorneys the law firm of Davis, Webb, of which Premier Davis used to be a partner and which is now headed by his son, Neil, and Ronald Webb, who was chairman of the local Progressive Conservative association at the time of the McLeod episode. The paper's publisher, John McLeod and Kerry Lambie, a Thomson assistant general manager, then met, and John was ordered to pull Judi off her beat. Although Slaight says Thomson papers are used to turning a deaf ear to pressure, the *Daily Times'* position regarding the McLeods was contradictory. If, as Slaight says, her stories were not regarded as objective, she should have been pulled off the beat far earlier. He says that Mlodecki had already spoken to John McLeod several times about her coverage.

In any event, two months later, both John and Judi were fired after John had reinstated her on the grounds that the editor, and not the publisher, traditionally hires and fires. Ironically, Judi had won a Western Ontario Newspaper Award just one week earlier for coverage of her beat. Part of the reason for her selection may have been that the award's winner was chosen by the former associate research director of the Kent Commission, which had been so critical of Thomson Newspapers.

It took the McLeods six months to find new jobs. Part of the problem was that newspapers in general were undergoing a hiring freeze, but there are contradictory versions of their unsuccessful applications to the *Toronto Star*, Toronto's largest-circulation paper. Judi says she made arrangements to write some freelance stories for the paper on the basis that they might lead to a full-time job. When none of her stories appeared, she says she was told by the then regional editor that the paper's city editor at the time had directed none should be published. Subsequently, she spoke to an acquaintance, the managing editor of the *Windsor Star*, Bob McAleer, and asked him to intercede on her behalf with the *Star*'s managing editor, Ray Timson. One of her stories, about an elderly widow stuck with a poorly built home, was then published, but after that she had no further dealings with the paper.

John McLeod says he spoke to the *Toronto Star*'s assistant managing editor, Gerry Barker, about a job but that after Barker spoke to Thomson's Kerry Lambie, Barker was no longer interested and did not return McLeod's phone calls. For the purposes of this book, written confirmation or denial was requested from McAleer and all the individuals at the *Toronto Star* to whom the McLeods spoke. Their responses were diametrically different. McAleer replied about Judi: "Essentially correct. As for Judi having no further dealings, I can't say why." Replying on behalf of all the *Toronto Star* people, Timson said, "The information given you in this regard is totally inaccurate."

After six months, the McLeods were hired by Toronto's third daily paper, the *Toronto Sun*. She was a court reporter and he was an assistant business editor. Then, exactly one year to the date after they were fired by the Brampton *Daily Times*, the McLeods launched a rival newspaper, a sixteen-page free weekly called the *Bramptonian*, initially distributed to 40,000 households in the Brampton area and depending on local advertising for revenue. The McLeods own 40 percent of the paper and say the idea for it came from the 60 percent owners, a former classified-advertising employee of the *Daily Times*, who had been discontent over not being promoted into display advertising, and her common-law husband, a Brampton food broker. John McLeod is the *Bramptonian*'s editor-in-chief, and his wife is associate editor. They claim the timing of the paper's start was not deliberate but merely an "ironic coincidence." Their long-term goal is more frequent publication of the paper and paid, rather than free, circulation.

The Lethbridge and Brampton incidents resulted in further bashing by media rivals and critics of the Thomson chain. But as it marks the fiftieth anniversary of Roy Thomson buying his first paper in 1934 in Timmins, the newspaper empire is at its peak in wealth. The collapse of the proposed newspaper act leaves the door open for it to expand in Canada. However, Slaight says all that the chain contemplates in Canada is changing some more of its weeklies into dailies, the continuation of a process started twelve years ago. There are more buying opportunities in the United States, and acquisitions there plus the rate of inflation should push Thomson Newspapers over $1 billion in revenue well before the end of this decade.

CHAPTER

10

FIGHTING BACK

IN RECENT YEARS, a few of the mice within the North American Thomson newspaper empire have started to roar. Employees, angered at low wages and the company's frustrating their efforts to form unions, have fought back through strikes or starting alternate papers. When the mice have roared, they have either won higher wages or their alternate papers have become strong competitors to the Thomson papers. Their success has not triggered a tidal wave of revolt within the empire because other Thomson employees either are happy or realize that these few rebels benefited from unique circumstances. In each case, the strikers lived in strong union communities and could count on the support of the residents as fellow union members. Also, the recent death of one such alternate paper, after three and a half years of taking away circulation from the Thomson paper, shows that without sufficient financial backing, such papers have a slim chance of surviving.

Thomson Newspapers is regarded by union leaders as one of the toughest chains to organize in Canada and the United States. In the unionists' view, Thomson is prepared to shut down a paper and lose millions of dollars in advertising and circulation revenue in order to keep the unions out because union salaries, which are often higher than those at nonunionized small Thomson papers, are regarded as a long-term drain on profit. "Once a paper is organized, Southam Incorporated takes the stance of let's deal with the union, but Thomson . . . ," says John Bryant, executive director of the Southern Ontario Newspaper Guild. (The guild represents reporters.)

Bryant's assessment is shared by Robert Eccles, executive director of the Canadian branch of the International Typographical Union (ITU), which primarily represents composing-room workers but is edging into representing clerical, advertising and editorial employees at smaller Canadian papers. The ITU has organized about half of Thomson's Canadian papers, but only two encompass all workers and not just compositors. "Thomson is the worst newspaper employer to deal with in Canada," Eccles says. "When we go into negotiations with Southam or the Irving chain, the company answers our proposals on all matters with counterproposals. With Thomson, they specify the items which they are willing to discuss and then they don't negotiate properly. They just say no. Nothing has changed since the Kent Commission."

The chain's reputation with unions is just as bad in the United States. "On a scale of one to ten in toughness, they rate a seven or higher. Only the Gannett chain, which has more papers, is harder to organize," says a senior executive of the International Printing and Graphic Communications Union. "Both Thomson and Gannett can keep out unions because their papers have a small staff and workers are afraid of losing their jobs, especially as this is a time when many papers are going out of business or cutting back. It's easier to replace a handful of workers at a small paper with scabs than the large staff of metropolitan papers."

Nevertheless, despite these odds, some of the mice have fought the lion. The rebels are an intriguing group. They are not young firebrands, fresh out of college, but instead are mostly middle-aged and older people who previously were of a conservative mentality, mostly voted Republican, believed in the American Dream, and never considered supporting a union, let alone join one. Their radicalization came only after years of putting up with extremely low wages.

The first paper ever to win a strike in the United States against Thomson was the *Valley Independent* of Monessen, Pennsylvania. In 1970, less than a year after Thomson bought the then sixty-seven-year-old paper (circulation 16,000), the employees went on strike for seven and a half months to get higher wages and a closed-shop clause, meaning that the paper could not hire nonunionized people. There was peace until 1979, when employees struck again for more money. That strike lasted fourteen months, with the success of a weekly paper started by the strikers forcing Thomson Newspapers to settle. It agreed to raise the top minimum salary for reporters and advertising salespeople by $120 over a three-year period, to $310 a week—a substantial increase but still well below salaries on metropolitan papers.

The strike was not led by a flaming radical. The union's local chairman, Steve Menzler, has been a display advertising salesman at the paper for thirty-seven years. But his mild voice hardens as he talks about the Thomson company. "They preferred to spend on bringing people in to run the paper and paying for their housing rather than settle. Thomson is willing to spend $1,000 to keep its workers from making $10 more."

The tactics of the Monessen strikers served as a role model for a strike that broke out at the *Oswego Palladium-Times* in Oswego, New York, near Syracuse, shortly after the Monessen staff returned to work. But the Oswego strike had a different outcome. Whereas the Monessen strikers returned to their paper, the Oswego strikers grew to like running their own paper, the *Messenger*, and opted for a small lump settlement rather than return to the *Palladium-Times*. But their venture was ill-fated. The *Messenger* was always a shoe-string venture run by people with meagre savings and no independent sources of income. Moreover, it was started at a time when the number of two-newspaper cities in the United States was shrinking drastically. Oswego (population, 19,000) was the smallest city in the U.S. with two newspapers, and whereas Thomson Newspapers had the financial resources to sit out a bruising war for circulation, the *Messenger* did not. Despite cutting into the *Palladium-Times'* circulation by close to 4,000 readers, the *Messenger* was never able to get sufficient advertising revenue, and in April 1984 it folded after nearly four years in operation.

The *Palladium-Times'* dispute had all the classic ingredients of small town folks taking on the big corporation. The strike's leader, Don McCann, was fifty-eight when the strike started. He would never qualify as a spellbinding orator, but in 1979, after twenty-five years at the paper, his anger finally erupted over the fact that although he was the highest-paid reporter, he was making just $250 a week. Like McCann, about two-thirds of the eventual sixteen strikers had worked for the *Palladium-Times* all their working life. This older group had always lived in Oswego and were the sort who flew the American flag outside their small frame homes and never rocked the boat. They had received low salaries before Thomson bought the paper in 1970 but had not complained because Oswego's economy was depressed and jobs were scarce. Moreover, there had been a feeling of camaraderie with the publisher-owner because he, too, lived in Oswego.

That sense of the paper being a family affair vanished when Thomson Newspapers bought it. The company instituted a pension plan in 1972, but employees could not qualify until ten years after the plan was implemented. The old-timers began to become concerned about job security and their pensions as they saw that other employees with up to forty years at the paper were let go just before their scheduled retirement. The remaining veterans were also upset because at a time when inflation was 9 percent, Thomson was offering 4 to 5 percent raises.

The younger staff members, many of them just out of college, were disturbed, too. Their fears that Thomson would not promote from within were aggravated when the company parachuted in an outsider as managing editor rather than promote staffer Russell Tarby, who had been acting managing editor for six months. Tarby was upset by the company's "obsession" with story counts, the routine measurement at newspapers to check how much information is being provided readers. Says Tarby: "When I was editor, I had a decent story count, but I often sacrificed additional items in favor of good design and better display. When Thomson brought in my successor, a company man who had worked as a scab for one of their papers in Pennsylvania, he redesigned the paper so that it had hundreds of little one-column stories. It looked terrible, but it brought his story count way up above mine. Thomson understands numbers, not quality."

Other young members of the staff were distressed over Thomson's tightfisted financial controls. Says Carol Wilczynski, who became managing editor of the *Messenger* and had been chief of the *Palladium-Times'* one-person bureau in Fulton, near Oswego, before the strike: "I had no bureau budget. If I wanted supplies, I had to go to Oswego and would be handed one pencil. We weren't allowed to buy reporter shorthand books but instead were given scrap paper. After five years, I was one of the highest-paid reporters but was only making $225 a week."

Not only were the workers greenhorns in industrial relations but the union to which they turned to organize them as a local had had no previous experience in newspaper negotiations and knew nothing about the Thomson organization. Normally, it is the Newspaper Guild that organizes a newsroom, but Tarby says the guild never replied to the workers' inquiries. McCann, who had reported on local labor issues, suggested an alternative: the Service Employees International Union, a public service union. The SEIU placed responsibility for organizing the workers in the hands of an unseasoned organizer, Chris Binaxas, with the unlikely credentials of being a folksinger. Binaxas's first step was to contact the SEIU's head office for information on what the Thomson organization was.

Binaxas organized the union, with all but six employees joining. It included the son of the former owner, who sold advertising. Thomson had retained the owner as publisher, but fired him because he had not stopped the unionization. Negotiations started in April 1980 between the SEIU and Thomson corporate attorneys flown in from head office in

Des Plaines, Illinois, and dragged on for more than six months with no progress. Discussions over wages, job security, seniority and arbitration rights bogged down in debates over the definition of terms such as "seniority" and never got to financial issues.

Finally, in October 1980, the union went on strike and, based on Monessen's strategy, set up the alternative paper. The offices of the *Messenger* were opened in a condemned building with $12,000 of their own money and $15,000 borrowed from a local businessman. Some office equipment was donated to them and other pieces they built themselves or obtained in return for not charging for advertising. "We went on strike on a Saturday and had our first paper out the following Monday," McCann says.

Half the strikers drifted away over the succeeding months, due to a combination of being unable to survive on the paper's $25-a-week salaries and internal power struggles. Others, however, who had complained bitterly about the low Thomson salaries, stayed, compensated by the excitement of being in charge of their own paper and getting by financially through moonlighting at other jobs. In September 1981, with the walkout nearly a year old, the strikers decided they would never be interested in returning to the *Palladium-Times* and waived their right to reinstatement in return for the $45,000 lump settlement, which worked out to under $3,000 per striker. "That's chicken feed to a company the size of Thomson," says Mimi Satter of the Syracuse law firm of Blitman and King, the SEIU's law firm. The workers also received unemployment insurance but only after the SEIU's lawyers appealed to the New York State Unemployment Commission to force Thomson Newspapers to pay the money, for which strikers in that state are eligible after seven weeks.

Oswego is a strong union town and the *Messenger*'s advertising revenue was boosted by the city council's switching its legal advertising from the *Palladium-Times* to it. However, the *Palladium-Times* was still the largest-selling paper. It never stopped publishing during the strike, having first imported workers from other papers and then hiring new employees. While it lost the city's advertising, it retained the advertising from major retailers in Oswego who refused to advertise in the *Messenger*. But the *Palladium-Times*' trump card was that the Thomson millions were always behind it. For the seven middle-aged rebels who remained from the original strikers, the shutdown of the paper was a bittersweet ending, with pride that the *Messenger* had lasted so long and sadness at its death and the end of their dreams.

In Canada there have been several strikes over wages at two Thomson-owned papers—the *Sudbury Star* and *Oshawa Times*. In both cases, the strikers were backed by their communities, which are strong union towns: Sudbury is the home of the world's largest nickel producer, Inco Limited, organized by the United Steelworkers of America, and Oshawa has the main Canadian plant of General Motors, organized by the United Auto Workers.

But a strike by 35 of the 104 employees of the *Welland Evening Tribune*, started in October 1982, will probably never result in a settlement because the strikers started an alternate paper and, like their counterparts in Oswego, enjoy running their own show. The paper, the *Guardian Express*, located a few blocks from the *Tribune*, is receiving financial support from the International Typographical Union. It is the first time the ITU has taken such action, which is part of its stepped-up campaign to sign up editorial and front-office employees as members in the face of the declining membership in their original constituency of composing-room workers. The compositors have decreased substantially in number as newspapers have become more automated. The ITU gave the *Guardian Express* $5,000 weekly, paying up to $250 of a person's former earnings, for close to a year until the paper made a profit.

The *Tribune* maintains that the union demanded a wage increase based on a recent contract signed with the Thomson-owned *Peterborough* (Ontario) *Examiner* and then rejected the offer despite its matching the *Examiner*'s 10 percent wage increase. The strikers say that the amount offered was too little because their salaries were so low that the increase would not have made much difference. According to them, a fourteen-year advertising employee was earning $185 a week. The ITU also says that the *Tribune* is giving a misleading view of how many of its workers did not join the strike. The ITU's Eccles says that while the *Tribune* has 104 employees now, at the time of the strike it had only 68 workers, half of whom went on strike.

The dispute in Welland is unfortunately colored by the personal antagonism between the strike's leader, Ted Thurston, and the *Tribune*'s publisher, John Van Kooten. Thurston, who worked for the *Tribune* for twelve years, sarcastically mimics Van Kooten's Dutch accent when he says the publisher "is 70 percent responsible for what happened." Among his criticisms are charges that the *Tribune* had no office-supplies room, but instead staff were given scrap paper for making notes; no carbon copies of stories were allowed to be made—a traditional safety precaution against misplacement—because this was regarded as "too expensive"; the paper had only an "old beat-up dictionary" and an old camera; the gasoline allowance was only half the actual cost per mile; and the lunch allowance for sources was "$1.50 a week."

Thurston also gleefully recounts how the *Tribune*'s sports editor was duped into writing stories for more than a year about a nonexistent Canadian soccer team based on phone calls from a local teenager who had invented the team. The hoax was uncovered when the teenager claimed to have kicked the winning goal in a match between his fictitious team and one in Australia and reporters in Australia said they had never heard of such a tournament. The Welland sports editor had accepted the stories at face value and had never sought confirmation.

In turn, Van Kooten says he and Thurston would both describe differently the picture of a red car on Van Kooten's office wall. "His statements about me and the paper have been deceitful," he says. "For example, he said we were guilty of sex discrimination because we paid a brother and sister working in circulation different salaries. What he didn't mention was that the brother had worked longer for the paper."

The duel between Thurston and the *Tribune* went far beyond words. Their battleground moved from Welland to the Toronto offices of the Ontario Labour Relations Board when Thurston charged that he was demoted from district editor to reporter and was not given a promised merit pay increase after he applied to the ITU for certification of a union at the *Tribune*. The board supported his contention in a 2 to 1 ruling. According to the board's January 1983 report on the charges, this was the chain of events: Thurston became district editor in 1979. He was the first person to contact the ITU in February 1982, and at noon on 29 March 1982 he was elected to the bargaining committee of the newly formed union local. Three days earlier, shortly after Thurston had posted the nominations for the bargaining committee, the managing editor, James Middleton, gave Thurston a memorandum pointing out errors in the pages for which he was responsible in the previous day's paper. On March 30, the day after the election, Middleton informed Thurston he was being moved from district editor to a district reporter. Van Kooten and Middleton told the board that Thurston was reassigned because his job performance was unsatisfactory.

But the board said Thurston's March 25 pages were not the only ones with errors. The city page, for example, contained two major stories for which the headlines had been reversed, and the sports pages contained both spelling errors, including instances of people's names being spelled differently within the same story, and grammatical errors. However, there was no evidence that either of the editors responsible for these pages had also received written reprimands. As a result of the inconsistencies, the board found that Thurston's demotion was "motivated at least partially by his active support" of the Welland Typographical Union and that the demotion, therefore, contravened the

Ontario Labour Relations Act, which prohibits employers from discriminating against union members.

In all fairness, it should be noted that the staff of some papers are happy after they are bought by Thomson Newspapers. One such instance is the *Waukesha* (Wisconsin) *Freeman*, where the employees' attitude has taken a 180-degree turn from panic and loathing when Thomson bought the paper to one of astonished relief and pleasure that none of the deadening changes they feared have occurred. However, it remains to be seen whether the lack of change is due to Thomson owning the paper for less than two years.

Thomson Newspapers bought the *Freeman* in February 1983 for $9 million (U.S.) from the Des Moines Register and Tribune Company, against whom Thomson had unsuccessfully bid for the paper in 1979. Thomson's interest in the *Freeman* was understandable, as it was buying a paper with a long-established presence in a district whose population is rapidly growing. Moreover, the paper's then circulation of 25,380 made it the seventh largest among Thomson's eighty-six U.S. papers. It also offered another plus: it was not unionized.

Waukesha (population 52,000) is located about thirty miles west of Milwaukee. In its early days, the community made its money as a health spa resort because of a hot spring nearby. Now, its main claim to fame is that it is the farthest-west point in the United States to have machine-tool foundries. The community is also the county seat of Waukesha County, the fastest-growing county in Wisconsin in terms of population and the second most affluent, with an average household income of $32,000. In recent years, as the middle class has found housing too expensive in North Milwaukee and too "blue collar" in South Milwaukee, many families have moved to Waukesha, attracted by the comparatively low property and school taxes.

Although it has become a bedroom suburb, Waukesha still has the quiet appearance of a small, prosperous Midwest town. There are few stoplights and no high-rise office towers or apartments. The streets are wide; the houses have spacious lawns; and the downtown is spruced up, due to a cleanup campaign by the paper, *Freeman* staff like to say. The quiet at dusk is occasionally ruptured by teenagers using the main street as a drag strip.

The *Freeman* has been a part of the changing face of the community. Since its establishment in 1859, the paper, like Waukesha, has changed with the times. It was started just before the Civil War by abolitionist Republicans opposed to slavery. But today, Waukesha County provides the third-largest number of Democratic votes in Wisconsin and the *Freeman* is pro-Democrat now, too.

With Waukesha County's population projected to reach 400,000, an increase of 80,000, within a matter of years, *Freeman* employees could understand why Thomson wanted their paper so much. But at the same time, they wondered about the purchase, since there is a dark side to the growth the area is experiencing. There is concern among Waukesha leaders that the population may grow faster in the southern part of the county than in the north where Waukesha is, and they are also perturbed that as Milwaukee residents move to Waukesha, shopping malls will follow them and siphon off business from the downtown area. If these pressures, which could affect circulation and advertising, occur, Thomson Newspapers could come to regret buying the *Freeman*. The paper's circulation and advertising are already being stalked by the two Milwaukee papers through increased coverage of Waukesha County news. But the challenge of running a small town paper in the shadow of a big city is old hat to Thomson Newspapers, since it has such papers in the ring of communities around its home base of Toronto.

The reaction of *Freeman* staff to the Thomson takeover has altered dramatically from their initial horror. The staff, proud of the paper having recently won several awards for its stories, were worried about potential damage to the *Freeman*'s quality, and one anonymous staffer was quoted in the Milwaukee papers as saying that "Thomson's is the K-Mart of journalism." The Milwaukee papers kept asking the publisher imported by Thomson, Steve Hollister, formerly an assistant general manager at Thomson's U.S. headquarters in Milwaukee, about what changes he was going to make. He said none, but nobody, including the *Freeman*'s staff, believed him.

Their gloom deepened when Thomson Newspapers sent in a series of brown-suited, brown-shoed whiz kids to examine the paper's accounting records. The group came and went silently, heightening fears. Then there was the behavior of Frank Miles, Thomson's general manager in the U.S., who did not even introduce himself to the staff, but just huddled over the books. Although Hollister gave what the staff describe as "Dale Carnegie–type" pep talks about his commitment to a good paper, they wondered about his sincerity, as he continued to live in Chicago and commute the three hours' drive to Waukesha several days a week. They fretted that staff would be fired, promotions from within would stop, staff who left would not be replaced, and that Hollister would drop several syndicated columnists they carried as well as their wide variety of news services. They were contemptuous when the Thomson bureau in Washington, which serves all Thomson papers, sent "simplistic rehashes of old news, embargoed for publication until several days later."

But by the summer of 1983, the staff had calmed down. The shoe that they had expected to be dropped on them had not fallen. Only one reporter had left, and she had departed on her own initiative and was replaced. The news editor also left of his own volition, and instead of bringing in an outsider, Hollister promoted a longtime staffer. None of the columnists, nor the news service, were dropped. By a year after the purchase, *Freeman* staff were bewildered. Veterans who had been expecting "all sorts of terrible things" under Thomson were pleasantly surprised to find their expectations unrealized. "Everybody is happier than under the old management and that's not the way it is supposed to be at Thomson Newspapers," said a staffer who had been especially unhappy over the Thomson purchase.

With Hollister's encouragement, the paper was pushing the Washington bureau for more stories and getting them. When Hollister first joined the *Freeman*, the staff felt under pressure to put Chamber of Commerce and service club stories on the front page, but when they resisted by putting such stories inside the paper, Hollister did not argue. Not a lot of money, but at least more, was made available to hire stringers in nearby communities. A request by the staff that a "shopper" be started—an idea rejected by the Des Moines paper—was accepted by Hollister. (A shopper is a weekly paper distributed free to all residents, not just subscribers. It primarily contains advertising plus a few stories lifted from the regular paper's past week's editions.) *Freeman* employees had pressed for the shopper as a way of competing against the Milwaukee papers.

Despite initial concerns that the Milwaukee papers would eat into the *Freeman*'s circulation, paid subscriptions to the paper climbed under Thomson. This helped boost the staff's morale and their support of Thomson, while at the same time justifying the decision of Thomson Newspapers to buy the paper. In 1982 the *Freeman*'s circulation had dropped by 298 subscribers from its peak, despite the influx of new residents, but by the end of 1983, the paper's circulation had rebounded by 122 readers. In view of their rejoicing that the worst had not happened under Thomson, it would be expected the staff would be willing to be quoted. Instead, the opposite is the case. "It's embarrassing in the profession, in view of Thomson's bad reputation, to say that things are better with them than with the previous Des Moines owners," says one staffer. The loathing may have disappeared at the *Freeman* but some kind of fear still remains.

CHAPTER

11

SHOWDOWN ON FLEET STREET

NOTHING THAT HAPPENED at the *Times* (of London) and the *Sunday Times* between 1978 and 1981 was unusual for the newspaper industry. Other papers have been shut down in an effort by newspaper owners to break the unions, as Kenneth Thomson did with both the *Times* and the *Sunday Times* between November 1978 and October 1979. And other owners have also sold their papers, as Thomson did with both papers in February 1981.

But the *Times* and the *Sunday Times* are no ordinary newspapers. They stand for Tradition, Influence and Prestige, and are regarded as ranking among the top five of the world's greatest newspapers in terms of quality of writing. That guaranteed the dispute coverage in newspapers around the world, whereas strikes at Thomson papers in small Canadian and American communities have been scarcely noticed even by neighboring towns. It cannot have helped either that the participants were all highly articulate, speaking with the acidity of British satirist Jonathan Swift. Their clever comments were greatly amusing to nonparticipants, but tended to inflame already edgy nerves rather than act as soothing balm. Moreover, a complicated situation was made even worse by labor and management being fragmented into hawks and doves within their own ranks.

But despite the charges and countercharges flying back and forth between labor and management in ever-so-polite letters, and despite the late arrival on the scene of the star of the show, Kenneth Thomson, the outcome was crystal clear from the start. Although the dispute dragged on inconclusively for eleven months in 1978 and 1979, management did in the end what newspaper management in the U.K. has done for years: it gave in to the unions. And then Kenneth Thomson did what an owner who is fed up with a prize stallion that bolts once too often does: he said he would close the newspapers if a buyer were not found. An unlikely suitor charged to the rescue— Australian-born newspaper mogul Rupert Murdoch, whose ownership of a number of sensational newspapers in the U.K. and U.S. and hardline labor relations have earned him even more of a black-sheep reputation in journalism than the many low-quality North American Thomson newspapers (which, while often criticized for being weak and bland, at least are not sensational) have earned Thomson.

Although the problems at both papers exploded under Kenneth Thomson, they actually began to fester under Roy Thomson, who refused to raise wages to the Fleet Street norm and was unable to defuse rivalry between his two prize papers. But Roy died in 1976 before new equipment that made fewer production workers necessary became widely available in the newspaper industry. Kenneth Thomson was only one of the many newspaper owners around the world who embraced the equipment as a modern cost-saving measure and subsequently became locked in mortal combat with the unions. While those *Times* executives who admired Roy believe he would not have done what Kenneth did, the vastly changing circumstances in the newspaper industry between 1976 and 1980 might have pushed him to do the same.

Despite its small circulation of just over 300,000, the *Times* has always wielded influence disproportionate to the size of its readership. While the lack of advertising has been the bane of its owners, its elegant, analytical prose and polished gems of stiletto wit are must reading among politicians, civil servants, and prominent businessmen at their offices, homes or clubs. The *Times* was founded nearly two hundred years ago, in 1785, under the name the *Daily Universal Register* and was renamed in 1788. At that time, newspapers received money either from the government or the opposition for their support, and at first the *Times* was no better than the rest. But by the early 1800s, circulation and advertising had risen sufficiently for these bribes to be rejected. By the time of Queen Victoria's reign, the *Times* had the largest circulation of any U.K. newspaper, its editor was regarded as the most powerful man in England, and its ringing editorials earned it the sobriquet of "The Thunderer." This prompted the *Saturday Review* to write in an 1861 article:

> No apology is needed for assuming that this country is ruled by
> *The Times.* . . . It is high time we began to realize the magnificent

spectacle afforded by British freedom—30 millions governed by a newspaper.

The 1900s were less kind to the *Times*, however. Although it retained its elitist position on Fleet Street, it faced growing competition from other quality papers, such as the *Guardian* and the *Daily Telegraph*, and was beset by labor problems. By 1966 the *Times*, then owned by John Jacob Astor, was in the red. Nevertheless, the prestige of the paper appealed to Roy Thomson, then an outsider who wanted very much to be on the inside of the British Establishment, just as it would fifteen years later to another outsider, Rupert Murdoch. Because Thomson already owned the hitherto unrelated *Sunday Times*, his purchase of the *Times* was referred to the U.K. Monopolies Commission, which gave quick approval.

The *Sunday Times* was started in 1822 and built up its popularity through fictional serials on high society and its unabashedly nationalistic coverage of the theater, in which it heaped praise upon U.K. productions and scorn upon imports. Its long series of owners included two eccentric women who owned the paper in quick succession in the late 1800s. The first, Alice Cornwell Whiteman, was known as Princess Midas after the Australian gold mine of that name, which she had personally developed and on which she had struck it rich. Her other accomplishments included forming the first U.K. dog club exclusively for women dog-owners. Princess Midas was followed by Rachel Beer, a brunette beauty whose husband owned both the *Sunday Times* and its rival, the *Observer*. Her idiosyncrasies included dressing her footmen in brown liveries with gilt buttons showing the Beer crest of a pelican feeding its young, and clipping the back of her poodle in the design of the crest. Although her husband was the proprietor, it was Mrs. Beer who was in charge, writing and editing both papers.

Because the *Sunday Times* was a weekly, for years it had no full-time staff, but it did retain people long after they reached age sixty-five. Although this practice is not as widespread today at the paper, it does continue, with the eldest employee being eighty-six years old, and his assistant eighty.

Roy Thomson's predecessor as owner of the *Sunday Times* was Gomer Berry, then known by his title of Lord Kemsley. Kemsley and his brother, William (Lord Camrose), jointly owned the paper, as well as a chain of regional newspapers and the *Daily Telegraph*, from 1915 to 1936, when they amicably split because of concerns over inheritance difficulties, especially as each had large families. Camrose kept the *Daily Telegraph* and Kemsley took the *Sunday Times*.

Under Kemsley the circulation of the paper rose to nearly one million, but he was best known among his employees for living in the ostentatious style of New Money. He came from very humble origins in Wales; yet he was more of a stuffed shirt than many blue bloods who inherit a title. He never carried his own briefcase; this was done by an assistant or servant. His Rolls Royce, with black glass windows, would wait for him at a private entrance to the *Sunday Times* building. Although his moustache was thin, there was something about him that reminded people of Groucho Marx, a name that some called him behind his back. This apparently bothered him so much that when an editor who was unfamiliar with the situation suggested that Groucho Marx, who was in London, be interviewed, it was one of the rare occasions Kemsley lost his temper. One of his closest acquaintances at the paper was Ian Fleming, who interspersed writing his James Bond books with stories for the *Sunday Times*.

"Kemsley was Victorian in all his attitudes, a High Tory even though most of the people from where he came in Wales were strong Labour party supporters," says Denis Hamilton, who was Kemsley's personal assistant from 1946 until Kemsley sold his chain to Roy Thomson in 1959. "He ran his papers with very severe central control and a strong right-wing political flavor and he didn't particularly like change. When the commercial TV era came to the U.K. in the 1950s, he was ill-prepared for the great switch of advertising from papers to TV. The upshot was that with his growing older, the ill health of his wife, and the incapacity of some of his children, he sold to Roy Thomson."

In 1959 the sale was made abruptly without Kemsley consulting any nonfamily members of his board of directors. In 1967 the *Sunday Times* was amalgamated with the just-purchased *Times* to form Times Newspapers Limited. But although the two papers had the same parent, away from the public eye they often seemed to get on no better than Cain and Abel did. Because the *Sunday Times* was profitable and the *Times* lost money, the *Sunday Times* employees felt the *Times* lived off their paper and the *Times* workers were under the constant threat that their paper was financially endangered. The prince-and-the-pauper difference was further heightened by employees at the *Sunday Times* getting higher wages than those at the *Times*.

The simmering conflict this created was aggravated when the *Times* moved in 1974 from its crowded Fleet Street district quarters into a building adjacent to the *Sunday Times* located about a mile away. Although each paper's reporters were still physically separate, the compositors of the two papers were now working near one another. The daily reminder that one paper's compositors were making more than those on the other became a slowly ticking time bomb. "It was a recipe for ill will and the Thomson executives either didn't recognize the importance of the pay differential, or if they did, they didn't do anything about it," says Jacob Ecclestone of the National Union of Journalists.

Further potential dynamite was added by wage levels at the *Times* not only being less than at the *Sunday Times*, but also being way below those of some other Fleet Street newspapers, which were paying twice the limit the Labour government had set for wage increases. Thomson management was reluctant to do the same for the *Times* because the government had threatened to crack down on companies that paid more and had already taken away the export credits of one company that had exceeded the wage-increase regulations. Thomson executives were nervous because their North Sea oil fields came under government regulation and their regional newspapers relied heavily on revenue from government advertising. However, under the wage restrictions, if a company increased its efficiency enough to pay above the 10 percent ceiling without raising prices, it could do so, and the *Times* employees were convinced the paper could have done this.

But the Times newspapers were not alone in their labor problems, as a general malaise struck newspapers in 1978. In the U.S., the three New York City daily newspapers went through an eighty-eight-day strike that cost them $150 million in lost advertising and circulation revenue. In England the *Daily Telegraph* failed to appear for weeks because of labor problems and the *Guardian* had been losing millions of pounds each year for a decade. The issue at all the papers was the opposition of production workers to new technology that reduced the papers' costs but also wiped out many jobs.

The printing unions are much more powerful in the U.K. than in North America because they date back several centuries and have grown up, like a vine around a beanstalk, with the newspapers. U.S. national newspapers are less vulnerable to disputes, since they are printed by satellite from a number of locations, whereas U.K. national newspapers are produced in one building in London and are then sent across the country by truck, train or plane. In addition, as most Fleet Street proprietors own more than one newspaper, owners tread very cautiously for fear that a dispute at one paper might spill over to another. In the U.K., everyone working at a paper, including secretaries and tea servers, must belong to a union, and there are separate unions for the printers, compositors, journalists, electricians and engineers, as well as the catering, transport and general workers. Each union is further divided into sections called chapels. One paper can have up to seventy different chapels, making negotiations as complex as if treaties had to be signed with seventy countries, all of whom barely tolerated the others.

Because Fleet Street is so competitive, with five tabloid morning papers and four "quality" papers, newspaper owners have traditionally caved in and paid workers very high wages, since the alternative of shutting down costs them millions. "Every day we could not put out a paper would cost us £150,000," says Hugh Lawson, general manager of the *Daily Telegraph*, the biggest-circulation quality newspaper (it has 1,270,000 readers, compared with the *Times*' 340,000). In addition, the market for Sunday newspapers has been dropping, as readers cut back on their traditional habit of buying three or four to just one in order to save money. Fleet Street's philosophy of survival at any price has resulted in what the owners berate as grotesquely high salaries for newspaper workers. The average annual salary for a journalist is £17,000, twice what a regional U.K. paper pays, and linotype operators can get an extraordinary £734 a week even though linotype machines have about one-sixth the productivity of a computer-operated photocomposition machine.

The Times Newspapers showdown exploded after years of trouble between management and the unions. In 1974, after the *Times* moved to its new building, Times Newspapers' managing director Marmaduke Hussey threatened suspension of publication unless an agreement was reached on new procedures that would lead to some reduction in overmanning. A compromise was reached before the deadline, and the situation settled down until January 1977 when the *Times* failed to appear for a day because of a dispute over the contents of an article in the paper. Then in March of that year, publication of the *Times* was halted for a week due to a stoppage by machine-room workers, who returned to work only after the national office of their union threatened to expel them. There were no shutdowns by the unions after that, but minor disruptions frequently delayed editions and resulted in the loss of copies. Between January and November 1978, Times Newspapers' management reported that about 12 million copies were lost because of union disruptions, resulting in a loss of £1.16 million in profit. Disputes had stopped the printing of the *Times* twenty-one times and the *Sunday Times*, nine.

Times Newspapers' executives were concerned that the constant interruptions were causing advertisers to take their money elsewhere, and they shared in the despair of Fleet Street owners over what they regarded as the unions' intransigence. But changes within the Thomson empire were also influential in causing the shutdown of the papers. By

1978 the empire was far different from what it had been at its infancy in the U.K. It was no longer solely dependent on newspapers but was a multibusiness empire in which the Times newspapers were a prestigious, though tiny, component. When Roy Thomson bought the *Sunday Times*, there was no Thomson Organisation (the original name of ITOL). When he acquired the *Times*, the Thomson Organisation had only begun branching out from newspaper publishing into travel and books. In 1974, when the *Times* moved next door to the *Sunday Times*, Roy Thomson had just invested in North Sea oil. Thus, when Roy Thomson bought the money-losing *Times*, he promised that he and his family would meet any losses so that they would not affect the dividends of public shareholders of the Thomson Organisation. Under the terms of the agreement, however, financial responsibility could revert to the Thomson Organisation upon either side giving six months notice.

The industry was tipped off that the company was going to take a hard line by two separate events in 1977: the family cut back the notice period to one month; and Gordon Brunton told a meeting of Thomson executives that a six-month closure of papers was quite likely in 1978 or 1979 as a way of curbing the unions' power. Early in 1978, the hardball tactics gained momentum as the financial responsibility for the papers was handed over to the Thomson Organisation, a signal to the unions that the family was no longer willing to absorb the losses *ad infinitum*, even if they were for one of the world's greatest papers. The losses came from the *Times*—the *Sunday Times* was still profitable. Between 1966 and April 1977, the accumulated loss borne by the family was £10 million, and understandably, their patience was wearing thin. Ironically, however, the 1978 clash occurred just when the *Times* was moving back into the black and the *Sunday Times*' revenue was growing.

But following the tossing of the papers by the family to the Thomson Organisation, events snowballed to such an extent that avoiding the inevitable shutdown was as hopeless as stopping a runaway train. The family further divorced itself from the U.K. by converting the British-based Thomson Organisation into the Canadian-based ITOL. Next, early in the spring of 1978, Marmaduke Hussey was ordered by the board of Thomson British Holdings (as the U.K. division of ITOL was then known) to do something quickly to stop the chain of work stoppages. On April 10, he wrote all employees saying the situation was "disturbing." On April 26, he wrote the general secretaries of the unions that he would suspend publication of the papers on November 30 unless the unions agreed to a new disputes procedure, no "arbitrary work restrictions," more-efficient manning levels and a restructuring of the wage system.

But although his ultimatum in effect would have overhauled and revolutionized labor relations at the paper, no specific proposals had been drafted as to how this would be accomplished. This put management and labor under an impossible deadline, especially as it was not a matter of drawing up just one agreement between management and one union. There would have to have been fifty-four agreements between management and the papers' different chapels. This tended to make the unions believe that management's true goal was to shut down the papers rather than reach a settlement. In any event, agreement was not reached with all the unions, and on November 30 Hussey issued a six-paragraph statement saying publication of both papers was being suspended. The *Times* announced the shutdown by saying: "There will be an interval." That Times Newspapers executives were willing to shut down during the Christmas season, when advertising is traditionally at a peak, was viewed by many as showing their determination.

The tough stand by management soon eroded as two camps of doves and hawks emerged at a time when unity was essential. The hawks were Hussey, general manager Dugal Nisbet-Smith, and the *Times*' editor, William Rees-Mogg. The doves were Sir Denis Hamilton, editor-in-chief of both papers, and Harold Evans, editor of the *Sunday Times*. But the position of the two key players—Kenneth Thomson and Gordon Brunton—was cloudy, vacillating between the two extremes except at the end when they veered towards the doves.

Marmaduke ("Duke") Hussey was fifty-five at the time of the dispute. He had lost one leg as a result of being wounded at Anzio during World War II and had been hospitalized for much of the following five years. In 1949 he joined the *Daily Mail* and eventually became group managing director. He moved to the Thomson Organisation in 1971. His wife was a Woman of the Bedchamber to Queen Elizabeth II at the time of the dispute at the papers. It was Hussey who was in the front line during the showdown, and his personality is described in contradictory terms by the heads of two of the unions involved. "He was generally a respected employer who was regarded as being wrong on this occasion," says Owen O'Brien, general secretary at that time of the National Society of Operative Printers and Media Personnel. "He was old-fashioned and patrician with no common touch," says Jacob Ecclestone, who was head of the *Times*' chapel of the National Union of Journalists during the dispute.

Dugal Nisbet-Smith was a New Zealand journalist who moved to England in the late 1950s and worked for the Mirror Group, setting up their paper in Jamaica and then becoming managing director of the *Glasgow Daily Record* in the early 1970s. A November 1978 memo from the paper's members of the National Union of Journalists to the union's London head office described him as

> hard, clever, and arrogant. . . . Basically, Smith believes in increasing profits by cutting down on spending money. Great in the short term—but let me give you an example. Glasgow had five press units. Smith saved money by using only four and cannibalising the fifth press to provide spares. Now, Glasgow will have to spend more than £1 million to buy a new fifth press unit. Smith, of course, has moved on.

Rees-Mogg, however, provides a more flattering description of Smith as being "a staunch, effective, competent manager."

Rees-Mogg, whose formidable intelligence and scintillating conversation can stimulate people out of any fatigue they might be suffering, led a charmed life until the sale of the *Times* cut short his journalistic career. When Rupert Murdoch bought the *Times*, Rees-Mogg was only fifty-three; he left the paper and opened a rare-books store on Pall Mall in London. Rees-Mogg started at the *Financial Times* and then became financial, political and city editor of the *Sunday Times* and, in 1967, when he was just thirty-six, editor of the *Times*.

Rees-Mogg had a major impact on both papers, developing the *Sunday Times'* business news section and writing elegant, pontifical, proestablishment editorials for the *Times* that tended to support the Conservative party. In return, Prime Minister Margaret Thatcher recently showed her appreciation by making him chairman of the British Arts Council. Ecclestone, who has little that is nice to say about anybody at Times Newspapers in 1978, saves his most acid comments for Rees-Mogg. "He is a product of the British ruling class, a person who was born into lots of money and was clever academically, but was unable to relate to the world of ordinary people, who didn't have servants or nannies or go to private schools. He traveled around by chauffeured-driven car or taxi, never by public transit. He was an old-fashioned High Tory. He was pleasant to be with, although he got cross if you disagreed."

Denis Hamilton, a dove during the dispute, had had the most impact on the papers of any of the people involved. Diplomatic, disarming and dashing, with a pencil-thin moustache, Hamilton puzzled his staff with his mercurial mood changes, from briskness and frankness one day to remoteness the next. He was best known for his long pauses in conversation, particularly on the telephone, making the person on the other end think the line had gone dead. But former employees also describe him as gallantly courteous, willing to delegate, and innovative. Today, he is chairman of both Reuters and the British Museum and is largely responsible for the museum's vast ancient Egyptian collection.

Hamilton, born in 1918, wrote for a number of the Kemsley regional newspapers before World War II, and after being demobilized from the army, he became Kemsley's personal assistant. When Roy Thomson bought the Kemsley chain, he persuaded Hamilton to stay on as editor-in-chief of the *Sunday Times*, and when he later bought the *Times*, Hamilton became its chief editor, too. Hamilton extensively refashioned the *Sunday Times*, including creating the business news section; developing the color magazine—the first among U.K. papers; hiring Lord Snowdon as artistic adviser to the magazine in 1962—which caused an uproar but also brought the magazine welcome publicity; establishing "Insight," an in-depth essay on a major news event or social trends; and enlarging the paper's size by about thirty pages. All this resulted in a big jump in circulation.

Hamilton, who was on Field Marshal Montgomery's staff during World War II and has a bronze statue of the war hero in the library of his London flat, tends to speak in military terms. "Since 1946, I have had a ringside seat with all the great warriors of Fleet Street," he says. During the dispute, Hamilton would say a company's chief executive officer, like an army's commanding officer, should get plenty of sleep in order to make the right decision and that corporate leadership, as in the military, should be from the front of the battle.

"The closing of the papers would have broken Roy Thomson's heart," he says. "He did not view the new newspaper technology as leading to a reduction in employment but instead as creating opportunities for new magazines and newspapers. While there is acceptance of change in new industries, the older industries tend to resist technological change until it is too late for that industry. The opposition of the printers to computer technology is akin to the hostility in the last century to the introduction of the spinning wheel."

Harold Evans, the other dove, had as meteoric a career rise as Rees-Mogg. Evans was handpicked by Hamilton to become editor of the *Sunday Times* in 1967, when he was thirty-six, over a number of other seemingly more likely candidates cast in the traditional sedate mold of *Sunday Times* editors. But Hamilton chose Evans, previously the editor of a number of regional papers, for the very reason that he was a tradition-buster who would bring new vitality to the paper. Under Evans, the paper scooped its rivals in revealing that Kim Philby, a member of the British Secret Intelligence Service, was a Soviet spy, and began to spin off some of its long series into books. Evans also encouraged the paper to pursue a more liberal editorial policy than that of the *Times*. For example, the *Sunday Times* was for abortion law reform, while the *Times* was opposed.

Considering their opposite approaches and that both are described by acquaintances as being well aware of their cleverness, it is not surprising that Rees-Mogg and Evans did not get along. Rees-Mogg is tall, lean, cool, profound, and immaculate in three-piece suits. Evans is bantam-size, works with his shirt-sleeves rolled up, and creates a tornado in his wake. Rees-Mogg is Old Money; Evans's father had been a railway driver. "Rees-Mogg was academic in his style, whereas Evans was flamboyant and a self-publicist for himself and his paper," says Hugh Lawson of the *Daily Telegraph*. Evans's style was a daily enactment of the screaming mayhem of the film *Front Page*. As former *Times* reporter John Carter recalls: "Evans played the part of an editor. Every Saturday night he would slash away at the makeup editor's page layouts in loud shouting bouts. He delegated me to run interference with Randolph Churchill, whose book about his father had been serialized by the paper and who would often be drunk when he called."

After Murdoch bought Times Newspapers, Evans was made editor of the *Times* and upset its readers by revamping the staid front page to resemble that of a regional newspaper with dramatic photos that often did not relate to news stories. He left in July 1982 for Goldcrest Films & Television, a division of Pearson Longman and producer of the 1981 and 1982 Academy Award winners for best picture—*Chariots of Fire* and *Gandhi*. That Evans left under a black cloud was shown by the *Times* waiting for two days to announce his departure and doing so in just two lines. Also, Evans had previously expressed the wish to edit the paper for another seven years, until he was sixty. "One of the sad effects of the shutdown is that neither Rees-Mogg, nor Evans, both of whom were high-class editors, are editing papers today," Hamilton says.

The two most influential people in the Times Newspapers disputes were also the least seen—Gordon Brunton and Kenneth Thomson. Brunton started off as a hawk and wound up as a dove, in line with Kenneth's changing attitude. But it was Kenneth who most puzzled, frustrated and infuriated the unions, who thought of him, as one member sardonically puts it, as "the invisible man." His not getting directly involved in the negotiations reflected the decentralized way he runs the empire. Moreover, direct involvement in the papers could have resulted in his having to move to London, which he did not want to do.

Sitting on a candy-pink chair in the study above his bookshop with a portrait of Alexander Pope gazing over him, Rees-Mogg equals the rapier epigrams of Pope as he describes his impression of Kenneth during the dispute. "The initial strategy was developed under Roy Thomson, who was highly aggressive and able to change situations to his own advantage. If he had been alive, he would have been able to introduce the new machinery without perhaps more than a week's stoppage. But success depended on having the proprietor in England and his having a tough reputation with the unions. The campaign had been conceived and was conducted by people trained in the Roy school, and it didn't suit Kenneth's fundamentally conservative character. He wanted order and peace and disliked face-on, brutal conflicts with the unions. In the middle of everything, he said to me, 'I never understand why you English hate each other so much.' Here he was facing a dispute at his expense in a country in which he had chosen not to live. Kenneth and John Tory were keen that something be done about the unions, but you mustn't make judgments based on what people want, because until a crisis develops, you don't know what they want. I have great regard for Kenneth Thomson, but he was not the man for this situation. It's a nuisance to have a bishop when you need a commander-in-chief."

Thomson was criticized for a lack of resolve when he agreed in June 1979, seven months into the shutdown, that the issue of new technology be settled separately at a later date. He also undermined the hard-line stand by Times Newspapers' management when he openly expressed his wish that publication be resumed. But if Thomson was viewed as wavering, his irresolution may have partly stemmed from Times Newspapers getting no support from other Fleet Street owners. That greatly embittered Times' executives, who felt they were fighting an industry-wide battle all alone.

"They didn't succeed because their competitors were not prepared to back them by also stopping production," says John LePage, deputy secretary of the Newspaper Publishers Association. "Their stand was understandable because they had been losing money and felt they couldn't afford to shut down. But what did upset Times Newspapers was that the other papers took advantage of the situation by printing extra copies to take away circulation. The unions gained considerable strength as a result because it showed that no paper could close down unilaterally and expect to beat the unions."

Owen O'Brien, who is now joint secretary of the Society of Graphical and Allied Trades, the largest newspaper union, and who supports single keystroking being introduced, is far more scathing than LePage. Anger and disgust filled his voice as he said: "It showed that every employer was only paying lip service to the need for new technology. When the Thomson management closed down the two papers to pressure the unions into accepting the technology, the other employers reacted like a pack of hyenas. They put on extra machines and picked up circulation. If they had really wanted to support Times Newspapers, they would have stabilized production, but by increasing pagination, they provided jobs for the Times' production workers and helped drag on the closure."

The gains made by the rest of Fleet Street were short-lived, since circulation returned to its original count for each paper after the dispute ended. The *Daily Telegraph*'s Hugh Lawson expressed the views of Fleet Street when he said that each paper must fight its own battles. "Fifteen years ago, Fleet Street might have supported one another, but we don't have the resources to lose £150,000 a day to support the *Times*, whereas the Thomson organization makes millions from North Sea oil, the Hudson's Bay Company and its many other companies. In November 1982, when we had a stoppage that cost us £1,700,000, we were entirely on our own."

The *Daily Telegraph*'s losses were miniscule, however, compared with the £30-million losses suffered as a result of the shutdown of the Times Newspapers. When the closure was finally over after management capitulated, the papers' wage bill increased by about 100 percent. The truce between management and the unions was soon broken by new disruptions. In August 1980, Kenneth Thomson's patience was stretched even thinner when the *Times*' journalists, seeking more money, went on their first strike in the paper's long history.

As far back as 1971, Kenneth Thomson was saying publicly that "the *Times* is just a drag on profits. . . . It is not reasonable to expect us to support such a loss indefinitely." Nevertheless, despite this realization of the cold hard facts, Kenneth's devotion to his father and his loyalty in perpetuating what had meant so much to Roy kept him pouring millions of pounds into the papers. But while the losses and labor problems convinced onlookers that it was a matter of when, and not if, Kenneth would sell or close the papers, he was still saying in 1979 that "the sale of the *Times* is one of those awful specters we would not wish to contemplate."

The journalists' walkout, continued production disruptions, and the fact that no agreement was reached on computer setting proved to be the final straws. It was the *Financial Times*—not Thomson or any of his papers—that actually said what Kenneth must have been thinking but never voiced: "Confronted with the astounding truth that a total expenditure of £70 million on Times Newspapers had resulted in hostility and ingratitude from the workforce and a prospect of unending losses, Lord Thomson had little option but to agree" when the Board of Thomson British Holdings decided that the papers must be sold. And so, on 22 October 1980, Thomson British Holdings announced that it would be withdrawing from publication of the papers and that if no buyer were found by March 1981, the papers would be closed.

On 13 February 1981, the surprise buyer was announced. Rupert Murdoch paid £12 million, a bargain price were it not for the fact that the *Times* was a steady money-loser, and signed an agreement specifying that he would not change the character of the newspapers. Employees insisted that this be done because of his reputation for buying newspapers and taking them "down market" to increase circulation, through the use of sleazy photos and sensational stories. The purchase made the then forty-nine-year-old Murdoch one of the most powerful Fleet Street publishers of this century, certainly more powerful than Roy Thomson had been. In the U.K., he owns the *Sun*, the *News of the World*, more than two dozen regional newspapers, and *London Weekend*. While Murdoch's *Sun*, which regularly carries a page 3 nude pinup, announced the purchase in a *Times*-like headline of six lines and twenty-two words, the *Times* carried a full page 3 photo of the nude Greek goddess of ecstasy. The photo was that of the figurine placed on the hoods of Rolls-Royces for seven decades with the ad inserted by Rolls-Royce's ad agency, Dorland Advertising.

The ad gave the transaction some humor, but the saga of the showdown at Times Newspapers had a grimmer denouement. Its goal of changing industrial relations on Fleet Street not only was not realized, but weakened the already palsied stand of management. Most of Fleet Street, including the *Times*, is still suffering crippling losses, wages remain horrendously high, the unions are as fragmented as ever, and no progress at all has been made towards technological change. The owner of the *Times* and the *Sunday Times* is new, but otherwise nothing has changed.

12

TURNAROUND IN THE UNITED KINGDOM

IT IS UNUSUAL for an industry leader to be depressed about its future, but that is the gloomy attitude at Thomson Regional Newspapers (TRN) in the United Kingdom. Kenneth Thomson is buying newspapers in the United States at the rate of at least four a year, but his U.K. chain is experiencing closures and stringent cutbacks in staff. Similarly, while magazine publishing by the young U.S. branch of the Thomson empire is at full throttle, the U.K. magazine operations have been shrunk. Only in information services is the U.K. side of the empire enjoying the same buoyancy as its U.S. counterpart.

Thomson's owns sixty newspapers in the U.K., with a total circulation of 2.7 million and revenue of £125 million. The chain includes the leading papers of Scotland (the *Evening News* and the *Scotsman*), Northern Ireland (*Belfast Telegraph*), and Wales (*South Wales Echo*), as well as newspapers in such major centers as Newcastle and Aberdeen. Several of its reporters have become bestselling authors, including Ken Follett and Anthony Holden, the biographer of Prince Charles and other members of the Royal Family. Yet, despite its pre-eminence, Thomson Regional Newspapers has become a scared rabbit in recent years as advertising, on which it depends for 70 percent of its revenue, has evaporated in the wake of high unemployment. The most recent substantial profit the newspapers had was 1979's £14 million. There were heavy losses in 1980 and 1981, and although a marginal profit was made in 1982, it was due to staff reductions rather than revenue gains. However, the company did have a valuable asset—a 4.73 percent interest in Reuters news agency, which it sold in 1984 for close to £50 million.

Regional newspapers traditionally derive most of their advertising revenue from employment ads, and these dried up as unemployment reached record levels in the U.K. Between the early 1960s and the late 1970s, the number of jobless rose from 300,000 to 1.5 million. Then in just the three years between 1979 and 1982, it soared to 3.3 million. No substantial decline is predicted for the near future. As a result, employment ads have been virtually wiped off the pages of all U.K. regional newspapers, knocking out their traditional props. Thomson Regional Newspapers, which had carried 37 million lines of employment ads in 1973, had only 8 million in 1981–82. Averaging out the cost of a line, the difference in revenue between 1973 and 1982 exceeded £20 million, about £15 million of which would have flowed through to the bottom line. The chain also lost more than £5 million due to industrial disputes in 1979–80.

Unlike Thomson's community newspapers in the U.S. and Canada, which are the only newspapers in town, the U.K. newspapers, while the only local paper, do not have a market monopoly. Instead, they compete for advertising and circulation with newspapers published in London but distributed nationwide, a task made easier than in North America because the U.K. is smaller and has only one time zone, compared with five zones in Canada and four in the U.S.

Making a bad situation worse for the regionals is the growing competition they face from free newspapers, which charge advertisers lower rates and which reach a wider audience, since they are circulated free to a community. They are cheaper to produce because they contain 15 percent editorial content compared with the 40 percent of paid-for newspapers, and consequently require fewer reporters, and because they are also printed under contract rather than by union shops. The lower cost base means lower advertising rates can be charged than those offered by paid-for papers.

Free newspapers started in the U.K. about twenty years ago but gained momentum in 1979, taking advantage of the weakened condition of the regionals. "They sprang up like mushrooms after the rain," says Jacob Ecclestone, now deputy general secretary of the 32,000-member National Union of Journalists. "In 1980, there were 100; now there are 600. Three years ago, they made about £60 million in advertising revenue; now they make close to £400 million." In some cases, the free newspapers were started by the regionals; in others, by local businessmen or real estate agents as a sales tool.

The trying task of steering Thomson Regional Newspapers through this stormy period is held by James Evans, who became managing director in April 1982 at the height of the chain's difficulties. His is not an enviable position, but Evans exudes relaxed calm as he munches cookies and smokes a cigar while ticking off in precise, measured tones the problems and how they are being handled. An indication of his rising status in the Thomson empire is his being chosen to head International Thomson Organisation PLC, the U.K. wing, as of this December (1984) when Brunton vacates that position as well as the presidency of the parent ITOL. Like John Tory, Evans is a lawyer and his well-organized manner reflects his legal background. Evans left private practice in 1965 to join the Thomson Organisation as its specialist in copyright and publishing law. He was the first in-house lawyer the *Sunday Times* had since it started in 1822. One of his assignments was defending the *Sunday Times* in a court case stemming from the paper's stories on how the drug thalidomide was resulting in the birth of deformed babies. The paper launched a campaign for greater financial compensation of the victims but ran afoul of the U.K. contempt laws. Evans fought a number of court cases "to get the issues out into the open" but lost in the House of Lords. He got this decision overturned at the Court of Human Rights in Strasbourg. Evans decided he would like to move into commercial work and became company secretary of the Thomson Organisation in 1976, a board member of Times Newspapers in 1978, and its chairman from July 1980 until its sale in February 1981. Subsequently, he became joint deputy managing director of ITOL in the U.K. and then moved over to TRN.

Because the recession is not lifting in the U.K., Evans says the only routes open for improving TRN financially are keeping a lid on wage increases (of about 4.25 percent in 1983), staff reductions, and starting up more free newspapers. Labor costs were a natural target because in the U.K. they average more than 50 percent of total expenses. So far, 500 of TRN's 7,500 employees, including 200 of the 300 head-office staff, have been let go, reducing costs by £5 million. Laid-off employees received the equivalent of four weeks' salary for each year of employment to a maximum of £25,000.

The National Union of Journalists' Ecclestone says these terms were better than those of other regional chains, which limited their severance allowances to two weeks' salary for every year of service. "Thomson Regional Newspapers has a reputation among the unions of being relatively civilized and easy to deal with, although the chain is not motivated by generosity but by the desire to get it done fast without any bother." In view of the notorious, unparalleled, unending and unbending adversary relationship between the newspaper unions and publishers in the U.K., this attitude is understandable.

In other moves, the head-office survivors of Thomson Regional Newspapers were transferred from London to Reading, about forty miles west of the capital, where the rent is much less than the £1 million paid in London, and Evans was able to decimate head office by two-thirds through rerouting some functions to the local newspapers, most notably in advertising. "Instead of a central London department handling copy from the advertising agencies and processing it to our different publishing centers, we now have the agencies deal directly with the papers," Evans says. "If an ad agency wants to place an ad in all our papers, they have to deal with each paper or the London representative for each district in which we have newspapers."

Evans and other U.K. newspaper executives are hamstrung by tough union opposition, backed up by crippling strikes, to the direct input of stories by journalists and of ads by telephone clerks, which would require fewer compositors and reduce the size of the production department. "The economies that direct input can provide are essential for the viable future of all U.K. newspapers," Evans says. He says TRN could move to this method within twelve to eighteen months but the unyielding position of the unions makes it unlikely that this will happen quickly.

Like other regional chains, Thomson Regional Newspapers has started a series of free newspapers, all in areas where it has paid-for newspapers, as a defensive measure to prevent the start-up of rival free papers. However, they contribute only a modest part of TRN's business. In 1983 their share was £3 million, or under 1 percent of the chain's total revenue.

While it is struggling to beat the recession, Thomson Regional Newspapers has a head start over its rivals because it is the U.K.'s largest regional newspaper chain. By contrast, International Thomson Publishing Limited, which publishes 19 business and 13 consumer magazines in the U.K., is dwarfed by its rival, International Publishing Corporation (IPC), a division of Reed International. Reed's other holdings include paper and packaging products and the Mirror Group of Newspapers (*Daily Mirror*, *Sunday Mirror*, *Sunday People*, *Scottish Daily Record*, *Sunday Mail* and *Sporting Life*). Reed's IPC Magazines is the largest U.K. publisher of weekly and consumer magazines, receiving about 30 percent of total advertising expenditure in this area. IPC Business Press publishes more than 130 business and technical journals, 22 directories, and 13 travel guides. It also owns 40 percent of Industrial & Trade Fairs Holdings, one of the world's largest companies in this field.

International Thomson Publishing has emerged from a rough few years of declining profits with new management, a new name, and a new publishing thrust. Its first director was Michael Mander, previously deputy chief executive and marketing director of Times Newspapers. Mander, forty-eight, is the son and grandson of newspaper advertising directors (his mother worked for Reuters and her father was on the *Morning Post*). He started his newspaper career at Associated Newspapers, which owns the *Daily Mail*, the *Mail on Sunday* and also a slew of regional newspapers. There, he developed secret plans to merge the *Daily Mail* with the *Daily Express* and the *News* with the *Standard*—both schemes code-named after swanky restaurants. Neither merger occurred. Mander worked for the *Mail*'s group managing director, Marmaduke Hussey, and subsequently became Hussey's deputy at Times Newspapers, emerging occasionally from the shadows during the 1978–79 dispute at the *Times* and *Sunday Times* as a substitute memo writer to the unions on Hussey's behalf.

Acquaintances describe Mander as a skilled marketing man who bravely criticized Roy Thomson's disastrous attempt, from 1967 to 1970, to increase the circulation of the *Times* at the expense of quality readers and advertisers. Still, considering the failure of the plan, Mander was not sticking his neck out foolishly. He also is a survivor, being the only senior member of the *Times'* management still working for the Thomson organization. In 1984 Mander was switched to Thomson Information Services Limited (the magazine and data communications group) as its director and was replaced at International Thomson Publishing by Malcolm Gill, formerly head of Thomson Business Magazines.

The name change, from Thomson Magazines, is cosmetic, as the division remains a U.K.-only venture. But the new directions in publications are more than skin-deep. The company is now concentrating on acquiring or starting magazines in growth industries and is paring away publications on topics for which circulation is declining. In 1981 International Thomson Publishing disposed of twenty of its less profitable magazines.

The crackdown occurred on the business magazine side, rather than the consumer magazines where there was not the same need to rationalize, since they are distributed over the counter by news agents and not by mail. However, with television advertising threatening the profitability of general women's magazines, a field that is flooded with publications, Thomson's is expanding into specialized leisure magazines to attract advertisers who do not normally use national media because of the limited appeal of their products. At the same time, there has been a heavy investment in two top-selling Thomson magazines—*Family Circle* and *Living*—which are both sold through supermarkets. Saturation radio promotions for the two magazines have boosted their circulations substantially.

In business publishing, International Thomson Publishing has traditionally concentrated on construction, farming and meat industries, textiles, and retailing, but it is now embracing health care as an explosive area of future growth. "The health-care market is the biggest technical and professional publishing sector in the U.K., with about £40 million in advertising revenue," says Andrew Shanks, marketing director of International Thomson Publishing. "Although most advertising expenditure is geared towards doctors, we do not think of health care in a narrow sense. In addition to general practitioners and hospital doctors, the sector includes nurses and midwives, paramedicals, social workers, pharmacists and technicians, all of whom support publishing markets.

"Health care has been growing quite fast over the last decade and seems to us to have good prospects for further growth over at least the next decade because of demographic factors. Growth in the number of people over seventy-five will be considerable during the coming years. There has also been a modest increase in the birthrate since the late 1970s, and it is the very young and the very old who make the most demands on our health-care services. Moreover, rising standards and needs are likely to override political and budgetary pressures to reduce the standard of services. There already is evidence that public sector cuts in the U.K. may well generate private sector expenditures to make up the gap."

International Thomson Publishing is not alone in pouncing on health-care magazines as a lucrative gold mine. In fact, it is turning its attention to what is already a field crowded with 200 medical publications, most of which are geared towards doctors, explaining Shanks's emphasis on the importance of other health-care professionals as potential readers. The company now publishes 4 journals, mostly dealing with hospitals, but plans are being hatched for publications on diagnostic medicine, geriatrics, social work, pharmacy, and medicine's use of computer technology, as well as for the launch or acquisition of a weekly medical newspaper.

The Thomson U.K. newspapers and magazines are long-established media industries trying not to get bypassed in the 1980s, but in information services in the U.K., the Thomson empire is right on track with present and future demands of business for high technology. Although the U.K. is often derided for its monumental labor problems and outmoded equipment, it is becoming a world leader in high technology. In Europe, Britain is already the number one supplier of databases as well as the largest single database market, with 1982 sales of $235 million, far ahead of the $150 million each that France and Germany logged. The good news for database firms like Thomson's is that the already buoyant market is expected to become even bigger, with growth projected to run at more than 20 percent a year during the rest of the 1980s.

The responsibility for seeing that Thomson's gets a large piece of this action has been handed not to a computer expert but to a longtime employee, David Cole, a former newspaper reporter who became chairman of both Thomson Regional Newspapers and Thomson Books. Cole, fifty-six, is described by acquaintances as "dour," "a cold fish," and somewhat narrow-minded. "When I left Thomson's to become head of the Book Marketing Council, everybody else at the company acknowledged that it was an opportunity to widen my knowledge of the book-publishing industry and gain greater visibility, but Cole couldn't understand this," Desmond Clarke says. "However, I've seen him since I left, and although it's still not easy communicating with him, he has been friendly and will accept suggestions."

The description of Cole as dour may have something to do with his dimly lit office, which seems as dark as a cave. But while a smile rarely cracks his face, he does have a dry sense of humor and enjoys waiting for people to realize he is joking. Cole was born in the coal valleys of Wales and "educated abroad—in England," an expression that he says is a traditional Welsh joke. Although his parents wanted him to attend university, he preferred becoming a journalist and "the conventional wisdom then was that journalists didn't attend university but went straight into a newspaper and learned from the bottom up." Cole started at the *Merthyr Express* in Merthyr Tydfil, a small town in the hills north of Cardiff. In his twenties, he became the features editor of a major Welsh and Manchester newspaper and at twenty-seven became editor of the *Western Mail*, Wales's national morning newspaper.

When Roy Thomson bought that paper as part of the Kemsley chain, he made Cole managing director of the paper and of a printing company he owned. In 1967 Cole stepped up to become managing director of Thomson's Newcastle newspapers, the biggest center then in its web of regional newspapers. After this nearly twenty-year apprenticeship, in quick succession Cole was named editorial, planning and circulation director of Times Newspapers, assistant managing director of these departments, and then, in 1972, managing director of Thomson Regional Newspapers.

Cole says he got this job at a time when the future of TRN was in doubt, just as it is now, and that therefore it was just coasting along, waiting for the worst. "There was a great feeling among certain people on the board of directors, excluding Roy Thomson, that there was not much purpose in investing much money in the chain, but I had a great belief in the chain's papers. If you batten down the hatches and wait to see what comes along, there won't be any growth, but if you believe that newspapers are valuable to a community, you beef up those aspects which are most valuable to the community."

This philosophical discourse gives the impression that Cole injected new vigor into the reporting of stories, but in actuality he is referring to TRN "not fully exploiting advertising and marketing opportunities." He squeezed out more advertising revenue by getting national and local advertisers to share the cost of an ad, a strategy common in North America but until then untried in the U.K. Cole says this boosted TRN's profit sevenfold between 1972 and 1979.

Although he has gone "abroad" to England, Cole retains close ties to his home country, sitting on the boards of nearly every type of public service committee, ranging from university to theater to sports. He chaired a two-year inquiry into the lack of nurses at many Welsh hospitals and was on a national tourism committee when it convinced the U.K. government to help finance regional tourism. He is also responsible for ITOL's support of a program in Neath, near Cardiff, to reduce the high unemployment and school dropout rates.

Thomson's has four database companies. Derwent Publications (chemical, pharmaceutical and electrical patent information), Eurolex (legal information), ESDU International (engineering), and Computacar (a matchmaker for sellers and buyers of used cars). While the Thomson empire moved into information services in the U.S. via acquisitions, in the U.K. it redirected existing companies from print into database publishers. Although the advent of cable TV in the U.K. provides a potentially glittering future for the databases of Thomson and its rivals, Cole says ITOL has no intention of becoming a cable operator: "The costs and risks are high, it takes a long time to get any returns, and the franchise period given by the government is too short."

Derwent, which was established in the late 1950s, is a classic case of how a print publisher moves into putting its information on computer. "Derwent originally specialized in doing searches of chemical patents to check if anyone else already held a patent and would send a letter to customers. Then it graduated into a card index, weekly bulletins, monthly abstracts, special alert bulletins, microfiche and, finally, on-line," Cole says.

By the time ITOL bought Derwent in 1966, it was highly profitable and had expanded into twenty-six countries. It now has a translating service because about 40 percent of the documents it receives are in Russian or Japanese. Derwent's database contains more than 5 million patents and can be accessed from computers in Santa Monica, California, Surrey in England, and Tokyo. It is broadening out into databases on a wide range of scientific and electrical topics, as well as such exotica as the keel design of the Australian boat that won the 1983 America's Cup.

Eurolex (an abbreviation of "European law center") was launched in 1981 with a hefty development budget of £7 million. It now contains about 500 million words dealing with British, European and Common Market law, including unreported cases, digests and abstracts, up from 135 million words in mid-1983. Unlike the long-established Derwent, which has a comfortable lead on competitors, Eurolex is a newcomer in an undeniably fast-growing, but also cutthroat, market. Its main rival, Butterworth's, is owned by Reed International and has a ready-made audience, since it is the largest legal publisher in the U.K. Butterworth's has the license for U.K. distribution of Lexis, an American-based service providing information on U.S. law.

Butterworth's head start and Eurolex's enormous start-up costs make Eurolex a long-range proposition, with Cole predicting it could take until 1988 for it to become profitable. Eurolex, however, has taken several steps in an effort to be in the black sooner. It is providing its data on nondedicated terminals, whereas Lexis-Butterworth uses only its own (dedicated) terminals. That makes Eurolex available to more people; Cole claims that 97 percent of U.K. office terminals can plug into Eurolex.

In 1983 Eurolex linked up with Westlaw, the largest U.S. legal data-base company, in an arrangement providing Eurolex and Westlaw customers access to both systems. Cole says similar arrangements are in the works with Australian, German, Italian and Dutch companies. The aggressiveness is paying off, with Eurolex well ahead of target in signing up subscribers. In its first two years of operation, its number of users soared from 25 to 375 in 1983, with its 1983 year-end target of 250 users reached in June—six months earlier than anticipated. Its blue-chip clients include the British Royal Courts, the House of Lords and the European Courts of Justice.

Cole is confident this pace will continue because it is becoming impossible for law offices to find space for the constant flow of legal tomes containing government regulations. "There are so many regulations from the European Economic Community alone, that it is impossible to index them other than on computer," he says. Recently, the EEC hired Eurolex to develop a European legal literature information service.

ESDU does evaluations of engineering design problems, such as the stress high winds would cause to the upper floors of an office tower. It is in a state of flux while Cole is deciding whether to shift from putting its information on compact discs or switch to online access, similar to that of Derwent and Eurolex, which would require a huge investment in mainframe computers. Nevertheless, the debate over technology has not stopped ESDU's sales drive. In 1983 it set up a U.S. sales operation and already has a number of U.S. military and commercial customers.

Posters for the fourth data-base company, Computacar, depict a girl in a low-cut, white T-shirt with the inscription I THINK WE'VE GOT JUST WHAT YOU'RE LOOKING FOR. The come-on has not been very effective, however, since Computacar, with £1 million in sales, is only marginally profitable. Notwithstanding, Thomson is holding on to it in anticipation of when cable TV becomes widespread in the U.K. and Computacar's car listings could be provided over the cable network.

ITOL acquired Computacar in 1977 from Unilever, which had started it just a few years previously. It was the world's first computer matching system for used cars, and the world was not enthused at its arrival. Unilever was eager to get rid of it and sold it to ITOL for a few thousand pounds. "ITOL bought it because it wanted to get into the computerized electronic medium," managing director Nigel Donaldson says. Because Computacar sells a relatively few 20,000 cars annually, it has scrounged around for other ways of making money. A fling at using its system to sell houses went nowhere, and now Donaldson is considering using it to sell motorcycles and boats. In the meantime, with few new ways of increasing revenue, the alternative is to cut costs through reducing telephone-answering staff. "We now list three cars per telephone call, which results in calls lasting up to fifteen minutes; the amount of time per call could be lowered if we listed only one car and mailed out a longer list," Donaldson says.

If Thomson's sticks with Computacar, it will not be the first time it has persevered with a company that has got off to an unpromising start. One precedent is its nearly twenty-year-old Yellow Pages business, which only now is showing hearty signs of life. The idea for Thomson's to enter this field came from Roy Thomson through his familiarity with the Yellow Page directories published in Canada and the U.S. by the telephone companies. No such directories existed in the U.K., leaving a gaping hole that Thomson rushed to fill. "It would be a public service that had long been needed, and throughout my career I have had a great liking for making a profit out of doing public service," Roy wrote in *After I Was Sixty*.

In the U.K., telephone directories are put out by the Post Office, which runs the telephone system, and Thomson persuaded the Post Office to sell advertising space in a separate Yellow Pages directory. He soon discovered that what did well in North America did not necessarily do well in the U.K. It took about eight years for the British public to accept the new concept; in addition, there were the usual difficulties that arise when private enterprise goes into business with the government.

The contract called for all printing to be done by Her Majesty's Stationery Office, the government printing agency, on a noncompetitive basis. Pricing policies fluctuated according to what government was in power, and were often imposed on political rather than commercial grounds. Thomson's also was often unwillingly caught up in industrial strife between the Post Office and the printing agency. "We learned a very important strategic lesson—the danger of having a major investment and profit center dependent upon divisions over which we had no ultimate control," Gordon Brunton says. In addition, the aggravation was not compensated for in huge profits. Thomson's made only £25 million during the fifteen years of its contract.

When its contract came up for renewal in 1980, Thomson's jumped at the opportunity to sever the connection, but it still had faith in Yellow Pages as a business and decided to launch its own directories in competition with the Post Office's. It formed a joint venture, called Thomson Directories, with Dun & Bradstreet, a U.S. firm specializing in business directories, with each firm investing £10 million. Unlike Thomson Yellow Pages, which was strictly a sales agent, Thomson Directories both publishes its own books and sells advertising space in them. The directories differ from North American Yellow Pages in devoting several pages to community information, ranging from local transport services to leisure activities and emergency household hints. So far, 136 directories have been published and they have quickly taken away one-fifth of the advertising previously received by the 26 Post Office Yellow Pages directories. Thomson Directories decided to publish five times as many directories as the Post Office in order to cover small areas not reached by the Post Office as well as households without telephones, not uncommon in the U.K.

Thomson's has been battered in its U.K. publishing ventures by the recession and by its own mistakes. Now it must wait and see if it has sufficiently corrected its weaknesses and errors.

13

DISCOVERING AMERICA

UNTIL 1978 James Leisy and his company, Wadsworth Incorporated, had never heard of the International Thomson Organisation. But after a whirlwind courtship by ITOL, Leisy dropped another takeover suitor for Wadsworth, then the twelfth-largest U.S. college publisher, at the altar in favor of ITOL. The takeover was important for several reasons. It marked ITOL's entry into the American market, from which it expects to have $500 million in sales and as much as half of its profit by 1988. By contrast, it took ITOL's other operations nineteen years, from 1959 until 1978, to reach revenue of $500 million. The Wadsworth acquisition also illustrates the disparate background of Thomson management as well as the empire's takeover strategy.

Leisy is both a trombonist and pianist in a Dixieland band and a co-founder of Wadsworth, which he started in 1954 with two former fellow salesmen at Prentice-Hall. Leisy sold college textbooks and Bibles for Prentice-Hall before leaving at the age of twenty-six. One of his partners was Dick Ettinger, the son of Prentice-Hall's founder. The trio chose San Francisco as their base because the New York and Boston markets already had many textbook firms whereas California, which was undergoing a population boom, had few college publishers. Within six years, the three recouped their original $1-million investment, and their astute choice of territory propelled Wadsworth (the maiden name of Ettinger's wife) into the number one spot in college publishing on the West Coast. At the same time, Leisy continued his music career, which he had started in college, and wrote several hit songs, including "Pinball Millionaire," "Please Tell Me Why," and "An

Old Beer Bottle." In 1967 he joined a West Coast Dixieland band that plays on Princess Cruises to Mexico and Alaska as well as at benefits. In 1976 Leisy and two of band leader Fred Waring's former performers started to write musical plays for children and are now the leading producers of packaged amateur shows for children in the United States. Their plays include a musical version of *Treasure Island*.

In 1977 Leisy and Ettinger had a difference of opinion (the third partner had already retired), and it was decided to sell the business. ITOL was not even in the picture as negotiations opened. As Leisy tells it: "We had about ten fervent suitors, including Harcourt Brace Jovanovich, the Times Mirror Company [owner of the *Los Angeles Times*], and Pearson Longman [owner of Longman Publishers and the *Financial Times*]. We signed a letter of intent to sell to Pearson Longman for $25 million and there was a story about the sale in the *Wall Street Journal*." But the negotiations were far from over because it was at this stage that ITOL became involved.

Leisy continues: "I had gone to New York to meet further about the deal and received a telephone call at my hotel from a Mr. Tucker of Brown Brothers Harriman, who asked to see me and told me ITOL was prepared to make a substantially better offer. I checked with my lawyer who said I had a fiduciary responsibility to Wadsworth's shareholders to listen to ITOL. I agreed to meet Gordon Brunton and Michael Brown in San Francisco. Brunton presented his case, speaking from notes, and a lot of careful work had gone into it. The tension of the situation had made me lose my voice, so I could only whisper. I had prepared thirteen demands which I thought would drive them away. The first demand was that they accept everything Pearson Longman had. The rest dealt with retaining management, our style of publishing and philosophy, and our name and board. It was around noon when my lawyer finished reading my list, and Brunton suggested we take a lunch break and meet again at 4:00 p.m. When we did, he said ITOL was still interested, but had a couple of questions of definition. These were settled the next day. Our demands were covered in a gentleman's, rather than contractual, agreement, and I have found ITOL scrupulous in living up to the agreement. There have been times when they have given in to us because we said we believed it had been settled in the agreement."

ITOL had not planned to enter the U.S. market until a year later, but Brunton decided to bid for Wadsworth after reading in the *Financial Times* that Pearson Longman was buying the company. "I phoned Brown Brothers and said we'd lost a good opportunity but was told that despite the announcement, a major shareholder had not been consulted. That was Ettinger, who owned 30 percent. We saw both

Ettinger and Wadsworth executives, although at first they didn't want to see us."

While Brunton and Brown maintain they avoid hostile takeovers, they are not averse to bidding wars as happened with Wadsworth. Brunton says: "I told Wadsworth that the Pearson Longman offer was totally inadequate and that we would pay them significantly more [ITOL paid $33 million—$8 million more]. I also promised they would have freedom of operation and that we would not withdraw dividends for five years. Instead, that money would go back into the growth of their business. We would give them a financial plan, but if they achieved their target, they would get financial incentives."

This pitch appealed to Leisy because with Wadsworth no longer publicly owned, management would not have to worry anymore about fluctuations in share prices. "The past five years have not been superb for the college industry, but instead of having to show earnings, we have been able to invest in our development. Not only has ITOL not taken out dividends but it has provided additional capital for new projects." Both Wadsworth and ITOL have benefited, with Wadsworth increasing its market share to climb up to fifth spot in college publishing. In the past few years, it has recorded some of the highest gains in the industry, rising from $42 million in 1981 to $58 million in 1982 and $65 million in 1983 partly on the strength of acquisitions it has made with ITOL's backing.

As the Wadsworth purchase demonstrates, Brunton and Brown like to personally do corporate takeovers. "We don't have a corporate development or planning department because I believe that is the chief executive officer's job," Brunton says. Adds Brown: "I do the acquisitions myself because they are the most important decision in business. In the last four years, we have bought more publishing companies in the United States than the rest of the industry. I have spent weeks in lawyers' and oil consultants' offices and at banks, insurance companies, and hospitals to get a better handle on each industry and find out what their information needs are, so we can buy or start a publication for which there is a market." Brown also says ITOL turns down far more prospects than it approves. "Every week ten items are brought to my attention, but we look at only one per month seriously and buy just three to four a year."

In 1976, before the Thomson empire had made a single cent from its investment in North Sea oil, it started planning how to spend all the money it was certain it was going to make. The advance planning was based on the hard reality that the empire should strike while it was rich. It would make a lot of money at first from the oil, but oil is a nonreplaceable, depleting resource. Although 80 percent of ITOL's profits now come from North Sea oil, Brunton predicts this will decline to under 20 percent by 1988. The company decided the solution was to be prepared for this dramatic change by pouring the oil money primarily into business-press publishing and information services in the United States and, on a more modest scale, into travel and oil and gas development there. Since it entered the U.S. market in 1978, ITOL has spent more than $400 million (U.S.) on acquiring American publications and another $36 million on new-product development.

As of the end of 1983, 5,000 of ITOL's 22,000 employees were in the United States and 25 percent of its sales—or $570 million—were there. Michael Brown says ITOL's U.S. sales should double every five years on existing products plus acquisitions, and he estimates that by 1988 there will be 10,000 employees without acquisitions and up to 12,000 with acquisitions. If the U.S. operations do contribute half of the group's profit by 1988, it would be quite an accomplishment in view of no profit having been made before 1982. Brown forecasts that by 1988, U.S. pretax profit will be $100 million.

Although ITOL is Canadian-owned, its executives see its future expansion, especially in its priority area of business publishing, in the United States. ITOL owns no business publications in Canada and has no immediate plans to enter the market. International Thomson Business Press president Richard Groves says he may launch Canadian versions of two ITBP publications—*Medical Economics* and *CableVision*—in two to three years, but an obstacle to ITBP in the Canadian market is the already high concentration of ownership, with Southam and Maclean-Hunter each producing about sixty trade magazines. "There may be areas they aren't touching; it's just a question of time until we go into Canada," Groves says.

The buoyant outlook for the U.S. business-press market explains Brown's optimism and ITOL's concentration there. By 1987 the electronic publishing field is expected to triple to $3 billion. The market for software programming for business and professional uses is predicted to reach $6 billion in 1987, compared with $660 million in 1982. Advertising dollars spent in the business press have more than doubled over the past decade, and profit margins as high as 35 percent are possible, substantially more than with consumer publications.

ITOL is also pinning its hopes on the United States both because of its large size and because its United Kingdom operations are encountering rough weather. "Its U.K. newspapers derive 70 percent of their revenue from advertising, and within that the largest segment is employment ads," says Julian Gamble, media analyst at the London investment firm of Philips & Drew. "The newspapers have therefore been hard hit by the high rate of unemployment. In addition, two new newspapers have been launched recently, increasing the rivalry for circulation and advertising. The U.K. trade and technical magazines have controlled, rather than paid, circulation and depend on advertising for the majority of their revenue. Consumer magazines, such as ITOL's, have faced increasing competition from the Sunday magazine supplements and for the past two years from Channel 4, the U.K.'s fourth television channel, an independent network which was established in November 1982. If cable television comes in, the competition will increase again."

While hungry for growth in the U.S., ITOL is not buying everything in sight. Instead, it has concentrated on businesses in which it was successful in the U.K. Its purchases are based on careful studies of what industries will grow during this decade and whether a targeted acquisition has the potential for multiple products, such as newsletters, microfilm, software, seminars, video, and looseleaf services, as well as the basics of books and magazines. In addition, the company must pass a number of other tests, according to a June 1983 memo by Michael Brown on "market sectors of special interest" to the empire. These criteria include medium-size companies in growing markets, high quality, strong market position, long life, potential for supplements or updating, being essential to the user, not being subject to intense competition, and being neither cyclical nor capital intensive. In addition, ITOL wants products for which the employer or business, rather than the user, pays the bill. As a natural consequence, the product can be sold at a high price, leading to good margins and cash flows. (In some cases, ITOL has as much as tripled a publication's cover price in its quest for 20 percent profit margins, double the traditional level for business publications.) A final yardstick is strong management. As yet, ITOL has not fired any U.S. management. Hostile takeovers are avoided, as are minority positions, because, Brown says, "we don't want to be just an investor but instead want to control our destiny."

With these criteria for takeovers in mind, ITOL identified six industries where it expects a boom and is buying and developing publications for these fields. The six are home entertainment and leisure, electronics, health care, energy, housing, and financial services. By buying now, ITOL hopes to be well positioned when the expected spending in these industries crests during this decade. For example, by 1990 health-care expenditures in the U.S. are expected to increase by more than $400 million over 1985 expenditures.

Over the past few years (1980–84), ITOL has put its money where its research said it should be spent. It now owns two educational

publishers—Wadsworth and Van Nostrand Reinhold—and five professional book publishers—Warren, Gorham & Lamont, Auerbach Publishers, a division of Warren, Gorham (information on computer
hardware and software), Callaghan and Company (commercial and
government law), Clark Boardman Company (immigration law), and
Richard De Boo (law). De Boo, based in Toronto, is ITOL's sole
Canadian professional book publisher.

While professional publishing does not attract the public's attention
as much as mass market bestsellers do, it produces steady profits
because its targeted clientele needs the books to keep abreast of their
field. In the United States, for example, there is a ready-made audience
of 500,000 lawyers and more than one million accountants.

ITOL is also well positioned in financial-services publishing. In 1983
it paid $86 million (U.S.) to acquire *American Banker*, the *Bond Buyer*
and several related data-based information services. *American Banker*
is a daily newspaper founded in 1836 for the banking industry, while
the *Bond Buyer*, also published daily, was established in 1891 and
specializes in tax-exempt bonds. *American Banker* is co-owner with the
Bank Administration Institute, a trade group, of *Innerline*, a computer-
based information service on banking news and money market rates,
which won the 1983 outstanding product award of the U.S. Association of Information Bankers.

Primarily through acquisitions rather than start-ups, International
Thomson Business Press, created in June 1980, has ballooned in size to
forty magazines, twenty newsletters, twenty directories, six data bases,
and more than $150 million in revenue, making it the fastest-growing
company in its field. Its publications deal with health care, energy,
consumer electronics, telecommunications, transportation, metal-
working and computers.

ITBP also owns a number of industry "bibles." *Ward's Auto World* is
considered the bible for the car industry; *Pacific Shipper*, the bible
for freight forwarders and maritime workers; and *Physicians' Desk
Reference*, the bible on pharmaceutical products. The latter book
alone sells one million copies annually, and its publisher, the Medical
Economics Company, is the world's leading publisher of health-care
and veterinary periodicals. ITBP also owns Titsch Communications
Incorporated, the leading U.S. publisher of cable TV and mobile-
communications magazines.

ITBP specializes in publications that lend themselves to being spun off
into data bases, which Brunton describes as "the great natural resource
of the twentieth and twenty-first centuries." For example, *Ward's Auto
Bank* gives car production, distribution and sales information; *Broad*

Run Enterprises, a division of Ward's, keeps repair information on domestic and foreign cars dating back to 1970; and Titsch is developing a data base that provides census information for every U.S. cable system.

ITOL was unknown when it entered the U.S. market, but its nonstop shopping binge, at top dollar, gained it speedy attention from the business press and investment analysts. "They have had the most rapid growth of any organization but have bought publications geared to today rather than in a helter-skelter fashion," says William O'Donnell, executive director of the American Business Press Association. Ken Noble, media analyst at Paine Weber Incorporated, says ITOL "paid top dollar but did not overpay in light of the growth that is expected. The market for their products is growing, and their products are adaptable to conversion to data bases. By 1990, the market for business information services is expected to reach $30 billion."

Other analysts, however, are more critical, charging that ITOL has indeed overspent and bought too many publications, especially in the field of health care. Brown is quick with a rebuttal. "If we were to sell everything, we would get triple our $400-million investment. It is difficult to overpay for a good company. Two years ago, the industry said we overpaid for health-care publications, but their earnings are now 50 percent higher. Health care is a growing field with the aging of America and more drugs and advances in hospital equipment. We were accused of paying too high a price but we bought when the stock market was down." Not only did the stock market prices make the purchases seem a bargain, but ITOL benefited from buying when the British pound was at peak levels. Consequently, ITOL had to change fewer pounds into U.S. dollars than it would have had to in 1983. "We bought when the U.S. exchange rate for British pounds was $2.25 to $2.45 compared with around $1.45 in 1983," Brunton says.

While the galloping consumption did not hurt ITOL's pocketbook, it did stretch management thin, especially as the acquired companies used ITOL's accelerated-development plan to buy more companies and launch new products. Wadsworth, for example, is triple the size it was when ITOL bought it. Consequently, ITOL designated 1984 as a year for management to catch its breath, absorb acquisitions, and concentrate on internal development projects. Brown stresses that the consolidation is the only reason for the slowdown, with no changes in management, the decentralized structure, nor any closures or selloffs contemplated. "By next year we will be ready managerially for another good push, depending on stock market values," he says.

Like ITOL, ITBP has a small staff. There are only fifteen executives at the Radnor offices, most of them financial and including an accountant who had been the youngest-ever partner at the chartered accounting firm of Touche Ross and the former number two financial man at the publishing firm of J. B. Lippincott Company. ITBP's youthful-looking president, fifty-five-year-old Richard Groves, formerly was chief operating officer and executive vice-president at the Chilton Company, a large business-publishing company for which ITOL unsuccessfully bid in 1979.

Chilton, owned by the Pew Foundation, a trust set up by the Pew family from their Sun Oil Company money, was put on the public auction block and attracted thirty bids. ITOL lost out by three dollars a share to the highest bidder, the American Broadcasting Corporation. "ABC made me president and chief executive officer of Chilton under a long-term, lucrative contract, but it was apparent ABC is primarily broadcasting oriented and not as interested in print publishing as I am," Groves says. His restlessness dovetailed with what he calls ITOL's "traumatization" in losing the bid for Chilton, and when Gordon Brunton and Michael Brown asked him to head ITOL's North American business-publishing venture, he accepted. Although ITOL has experienced publishing executives elsewhere in the empire, they ruled out parachuting one into the U.S. "Their philosophy has always been to hire people who know the local market," Groves says.

ITOL learned a painful lesson in the public bidding war for Chilton, and consequently, ITBP avoids such situations by moving in quietly on companies "where the owner doesn't know he wants to sell," Groves says. "Competitive situations get messy, and decisions are wrongly evaluated strictly on price." He says ITBP, in line with ITOL's thinking, only approaches companies that will be "compatible" with its style because it wants to retain management. The management of the acquired companies has remained, but ITBP's chief acquisition strategist, thirty-seven-year-old executive vice-president Peter Sprague, left as ITBP's galloping expansion slowed in 1984. Groves had brought Sprague with him from Chilton, where Sprague had been director of corporate planning and development. Previously, he was circulation director of the *Wall Street Journal*.

Despite the careful planning, ITBP has made some mistakes in its acquisitions. The most obvious was its 1981 purchase of the publishing interests of Litton Industries for $60 million (U.S.) even though the group had had a $1.1-million pretax loss the previous year. Litton had some strong properties, such as Medical Economics and Delmar Incorporated, an educational and vocational publisher, but also some troubled divisions, including the Canadian-based Fleet Publishers, the new name for the reconstituted Van Nostrand Reinhold in Canada. VNR's educational list was merged with Nelson Canada's and Nelson's trade list was merged with VNR's under the Fleet name. Although critics said that ITOL with its huge resources could afford to carry the money-losing Fleet, ITOL does not view itself as a philanthropic organization. "Most of its business was distributing books for other publishers, and the lists it represented were incompatible with one another and therefore did not lend themselves to a concerted effort by one sales force," Jack Fleming says. "Also, the recession hit at this time, and it is harder for smaller companies without their own product base to weather the storm."

All told, ITBP sold off about $20 million worth of the Litton publications. What is left is making a substantial profit, prompting Groves to do some fancy mathematical acrobatics to paint the purchase as a total gain for ITBP. As he explains it: "After selling off some parts and turning others around, our net cost was really $40 million. In our first year of ownership we made a pretax profit of $15 million, so instead of paying $60 million for a money-losing company, we paid $40 million for a $15-million operation."

The newly acquired ITBP companies are allowed to retain their management, but first ITBP puts them through a rigorous process of long-range five-year planning regarding acquisitions and new products. Groves says emphasis is placed on teaching the companies to be more selective. "A lot of the companies were used to launching perhaps ten new projects and, if five worked out, would regard that as a good batting average. We tell them to determine which two have the highest priority and potential and to develop them to the utmost."

How much a company invests in new-product development depends on the market outlook. In a mature business like automobiles, Ward's might set aside 2 percent of sales for new products, whereas in a thriving business such as consumer electronics, up to 10 percent would be designated. Publications that cover long-established products are urged to branch into related high-technology areas. For example, *Tooling and Production*, a machine-tools magazine, has started a section on industrial, computer-aided robotics, which eventually will be spun off into a separate publication.

Another hot high-technology business—office automation—is the target of ITBP's two-year-old International Thomson Technology Information (ITTI), which specializes in technology magazines. It is based in New York City and headed by Daniel McMillan, a former executive vice-president at McGraw-Hill Publications. The long title of the company gives the impression of tremendous size, but in actuality it consists of McMillan and a part-time secretary.

ITTI's first publication was *Management Technology*, launched in May 1983, which McMillan claims is the first aimed at managers involved in office automation. McMillan says ITTI chose this subject because while publishing about computers is a fiercely competitive business, it is also extremely lucrative. "The top sixteen business and professional computer magazines carry over 32,000 advertising pages from which they gross $115 million annually, and the top ten publications about microcomputers carry more than 25,000 advertising pages worth over $100 million." Despite what he calls the potential of a "big candy store" in sales for computer magazines, McMillan says ITTI will not rush out with a second publication but will wait a year to digest the cost of launching *Management Technology*. Although he refuses to divulge the start-up cost, McMillan points out that starting a magazine costs up to triple the price and time of operating an established publication.

While there are no plans to consolidate the magazines or book publications, some mutuality of effort is encouraged in production where it leads to economies of scale. Representatives of ITBP's cable, electronic and computer publications attend trade shows together, and Groves is considering joint typesetting by region and joint purchasing of paper. ITBP and its U.K. counterpart, International Thomson Publishing, are also considering joint publication or distribution of publications that have worldwide appeal. Their first international publication is *Computer Merchandising International*, a spin-off from ITBP's *Computer Merchandising*, a magazine for retailers of personal and small business computers. The international version, started in the fall of 1983, is published in French, German and Spanish. In other areas where each is dominant, such as in medical publishing, each country goes its separate way.

ITBP's umbrella group management for the U.S. business magazines is paralleled by a similar organization, called International Thomson Professional Publishing (ITPP), for its U.S. professional book-publishing companies and for Richard De Boo. ITPP was created in 1982 because the firms specialize in many of the same areas—banking, accountancy, finance, law—and can share their operating knowledge. However, decentralization is retained by each firm, maintaining its separate identity, board, and publishing program.

ITPP's first president was Art Rosenfeld, previously president of Warren, Gorham & Lamont. The organization was formed because its member companies have similar ways of operating as well as some mutual problems. All the firms are reference publishers and are subscriber supported rather than advertising based. Although they publish books on different topics, they often use the same production format. For example, both a law book and a taxation book may be published in loose-leaf and will therefore have the same manufacturing, marketing and fulfillment problems.

The firms also share the problem of small print runs. The typical publication, including periodicals, can print from as few as 2,000 copies up to about 40,000. But each firm puts out a lot of publications and updates them regularly. This creates the problem of having to update subscriber lists often, and too elaborate a system would be far too expensive in view of the frequency. Warren, Gorham & Lamont developed an economic system in 1978 that tracks whether subscribers have paid, as well as renewal dates, and their system has been adapted by other firms. Further, one company may assist another company move into new techniques. For example, Warren, Gorham, which is strong in telephone marketing, has helped Clark Boardman set up a telemarketing department.

Marketing, financial and production executives meet quarterly at ITPP's headquarters to discuss such issues as dealing with suppliers, maintaining economic paper sources, and keeping up with new printing technology. The firms have begun exerting group pressure to obtain better prices from suppliers.

Like ITBP, which encourages publications to grow through developing offshoot products, ITPP publishers are also told not to rely solely on books that perennially sell well but have a limited audience. "Professional reference books aren't like bars of soap for which market share can be readily enlarged," Rosenfeld says. "In a few years a professional publisher tends to achieve his circulation goal, and afterwards circulation remains at a plateau. The only way to grow is through creating new journals, newsletters, magazines or books on the subject. For example, Warren, Gorham now produces 170 publications compared with 16 in 1970."

Of the five ITPP firms, only Richard De Boo was losing money when it was acquired, and consequently, it is the only member company where senior management was fired and the structure was reorganized. There had been a total absence of usable records, and the staff was demoralized and mismanaged. Now that De Boo has been repaired, there are plans to expand its law and taxation publishing list and have it add accounting and real estate books.

The other ITPP companies, however, had expansion programs under way well before they were bought. One such example is Callaghan & Company, of which ITPP's head, Rae Smith, is chairman. Smith, who worked his way through university as a night watchman and started at Callaghan working on an addressograph machine despite his law degree, became the firm's chairman in 1979. He tripled the size of Callaghan's sales force, decentralized management so that half as many people reported to him as to his predecessor, and enlarged the publishing list. Smith says ITPP's major assistance to Callaghan has been making money available for expansion and familiarizing it with new technological developments in printing that speed up production and lower costs.

Discovering America has been highly profitable for ITOL. It will not be surprising if the Canadian-owned company and its British senior managers continue to pin much of their expectations for growth on the United States.

V

THE OTHER PARTS OF THE EMPIRE

14

FUELLING THE EMPIRE

THE THOMSON EMPIRE makes the lion's share of its profits from a business in which it does none of the work. It is one of the many contradictions of the empire that about 80 percent of ITOL's profits comes from North Sea oil, in which it is merely an investor and not the operator. Moreover, Thomson is only a minority investor, deriving annual profits of around £90 million from just a one-fifth interest in two fields in the North Sea. In effect, it gets to play the jukebox but does not have to make the records or sell the machine.

In a further contradiction, the empire has started to treat its oil investment as past history, even though it is far and away the largest financial tent pole among the many Thomson businesses. The empire is still heavily involved in North Sea oil and, indeed, even expanded its investment there in 1983. It has also redirected some of the money it has made from the North Sea into oil and gas development in the United States and Canada in the past few years. Nevertheless, oil is an irreversibly depleting resource, and when Thomson executives talk about the future, they get most excited about databases, not oil. "Over the next five years, oil will decline from providing 80 percent of ITOL's profits to under 20 percent," Gordon Brunton says. "Information technology will move from supplying about 10 percent up to 60 percent."

ITOL holds a 20 percent stake in two large North Sea oil fields, Claymore and Piper, located about a hundred miles east of Aberdeen. Its partners are three large U.S. firms: Occidental Petroleum (36.5 percent), Getty Oil (23.5 percent), and Allied Chemical Corporation

(20 percent). The actual exploration and drilling is done by Occidental. The consortium has had the sort of gold-plated success that would make Canada's much-troubled Dome Petroleum Limited drool with envy. After several decades of trying, Dome has yet to produce oil from the Beaufort Sea in Canada's Arctic, but Thomson and its North Sea partners struck oil in the third area drilled—the Piper field.

Not only did they strike oil, but they struck what the industry calls an "elephant"; the field contained 700 million barrels of recoverable oil. Recent studies indicate there may actually be more than 800 million barrels. It is not the largest field in the North Sea (the mammoth Statfjord field in the Norwegian area has at least 3.3 billion barrels), but the Piper field is no pipsqueak by oil industry onshore standards. For example, there is only one larger field in Texas. The Claymore field, located about fifteen miles from the Piper field and discovered in 1974, one year after Piper, is smaller, with 400 million barrels of recoverable oil.

There has been considerable criticism in North America over Dome's heavy use of other people's money through massive bank loans and government subsidies. But Thomson's involvement in North Sea oil has also been largely financed with other people's money. The initial Thomson family investment of $5 million eventually resulted in a financing requirement of more than $500 million to pay for the 20 percent Thomson share of two production platforms and an onshore oil terminal. Borrowing of this magnitude could not be supported by either the family or the empire's balance sheet, so the oil in the sea was used as collateral, with the banks taking the risk that oil would eventually be produced. The financing was also raised with no risk to the Thomson family or empire because the rate of repayment was geared to the rate of production, with no claim on the assets of the family or its businesses.

The investment has proved astute. Even though oil is a depleting resource, Piper and Claymore have averaged almost 300,000 barrels a day in production in recent years, equivalent to about one-sixth of the U.K.'s requirements. Thomson's share amounted to 22 million barrels, worth more than £400 million.

Producing that oil is a tale of high technical skills, dangerous operations, long working hours, and pampered living conditions. On the plus side, the temperature is bearable, ranging between 32 and 65 degrees Fahrenheit; on the down side, the pale green, translucent water can turn into a choppy, angry gray in a matter of minutes. High winds and thick fog are also frequent. There are warning signs everywhere about such safety precautions as not smoking on the deck of an oil rig and the importance of wearing a life jacket and safety harness. The deep-sea divers, who go down as far as 150 feet to inspect the underground part of the platform, are constantly monitored through a TV control room on the rig. Their breathing and the temperature of their suits are closely watched. The suit temperature is kept at 110 degrees Fahrenheit and must be watched closely because at 4 degrees warmer, a diver would be scalded.

The sea is not only a source of oil. Sea water itself is also important to the drilling operations. It is used to deoxygenate water in the pipes so that they do not rust, and to create pressure on the oil to push more out of the ocean bed. Another sixty tons are used daily for drinking, cooking, washing and laundering. Mud is another natural resource used a lot in North Sea fields like Claymore and Piper, just as it is in any oil operation. It is shipped in bulk to the fields, mixed with sea water, and then used to cool and lubricate pipes surrounding the oil-line drilling hole.

Keeping the crew happy gets equal attention. Piper has both male and female workers, but the smaller Claymore operation has only men. Both employ more than 200 workers. Each week at the Claymore field alone, the crew consumes more than 1,500 pounds of beef and steaks, 1,600 pounds of poultry, 2,000 pounds of vegetables, 1,500 pounds of dairy products and a quarter ton of sweets and soft drinks. For dinner, there is a choice of ten main courses and sixteen desserts. Each week, the crew also uses 600 bars of soap and 650 rolls of toilet paper; smokes 80,000 cigarettes and 1,000 cigars; and uses 3,000 sheets and 1,500 towels. The only item not allowed is alcohol. The crew members speak with a variety of accents, reflecting their polyglot backgrounds. Claymore's drilling superintendent, for example, commutes about six thousand miles from Provo, Utah. He spends twenty-eight days on the rig and then goes home for twenty-eight days.

Thomson's watchdog over its investment in this expensive but lucrative undertaking is wiry, cigar-smoking, sixty-five-year-old Bernard Roy Suttil. He signs his letters and memoranda with the unusual name of "Rab," which stems from his childhood nickname of "Bunny" being akin to "rabbit." Suttil, born in the U.K., worked for Shell Oil's overseas operations for thirty-two years, including a stint as managing director of the company's operations in the Persian Gulf state of Qatar. At Shell, retirement is mandatory at the age of fifty-five for overseas employees, but the company has a small department that tries to place them in new jobs. When Suttil registered with this clearing house, North Sea oil exploration was booming and he received seven job offers. He accepted a bid from the Thomson organization, even though it was the newest to oil development among the seven prospective employers. "I had a good pension, so my prime consideration wasn't the highest salary," Suttil says. The very newness of the Thomson involvement meant that Suttil was in on the ground floor and could build up his staff from scratch.

When he joined the just-formed Thomson North Sea in 1974, it had no employees with any technical knowledge of the oil business. Suttil was its entire technical staff. Since then, he has added two petroleum engineers, two geologists, an economist, and a commercial person to handle crude-oil sales. He recruited Thomson North Sea's managing director, Joseph Darby, from their mutual alma mater of Shell, where Darby had been a petroleum engineer for ten years. "Occidental is very sound technically, so there is no reason to duplicate it but only to check what it is doing," Suttil says. "As a result, we can deliberately keep our staff small in size."

The consortium's representatives meet semiannually to discuss finances, and a number of technical committees meet on an ad hoc basis, as does an advisory committee on policy. In the early stages, the chief representatives in the U.K. of the consortium used to meet weekly at Occidental's offices but now find monthly meetings sufficient. There also is an annual meeting to hash out the next year's operating budget. Membership in the consortium is not exclusive; other firms are allowed to participate on some rounds of government licensing of blocks of the North Sea. The four charter members stuck together until the sixth round. In the seventh round, Grand Metropolitan, a major U.K. company, entered the charmed circle, and in the eighth, the most recent round of licensing, neither Getty Oil nor Allied Chemical were involved. Under the consortium's master agreement, if one member gets an opportunity to farm into a nonconsortium prospect, it must offer a percentage of the deal to the other members, and if they are uninterested, the one firm can participate on its own.

Despite the huge output of the Claymore and Piper fields and their being in full production for only seven years, they are already in decline. Their current joint production of 300,000 barrels daily is equivalent to what the Piper field alone yielded in 1978. At the current rate of decline, they are expected to run dry by the year 2000. Although that deadline is sixteen years away, ITOL executives, watching their graphs on oil production inch downward, acquired more North Sea oil properties in 1983 to maintain a steady income from oil.

Those acquisitions were not meant as a one-time shoring-up of Thomson's North Sea interests. Michael Brown says a hunt is under way for other opportunities and that the early start while Piper and

Claymore are still big means the newcomers will provide profits in the late 1980s and in the 1990s as the two original fields wind down. The 1983 purchase, costing $14 million, was for an 8 percent interest in the Balmoral oil field of the North Sea, which is estimated to hold 70 million barrels of recoverable oil. Thomson is a minority partner in the venture with Clyde Petroleum PLC, a British company, to which Thomson will contribute $120 million of the development costs. The total project, including a floating production vessel, will cost about $700 million, and oil should be flowing from the field by 1987, which is when the Piper and Claymore fields are expected to drop substantially in output.

In terms of what Thomson invested in Piper and Claymore, the Balmoral investment is not "frightfully expensive," Michael Brown says. Thomson decided to buy into the venture because it did not have much luck in exploring for oil on its own and Balmoral is a proven oil field. Rebuilding ITOL's oil stake was only one factor in the timing of the purchase. Equally important was the chance to reduce the company's tax burden. The British government imposes a very steep tax on North Sea oil firms. In 1982, for example, the company paid £158 million in taxes, or £1 for every £2.5 it made in oil revenue. The Balmoral investment will result in ITOL getting back £52 in tax relief for every £100 spent on development.

Thomson North Sea's ventures still provide 90 percent of its oil revenue but an increasing proportion is expected to come from newer oil ventures in the U.S. and Canada, started in 1978 and 1983, respectively. The 1978 full-scale entry into the southwest U.S. followed some previous low-key dabbling in "teasers" in North Dakota that could not be developed. The company then formed a partnership, called Thomson-Monteith, with a longtime acquaintance, Ed Monteith of Dallas. Thomson agreed to put in 90 percent of the start-up money during Thomson-Monteith's first six years. When this initial commitment, which totaled $47 million, was completed by the end of 1983, Thomson agreed to make Thomson-Monteith an additional $15-million loan.

Investing such a large sum of money was an act of faith in Ed Monteith, but his background satisfied Thomson executives that they were doing the right thing. Monteith, sixty-two, does not live up to the stereotype of the backslapping, leather-booted, Stetson-wearing Texan. He is soft-spoken and wears white shirts and subdued ties. Instead of miniature derricks decorating his office, he has filled it with American Indian artifacts. But while he does not fit the popular image of the glad-handing Texan, Monteith has an encyclopedic knowledge of the industry, which he puts to added use as chief oil adviser to the Dallas TV series. He also has plenty of good ole' boy charm—so much, indeed, that he was able to pull off as a highlight of a tour taken of the oil and gas operations by Kenneth and his family the viewing of a rattlesnake captured from one of the oil fields and put in a barrel just for the Thomsons to see.

Monteith first met Thomson executives in 1973 when Michael Brown sought his assistance in the financing of Thomson's 20 percent interest in the Piper field. Monteith had moved to London in 1973 to become president of the newly formed International Energy Bank, a high-powered multinational financing consortium. Its members included the Bank of Scotland, Barclays, the Canadian Imperial Bank of Commerce and the Republic Bank of Dallas, the city's leading bank in petroleum financing and Monteith's employer. While running the International Energy Bank, he also retained his title as Republic's executive vice-president in charge of its petroleum and minerals department.

So new was the International Energy Bank when Brown called on Monteith that it was not yet capitalized or operating. The Piper field got the fledgling bank launched with a flying leap. Brown requested a $100-million loan, and simultaneously the leader in the Piper field's project, Occidental Petroleum, sought a $150-million loan. Later, Thomson borrowed another $100 million and Occidental another $175 million to finance their Claymore venture.

Monteith's transfer to London originally was intended to last only six months, but instead ran until 1976, when he returned to Dallas. Within a year, he decided he wanted to be directly involved in the oil business, rather than solely as its banker, and started scouting for a wealthy partner. While he was in London attending a meeting of the International Energy Bank's board of directors, Monteith approached Michael Brown with his idea. Shortly afterwards Thomson-Monteith was formed.

It began on a very small scale, staffed only by Monteith and his secretary of twelve years at the Republic Bank. There now is a staff of forty-seven, most of them in their early thirties. Half are in the Dallas headquarters, located across the street from the Republic Bank, and the rest are out in the company's fields in Texas, Oklahoma, Louisiana and Mississippi. Drilling for oil in these areas has as many dangers lurking for crew members as the "cruel sea," which is what the North Sea has been dubbed. The main U.S. site is at an unlikely location—on land leased from the federal government's air force base at Columbus,

Mississippi. The government is to get a one-eighth royalty on the field's revenue.

Employees must get security clearance from the base's guards before they enter the field and are not allowed to drive faster than twenty miles per hour because of the base's firing ranges, ammunition dumps, and bomber airplanes. There are other hazards, too. The exploration crew must slosh through swampy forest land in their search for gas and oil, and they must wear hip-high boots because the water is filled with such poisonous reptiles as cottonmouths, rattlesnakes and coral snakes. The snakes are shot on sight. Texans are known for telling tall tales, but they are not exaggerating when they say bumps from bites by the mosquitoes that also inhabit the base can swell to the size of golf balls.

In its fields near Tulsa, Oklahoma, Thomson-Monteith faces more hazards. There are some copperhead and cottonmouth snakes, but the major danger is the "chigger" or sand flea, which attacks people's feet. They cause huge welts and can lead to a high fever and death. Crews carry fingernail polish to apply to spots where the fleas have attacked because the polish smothers the insects.

Monteith's strategy was for Thomson-Monteith to begin by acquiring existing properties rather than the more risky avenue of exploring, since disappointment is more common than success in searching for oil. To date, $120 million (U.S.) has been spent on acquisitions, and Monteith says another $80 million will likely be spent by the end of 1985. He picked an ideal time in which to go shopping because many bargains were available. A downturn in oil and gas prices, starting in 1982, had forced the oil business to retrench through selling off properties. "We looked at 132 possible acquisitions in 1982," Monteith says. "We rejected most and analyzed only 34. We further narrowed down the number to 25 and then only bought 2."

The reason more were not bought was that Monteith was not alone in realizing the time was ripe to buy. There was a stampede by investors aware of the relative bargain price of oil fields. They included non-oil investors who put their money in drilling-fund syndicates, which attracted big money and therefore could outbid a small firm like Thomson-Monteith. As a result, Monteith has concentrated on "the detective game" of tracking down acquisitions that are not being offered on the open marketplace.

Since 1982, Thomson-Monteith has moved into actual exploration, but has spread the risk by being the minority partner in ventures with two other firms. One is Liggett Myers, owned by Grand Metropolitan, which already is associated with Thomson in North Sea drilling. The other co-venture is with another large U.K. firm, Trafalgar House. They are shrewd deals. In the arrangement with Liggett Myers, Liggett pays 65 percent of the costs for 55 percent of the revenue, while Thomson-Monteith pays 35 percent for 45 percent. The reason for its advantage is its oil expertise and the high 35 percent return on investment after tax that is predicted for the partners. In the deal with Trafalgar House, Thomson-Monteith gets 25 percent of revenues, while paying only 10 percent of costs, and a 25 percent return on investment after tax is forecast.

Monteith also has high hopes in five water-flooding oil projects (water flooding is a process used to flush out additional oil when a field has been depleted by conventional drilling). "They cost less to buy than primary properties, but their rate of return can be higher because their potential value far outweighs their purchase price," Monteith says. He predicts that all the projects he has set in motion will result in Thomson-Monteith's revenue increasing by $20 million to a total of $50 million by 1988 and that net income will quadruple to $26 million. If these projections materialize, Thomson's investment in the venture will have been more than justified.

In mid-1982, with Thomson-Monteith under full steam, Michael Brown suggested that a similar venture be launched in Canada. Although Canada is the home base of the Thomson empire, it had paid little attention to the country's oil patch, although the company had made a half-hearted, short-lived investment in a tiny oil firm, Star Exploration, which it made a division of its main book company, Nelson Canada. This odd decision stemmed from Thomson having no direct Canadian oil interests and Nelson being its chief Canadian operating company. Thomson did have an indirect interest in oil through its control of the Hudson's Bay Company, which has an interest in a medium-size oil producer, Roxy Petroleum Limited.

Canada's oil and gas became truly alluring to Thomson in 1982 after the Trudeau government introduced its nationalistic National Energy Program in late 1981. Aimed at increasing Canadian ownership of Canadian oil, the program offered financial incentives and more favorable treatment in granting exploration licenses to Canadian-controlled companies. Upset at the preferential treatment the Trudeau government was giving Canadian companies, many American oil companies were either selling their Canadian properties at fire-sale prices and fleeing the country or searching for a Canadian partner in order to receive the benefits being offered the Canadians. "It was only natural that we should want to get involved in oil and gas in Canada where we could utilize long-standing business contacts, friendships and connec-tions," Monteith says.

He suggested that the venture be headed by Richard Jensen, a Canadian then living in Dallas. Like Monteith, Jensen had a back-ground in banking, having headed the Royal Bank of Canada's oil and gas services department for many years. Jensen was already familiar with Thomson's oil operations and executives. While at the Royal Bank's head office in Toronto, he had assisted Thomson in financing its North Sea oil activities. He had met Roy Thomson when Thomson was on the Royal's board of directors, and also knew John Tory, another Royal director.

Jensen had left the Royal in 1978 to become president of Oakwood Petroleum Limited of Calgary, a growing independent firm. In 1981 Oakwood sent Jensen to Dallas to open an American division, a posting that was part of a southward trend by Canadian firms as the oil and gas industry plunged into confusion and despair following the announcement of the National Energy Program. Unfortunately, Oak-wood encountered financial difficulties and the money for its U.S. operations dried up.

Nevertheless, despite his precarious position, Jensen three times rejected Thomson's offer that he become their Canadian partner be-cause he did not want to move back to Canada, having made certain tax declarations before he knew Oakwood's U.S. operations would collapse. Sympathetic to his situation, Thomson officials agreed to let Jensen make Dallas the initial headquarters of Thomson-Jensen until he was able to return to Canada to live in the fall of 1983. During Thomson-Jensen's first year, Jensen became a familiar sight on the Dallas-Calgary plane route. In addition to waiting until Jensen wished to return to Canada, Thomson gave him a piece of the action, just as it had to Monteith. However, Jensen owns a smaller portion than the 10 percent slice received by Monteith.

It took fifteen months until Jensen made Thomson-Jensen's initial Canadian purchase. It was a big first step: $48 million for all the shares of Global Arctic Islands Limited of Calgary, which was owned by Global Natural Resources Incorporated of Houston. Jensen says Global Arctic was one of several companies he had considered buying, but while he had bid on others, the prospective seller got cold feet and decided not to sell. Global Arctic was a shrewd acquisition because not only did it produce 43 billion cubic feet of gas and more than 1 million barrels of oil annually, but its ownership of 80,000 more acres, mostly in Alberta, offered the prospect of more potential reserves.

In addition, the purchase enabled Thomson-Jensen to participate in exploration for oil in 13 million acres in the Arctic Islands by a consortium headed by Panarctic Oils Limited of Calgary because Global Natural was involved in the project. To qualify for the government's new oil incentives to Canadian-controlled firms exploring in the Arctic, Global Natural transferred its frontier interests to a newly formed company that qualifies for the payments because of Thomson-Jensen's participation in it. Thomson-Jensen is to receive a 50 percent interest in all of Global Natural's Arctic exploration lands plus an added lucrative bonus of a 10 percent interest in all previous discoveries where delineation drilling occurs.

This was only part of the hard bargain that Jensen hammered out. Global Natural had initially planned to sell only a percentage of Global Arctic to a Canadian firm in order to qualify for the government grants, but Jensen said his company was not interested in a minority position. "A minority position is not convenient in any partnership because there is no access to the revenue and profit," he says. Buying Global Arctic also provided Thomson-Jensen with an instant staff and an office. Previously, Jensen had worked out of his home; Global Arctic had had seventeen employees and Jensen hired three more people.

Being part of the Thomson empire gives a new division greater access to funds for expansion than a just-launched small independent, and Thomson-Jensen is no exception. Assured of primary funding from ITOL and backup financing from banks because of its rich parent, Thomson-Jensen is scouting for more acquisitions. "Global Arctic did not satisfy our appetite at all," Jensen says. "We are continuing to pursue more acquisitions."

Thomson North Sea, Thomson-Monteith, and Thomson-Jensen each have directors on one another's boards, but on a daily operational basis they are independent. The single time one branch directed a possible deal to another, it fell through. Thomson-Monteith had suggested that an independent Dallas oil company, which wanted to sell an interest it had in a North Sea oil field, approach Thomson North Sea but the talks collapsed.

The empire's reaching into North America may mark the beginning of a worldwide search for oil. Suttil says the strategy is to concentrate on one country at a time but that "in due course, we will get involved in other countries if the risks are low and the amount to be invested is limited." Although growing emphasis by Thomson executives on information services has pushed oil to a lower position in the empire's firmament, it should continue to fuel the empire's balance sheet for many years to come.

15

BUYING TROUBLE

WHEN THE THOMSON EMPIRE expanded in recent years into North American book publishing and information technology, it struck it rich. Its stretching into nonmedia businesses has not gone as smoothly, however, although both the expansion of Scottish and York Insurance into the United States in 1975 and the $640-million purchase of the Hudson's Bay Company in 1979 made good sense at the time. Scottish and York's entry into the U.S. market was logical in view of the exploding growth in the property and casualty insurance market. The purchase of The Bay was also logical because, in addition to owning Canada's largest department store chain, the firm, which was 309 years old in 1979, had the extra attractions of also being involved in oil, gas and real estate.

But both companies subsequently suffered substantial financial losses, management dissension, and the resulting departure of top executives. Mark Landis, the head of Scottish and York's U.S. operations, whose firm Scottish and York had bought as the basis of its U.S. operations, resigned under pressure, and Edgar Burton, the president of Simpsons, a firm acquired by The Bay just before it was bought by Thomson, was encouraged to resign because his credo of free services for customers clashed with The Bay's bottom-line style. "He who has the gold makes the rules," Burton says. His leaving was part of a general housecleaning of many top Simpsons executives by The Bay. None of the directors on Simpsons' board who had worked for Simpsons at the time of its takeover by The Bay is on the board today.

Following its mauling in the fiercely competitive U.S. market, Scottish and York has scaled down its presence there to a skeleton operation, retaining a toehold just in case the situation improves. The financial outlook is better for The Bay, as its results are bouncing back, but discontent continues to fester among many employees at Simpsons over their company being reshaped in The Bay's image. Moreover, the remodeling did not improve Simpsons' results; instead, it was still losing money in 1983 just as it had before The Bay bought it.

Both the Scottish and York and Hudson's Bay episodes brought John Tory, the Cardinal Richelieu of the Thomson empire, more into public view. In the case of Scottish and York, he was responsible for its slashing its U.S. activities to the bone after it had heavy losses. In the case of The Bay, it was Tory who suggested its acquisition. His power within the empire is underscored by his convincing Kenneth Thomson to break the tradition of avoiding bidding for publicly owned companies. The change of course paid off in victory, although the price of success was high because more money than originally planned had to be paid and The Bay's financial results declined to a record loss of $127 million in 1982. Making the loss even more dismal was the fact that The Bay's chief rival, Simpsons-Sears Limited, made a $32-million profit that year.

Scottish and York's troubles were a classic example of the domino theory, with each mistake sending the company reeling more and pushing it from a position of consistent profits into the unwanted new territory of losses for several years. It was a victim of being in vulnerable lines of insurance as well as of cutthroat competition, overexpansion, and tension in the boardroom between the U.S. president and the other directors, all living in Toronto. As the company's position deteriorated, the tension worsened, culminating in the president's resignation.

Today, Scottish and York's U.S. operation is a ghost of its former self. The head-office building has been sold and two-thirds of the 700 employees have been let go. It is a sad comedown from the bright prospects and instant success of the company when it entered the U.S. market in 1975, three years before ITOL bought Wadsworth, its first U.S. acquisition.

Scottish and York moved into the U.S. market by buying two small insurance companies, Lincoln Insurance and Guarantee Insurance. They were owned by Landis, a young New York entrepreneur, who was looking for a rich partner to inject large doses of capital that would make the firms a fairly big fish in the then-booming property and casualty insurance market. Scottish and York bought 80 percent of Landis's firms and also put several million dollars into enlarging them. Landis was given a five-year contract and a bonus arrangement, which was renewed for two years in 1980. Although he was a minnow compared with Scottish and York, he says he would not have become involved with the firm if it had not been owned by the Thomson family: "To me, the family's financial strength was the strong point of Scottish and York."

During the first five years, Scottish and York's U.S. operations thrived and consequently were expanded very rapidly—too rapidly, as hindsight later showed. U.S. coverage was increased from eighteen to thirty-nine states, and six regional offices were opened. The initial activity seemed to validate the expansion. The volume of business leapfrogged from $5 million in 1975 to $100 million in 1980. In the face of this remarkable growth, management ignored storm warnings that the bubble was about to burst for U.S. property and casualty insurers. The impact on Scottish and York was severe.

More than a thousand firms chase after the U.S. casualty and property insurance market and its annual 20 percent growth. The competitive brawl is knocking the stuffing out of small firms like Scottish and York, unable to withstand the inroads being made by the big companies through cutting their premiums. The sharklike competition resulted in U.S. property and casualty firms losing $8 billion in 1983 on top of a $6-billion loss in 1982.

Obviously, Scottish and York was in the wrong place at the wrong time, and it was making matters worse by committing mistakes when it was crucial to avoid extra troubles. It relied for much of its business on selling insurance to commercial truckers, a field that insurance analyst Mike Franquelli of the New York investment house of Salomon Brothers describes as "the single worst type of insurance in which to be involved because it is particularly competitive." The fierce rivalry erupted after the U.S. trucking industry was deregulated. Truckers began to treat their insurance policies as a profit center that higher premiums would hurt, and insurers were forced to respond by charging what they viewed as inadequate rates.

Scottish and York made other errors, too. It opened a subsidiary in Bermuda in 1982 at a time when many other bigger competitors were also looking for business in that market. Other slip-ups were selling insurance on motorcycles, traditionally not a very good business, and on spectators at public events, such as car racing, which Franquelli describes as "the most treacherous of insurance lines" because of the potentially high claims.

Scottish and York might have been able to stanch its losses earlier if it had not been caught in a six-month snafu with a new computer system. The installation was ill-timed because it started in late 1981 as the U.S. marketplace was deteriorating, leaving Scottish and York deprived of current data when it needed it the most. Scottish and York would not have been caught empty-handed if it had run its old computer system until the new one was operational, but in an effort to save money it had decided against keeping the original system. It was a painful lesson in the accuracy of the aphorism about being penny-wise and pound-foolish.

Nor was the computer Scottish and York's only bad buy. Around the same time, it also ran into immediate difficulties in absorbing the acquisition of Tri-American Corporation, a ten-year-old personal automobile insurer. Tri-American was bought for $12 million in April 1981 and sold just eighteen months later for $7.5 million.

The bad situation was made worse by lack of agreement among the board of directors over how to handle the problems. John Tory favored the company taking the route of borrowing more money as the cheapest way to obtain a much-needed infusion of capital. The money was needed so that Scottish and York would not fall below the ratio between volume of business and net worth required under insurance regulations. By contrast, Landis was opposed to further borrowing, arguing that it would be difficult for Scottish and York to meet its debt obligations in view of its declining earnings base.

Harmony in the boardroom was also unraveling because Landis's entrepreneurial nature clashed with his role as part of a huge corporate empire. "When everything is going well, business relationships can remain easy, if not comfortable, but when things deteriorate, the relationships become difficult," Landis says. He began to chafe under the impression that to Thomson executives, the U.S. operations of Scottish and York were very small in the overall scheme of the empire and that, therefore, not enough attention was being paid to it. Although Kenneth Thomson is a member of Scottish and York's board, Landis found it was John Tory who was much more involved in operational issues and so he discussed his frustrations with him.

These discussions made it clear that Tory and Landis had opposite views on what should be done. Landis believed the U.S. operations could be turned around. While Tory never came right out and said it, he gave Landis the impression that given the unchanging competitive market, the operations should be scaled down. This is what has been done. Landis says he offered to resign in the spring of 1982 but Tory refused to accept his resignation. By the fall, however, after the losses had deepened, there was no effort to retain Landis when he submitted his resignation again. "I resigned voluntarily but by the time I did, the Canadians were glad I did," he says. Scottish and York's Toronto-based chairman Richard Broughton says that until the cutthroat competition eases up in the U.S. and "marketing and underwriting sense returns to the U.S. market," Scottish and York will not be "actively involved in writing new business there."

Scottish and York's U.S. expansion was a small step for the empire compared with the far bigger one of buying the Hudson's Bay Company. This was a particularly major move because it involved the empire in one of the fiercest takeover contests in Canadian business history, even though the Thomson philosophy is to avoid such fights. But Kenneth Thomson was determined to win because the company is Canada's most historic, and because it has many eggs in its basket— retailing, oil and gas, real estate—all of which were doing well in 1979. The one-step shopping expedition was the first Thomson venture anywhere into retailing and real estate and its first in Canada into oil and gas. In addition, Donald McGiverin, governor and president of the Hudson's Bay Company, shares the passion of Thomson management for high profit margins through stringent cost control measures. It was as if Tweedledum joined forces with Tweedledee.

The mosaic that is the Hudson's Bay Company today is vastly different from its origins as a fur-trading company whose search for more beaver pelts resulted in the exploration of much of western Canada. The Bay dates back to 1660 when two Frenchmen, Pierre Radisson and his brother-in-law, Médard Chouart des Groseilliers, made perilous journeys into the northern forests of Canada and brought back a valuable collection of furs to Montreal. Failing to get the financial terms they wanted, they went to England and saw Prince Rupert, a cousin of King Charles II. Recognizing the trade prospects, the prince organized a voyage from England to test the reports of the two Frenchmen. The result was that in 1670 King Charles granted a charter to Prince Rupert and seventeen others to form the Company of Adventurers of England trading into Hudson Bay.

The charter gave the company, whose local chief representative was called the governor, exclusive rights of colonization, government and trade in what is now the northern and western portions of Ontario and Quebec, all of Manitoba and Saskatchewan, the southern half of Alberta, and the southeast corner of the Northwest Territories. All told, the territory, called Rupert's Land, covered 38.7 percent of what was to become the nation of Canada. The company's motto, *Pro Pelle*

Cutem, reflected its goals: it wanted the skin—*cutem*—for the sake of the fleece—*pro pelle*. Many of Canada's most famous explorers, including Samuel Hearne and David Thompson, worked for the company, mapping inland routes to be used in pursuit of beaver.

In addition to the hardships of nature and of discovering routes through beautiful but seemingly impenetrable terrain, the company faced stiff competition from the North West Company, an amalgamation of nine companies formed in 1784. It operated from Montreal and consisted largely of Scots who had settled in Canada. The struggle between the two companies was bitter. They often built rival trading posts and forts side by side, and the fierce economic rivalry led to violence and bloodshed. Eventually, because the normal breeding of animals could not keep pace with the number killed, the specter of ruination forced them to amalgamate in 1821.

In 1870, two centuries after The Bay's start in Canada, much of the territory, including the original Rupert's Land, was taken over by the three-year-old Dominion of Canada. In compensation, the company received £300,000 in cash and seven million acres of the land it had held. Those real estate holdings diminished substantially over the years, but the company has become rich from its other ventures. Its fur trade posts evolved into department stores, and over the past decade, it has diversified into many nonmerchandising areas. Nevertheless, the company has not broken with its past. Legal documents are still signed under the 1670 charter name. The company has also amassed eighty tons of archival material covering its three centuries. When the task of administering all this material and finding space for it finally became too cumbersome in the early 1970s, it was brought over from England and given to the Manitoba Provincial Archives in Winnipeg.

The choice of Winnipeg stemmed from that city—which had been the company's Canadian head office for over a hundred years—being named the corporate headquarters in 1970. Until then, the head office had remained in London. By the 1960s, however, the board decided this was unreasonable, since 95 percent of the firm's business and 98 percent of its employees lived in Canada. In 1982, as further proof that Canadians were in charge, the company bought out the minority interest held in London-based Hudson's Bay and Annings Limited, with the result that it owned 100 percent of all its fur auction houses.

Today, The Bay is still the world's leading fur auctioneer and continues to sell its famous "point" blankets (broad red, black and sometimes green horizontal stripes on a white background). Ironically, the price is often less at the rival T. Eaton Company department stores for similarly styled blankets.

But The Bay has become far more than a trader of furs and blankets. Besides owning Canada's largest group of department stores, The Bay has extensive oil and gas interests in western Canada through a 51 percent interest in Roxy Petroleum Limited, a medium-size firm, and wholly owns Markborough Properties Limited, a major real estate developer in Canada and the United States. It is a major travel agent and wholesaler of vacations, one of Canada's largest suppliers of automatic vending-machine products, and the only leading Canadian merchandiser that is also a liquor distiller. Other interests include a minority interest in a financial services company that sells insurance, mutual funds, and trust company services to customers through direct mail as well as in its own stores and those of its partner, Eaton's of Canada, owner of Canada's largest privately owned department store chain.

It is McGiverin who is responsible for the aggrandizement of The Bay. McGiverin, who turned sixty in 1984, is a transplant both from western Canada to Toronto and from Eaton's to The Bay. He startled the merchandising industry when he moved from Eaton's, where he had worked for twenty-two years, ending up as the western vice-president based in Winnipeg, to The Bay in 1968 as director of department stores. The move made sense because there was less opportunity for advancement at the family-owned Eaton's than at the nonfamily-controlled Bay.

McGiverin quickly transformed The Bay's dowdy, backwoods image by building a snazzy flagship store in midtown Toronto's exclusive shopping district, several miles from the competitive downtown department stores. Jazzy advertising geared to the working woman who reads *Cosmopolitan* was introduced. McGiverin also was responsible for the company acquiring its automatic vending-machine business, Zellers, Simpsons, and the interest in Roxy Petroleum. All these changes initially had a positive impact on the company's financial results. Between 1972, when McGiverin joined The Bay, and 1981, profits rose from $13 million to $386 million.

Although McGiverin became president of the company in 1972, he had to wait ten years to receive the top title of governor. The first Canadian governor of the company was George Richardson, who was appointed in 1970 after the transfer of the company's sovereignty from the United Kingdom to Canada. He was an obvious choice because the Richardsons are the most prominent and wealthiest family in Winnipeg, with extensive interests in agriculture, real estate, construction and insurance, as well as in one of Canada's leading investment houses, Richardson Greenshields Limited. After George's older brother James entered politics in 1968 and eventually became minister of defense, George became the head of the businesses started in 1857 by his grandfather.

The Bay's department stores' jingle is "It's hard not to think of The Bay." This certainly was the case at Thomson headquarters in 1979, as they became increasingly interested in The Bay's own empire of widespread interests. Six months before the actual bid, Kenneth Thomson and John Tory had approached their Canadian investment dealer, Wood Gundy, with the idea. Gundy's chairman, Ted Medland, says the trio then "bounced the idea around in a theoretical and philosophical way." When it was decided to make the bid, John Tory took over the implementation of the deal, giving instructions both to Wood Gundy and to his brother, James, of Tory, Tory, Des Lauriers & Binnington, the law firm used by Thomson's. James led the legal team in devising strategy.

Kenneth was battling for The Bay, Canada's only major nonfamily-controlled or -run retailer, against another of Canada's foremost families—the Westons. The Thomsons and the Westons had much in common besides each wanting to buy the Hudson's Bay Company.

Like Roy Thomson, the Weston empire's founder, Garfield Weston, built his businesses up from scratch. Starting with a bakery, Weston erected an empire across three continents. The Weston empire runs grocery, food-processing, fishery, and timber firms. The family-controlled Loblaws is one of the largest grocers in Canada, while its Associated British Foods is the leading British food-processing company. In turn, Associated British Foods controls the largest food processors in Australia and South Africa. Like the Thomson empire, operation of the Weston empire has passed into the second generation. Garfield Weston died in 1978, two years after Roy Thomson. One son, Galen, runs the Canadian businesses and the other, Garry, is in charge in London.

The takeover of the Hudson's Bay Company was part of the acquisition fever that raged across Canada in the late 1970s, as the undervalued share price of many companies prompted Canadian businesses to go on a rampage. In the nineteen months before it became the quarry, The Bay had been one of Canada's busiest corporate game hunters. In the summer of 1978, it bought one of the country's leading discount department store chains, Zellers, shortly after Zellers had merged with a leading West Coast discounter, Fields Stores Limited. Barely had The Bay swallowed Zellers, when in January 1979 it bid for Simpsons, a major eastern department store chain. That brought The Bay upscale women fashion customers, as surveys by merchandising analysts consistently showed that Simpsons was the favorite store of such shoppers. Both Zellers and Simpsons were kept operating under their own names in contrast to the wipeout of the Henry Morgan Company name when The Bay bought that chain, the third largest in eastern Canada, in 1960.

The Thomson family originally sought only a 51 percent interest in the Hudson's Bay Company at $31 a share. When The Bay rejected this offer as being too low, it was revised upwards to $35 a share for a 60 percent interest. Meanwhile, the Westons had offered $40 a share for a 51 percent interest. This bidding finally ended with the acceptance of a Thomson offer for a 73 percent interest at $37 a share.

Unfortunately, the many attractive features of The Bay blinded Thomson executives to operational problems it was experiencing. The Bay's astronomical expansion had masked the company's weaknesses in absorbing its acquisitions, particularly Simpsons. Consequently, when the recession hit in 1981, The Bay was like the Titanic steaming towards the fatal iceberg. Its problems had started with a failure to realize the difficulties that would be entailed in untangling the many ties between Simpsons and Simpsons-Sears Limited, which Simpsons had hitherto owned in conjunction with U.S. merchandising giant Sears-Roebuck Limited. The final break did not occur until late 1983 when Simpsons moved out of a store in Halifax that was owned by Simpsons-Sears and into its own building.

Longtime employees and customers were unhappy as The Bay remade Simpsons' sedate, service-oriented slant into a reflection of The Bay's trendy, charge-for-every-service approach. Old-timers on Simpsons staff joked bitterly that "Simpsons' slogan 'Simpsons has it' should be changed to 'Simpsons hasn't it.'" All the changes led to an inevitable conflict between old and new management, and old management soon departed. The Burton family had run Simpsons on a credo of service. But in The Bay's cold-eyed appraisal, the free services were largely responsible for the firm's being heavily extended financially. Allan Burton, Simpsons' chairman, was at retirement age when the company was bought by The Bay, but he became a director of the Hudson's Bay Company and held the position until 1981. His nephew, Edgar (Ted), now forty-nine, who had been with the company for twenty-six years, and The Bay's executives clashed, however, with the inevitable result being Edgar's departure. "Both they and I spotted that I was not capable of sacrificing service to the customer or convincing people to do business another way," Burton says. He now works full time at his farm north of Toronto. His replacement, Charles MacRae, has worked at Simpsons for more than two decades and was an early proponent of the company relying more on computer systems, a hallmark of The Bay's management style.

For Simpsons' employees, the split from Sears was like the breakup of a long, happy marriage. Employees had been able to shop at either store at discount rates. By contrast, no mutual discount is provided for employees of Simpsons and The Bay. Other crackdowns bothered the employees, too. The Bay told Simpsons' executives that Simpsons' employees were no longer to receive a five-dollar bonus when signing up a new Simpsons' credit-card user.

Another dictum had an even stiffer impact on their earnings: in the old days if a customer returned an appliance, the salesperson still retained the commission from the original sale even if a new item was sent to the customer by way of replacement. After the takeover, the commission from the original sale was to be retained by the company. Employees grumbled that, as a result, it was no longer possible to estimate in advance what their paycheck would be and to make purchases on that assumption. After a year of complaints, the company relented and refunded the money, which in the case of some employees amounted to as much as $15,000. The change in policy may have had another motive besides relieving the employees, since it was instituted around the time that store clerks at a branch of Eaton's became unionized, the first time this had happened at a major Canadian department store and something that neither company wanted to become widespread.

Another indication of the company's desire to keep out unions and to mollify employees occurred in October 1983 when a company-wide survey of staff morale was conducted for the first time. It found that there was widespread dissatisfaction with the lack of communication from management and that one-third of the staff were worried about job security. Management's response to the situation was interesting not so much for how it responded, but because it did anything at all. Early in 1984 a nine-page memorandum was distributed to employees promising better communication, and meetings with the staff were held in small groups to demonstrate a commitment to the personal touch.

"Your concerns regarding the changes in systems at Simpsons in the last two years are well founded since it appears obvious that we failed to communicate these changes effectively," the memorandum said. To rectify the situation, management promised to distribute more information to employees both through newsletters and a possible quarterly in-house publication. No pledges, however, were made about job security. This was dealt with only in one sentence that said "a more stable and secure atmosphere" depended on "improved profitability."

The biggest upheavals at Simpsons have been in appliances and home delivery. When Simpsons still was an owner of Simpsons-Sears, Simpsons had sold Sears' "Kenmore" line of appliances: now it sells the Bay's private label, the "Beaumark" line. During the first four years after Simpsons was bought by The Bay, the furniture, appliance and television departments of the two firms functioned separately, although both sold Beaumark. Then early in 1984, an umbrella company, Beaumark Limited, was formed to buy supplies, sell them to The Bay and Simpsons, and perform centralized administrative functions for both companies.

This made sound economic sense, but for the employees there was an unsettling repercussion. The Bay insisted that all furniture, appliance and television salespeople at The Bay and Simpsons, including top-notch money-makers, take product courses, with the understanding that those who failed a subsequent exam would lose their jobs. The edict both infuriated and scared employees. They were angry because they felt they already knew their jobs and because such exams were unprecedented in Canadian department stores. Sears, for example, relies on product-knowledge meetings for its staff. The fear arose from apprehension about being fired, especially as staff already was being reduced through early retirement and an increasing number of part-time help was being hired as a way of keeping the unions from organizing employees.

The transformations at Simpsons have been wrenching for longtime customers, too. Simpsons used to do watch repairs on the premises. Now, the repair work is subcontracted and it can take up to three weeks until Simpsons gets these items back. Because The Bay does not sell pianos, other musical instruments, or sewing machines, Simpsons was instructed to stop selling these items. Shoppers would expect to get such items at a department store and they still can at Simpsons' and The Bay's competitors, Eaton's and Sears.

Despite both Simpsons and The Bay selling Beaumark, added convenience has not been the result for the customer. Instead, the opposite has happened. The old convenience of buying either at Simpsons or Sears when Kenmore items were on sale has not been duplicated with Beaumark because Simpsons and The Bay do not hold their sales simultaneously. Because there are more suppliers of Beaumark items than there were of Kenmore, it is harder, salespeople say, to keep track of product defects. The rival department store chains of Sears and Eaton's have their own in-house service repair sections, but to eliminate the expense of hiring repairmen, The Bay, and now Simpsons, farms out repairs of Beaumark appliances to a subcontractor, which has led to longer waiting times for repair work to be done. Installation of appliances is also farmed out now, and the subcontractor charges twice Simpsons' previous fee and Eaton's and Sears' current charge to install washers and dryers in customers' homes.

To reduce the high cost of warehousing, Simpsons was instructed to trim its inventories substantially. That made economic sense, but it also created a number of disgruntled customers during sales because they had to wait several weeks for delivery due to Simpsons' not putting through the orders until a prescribed number had been reached. Delivery of merchandise has been affected in other ways as well. Simpsons never used to charge for delivery, but now it applies the same two-dollar charge as The Bay, which initiated such a charge by Canadian department stores.

In another cost-saving measure, it was decided to reduce the number of separate warehouses used by Simpsons and The Bay by storing similar items, such as TV sets, in the same place and keeping a record as to which company owned what. To reduce the number of delivery trucks, an intercompany trucking operation was created. Under the new system, delivery dates are no longer promised by Simpsons because delivery is not made until enough orders are made up to fill the number of trucks designated as economic to use.

The changes in the stores were only a small fraction of the overhaul of Simpsons by Bay executives. Equally significant was the behind-the-scenes introduction of sophisticated financial control systems, an area pretty much neglected by Simpsons' old management. A joint computer processing system for The Bay and Simpsons was developed to cover accounting, payroll and, most importantly, merchandising. "It keeps track of inventory, does automatic reordering, and can tell you how many costs, for example, are in each store and what the sales have been over the last year," says Rolph Huband, vice-president and secretary of the Hudson's Bay Company.

Over a four-year period, a centralized credit authorization and transaction recording system was phased in. Simpsons' former "country club" billing system, in which customers were sent copies of every sales slip with their statement, was replaced with The Bay's "descriptive" billing, in which the bill lists all purchases but no sales slips are sent. The savings from descriptive billing are substantial because there is less paperwork and postage costs are lower. Under Simpsons' old system, the stack of paperwork was, as employees describe it, "as high as Toronto's CN Tower" (the world's tallest structure), and statements went through twenty-seven processing steps before they were mailed to customers. Now, accounts are processed in one step by computer.

As at Scottish and York, both Kenneth Thomson and John Tory sit on the Hudson's Bay Company's board of directors, and again as at Scottish and York, Tory is the more active director, sitting also on the board's smaller executive committee. But Bay executives stress that they are left alone to run things as they like. The executive committee of the board meets rarely.

Kenneth is said to act like any of The Bay's other seventeen directors rather than as the owner, and to treat The Bay as an investment rather than as a business directly under his wing. "Although it turned out to be not that good an investment in recent years, there has been no noticeable change in his attitude or that of John Tory," Huband says. Still, executives at The Bay no doubt would feel more relaxed if the company were more profitable. Kenneth Thomson and John Tory would feel better, too, because The Bay was their very own idea and one which marked a departure for the empire. It would be an embarrassing loss of face if The Bay were to continue not to do well. Thus, the fortunes of The Bay will be closely watched by both friend and foe of the Thomson empire.

VI

CONTRADICTIONS IN THE EMPIRE

CHAPTER

16

THE PARADOX

THE THOMSONS are by no means the only newspaper magnates who are no longer content to make their money from newspapers alone. On both sides of the Atlantic, media empires are rapidly turning into communications empires or, in an even sharper change of course, into conglomerates in which communications businesses are only one slice of the corporate pie.

In Canada, the Thomsons' chief media rival, Southam Incorporated, owns close to sixty business magazines and has an interest in cable television as well as being the sole English-language newspaper publisher in most of the country's major cities. In the United States, the Gannett Company owns a research pollster, Louis Harris & Associates, and television and radio stations in addition to its newspapers. The New York Times Company also owns several television companies, more than fifty cable franchises, and a book-publishing firm, Times Books. The Times Mirror Company, publisher of the *Los Angeles Times*, is involved in cable television, book publishing and television broadcasting, and also produces training material charts for engineers and pilots. McGraw-Hill Incorporated, in addition to producing eighty business, professional and technical publications, as well as Standard and Poor's financial rating service, owns several television stations and computer data information systems.

British media firms are branching out at a fast clip, too, including moves into other countries, unlike the Americans. Pearson Longman owns Penguin Books, the largest book publisher in the United Kingdom, Longman Books, the *Financial Times*, and Goldcrest Films and

Television (producer of *Chariots of Fire* and *Gandhi*), in addition to being one of the largest regional newspaper publishers. Like the Thomson empire, Pearson Longman has gone abroad and is now active in Africa, Asia and Australia, as well as in the United States where it owns Viking Press, a major book publisher. Reed International, owner of the Mirror newspapers and 130 business journals, is also a leading trade-show manager, paper manufacturer, and supplier of building and home improvements.

Pearson Longman and Reed, however, have remained in communications. Two other U.K. firms—Trafalgar House and the Associated Newspapers Group—have paralleled the widespread diversification of the Thomson empire. Trafalgar House bought the Beaverbrook newspapers, including the *Daily Express* and *Sunday Express*, in 1977 and is also active in construction (its main earner), shipping, aviation and hotels. Associated Newspapers, publisher of the *Daily Mail* and a number of regional newspapers, also has interests in North Sea oil development, several theaters, a cab company, wharf storage, real estate, radio stations, forest products, and opinion polls. Notwithstanding, it is by no means a close rival, in terms of sales volume, to ITOL, whose revenue is five times greater.

The heads of these other empires are little known to the public, especially as many such empires do not bear the names of their owners. The exception is today's Roy Thomson—Rupert Murdoch, to whom Kenneth Thomson sold the *Times* (of London) and the *Sunday Times*. Like Roy Thomson, Murdoch had built an empire through buying financially sick papers, but his approach has been different. For the most part, Thomson bought papers in small towns and did not interfere in their editorial stand, a policy continued by Kenneth. As a result, the papers have neither necessarily worsened nor improved. Conversely, Murdoch buys ailing papers in major cities, such as the New York *Post* and Boston *Herald*, and puts his distinctive stamp on them—an emphasis on sex, violence and sensationalism. While most journalists decry the changes, the formula evidently works, because circulation subsequently grows. Despite the diametric differences, the end result of the noninterventionist Thomson approach and the interventionist Murdoch style has been the same: the journalism profession generally despises the deadening impact of both.

The Thomson empire has been in the vanguard among media empires in branching into nonpublishing ventures, but it is a member of the pack, not the leader, in today's mecca for the press lords—information services. Their enthusiasm is understandable, as information services is regarded as the 1980s equivalent of the last century's gold rushes. By 1990 information services could be generating $70 billion in revenue, and already the stocks of such information companies as Prentice-Hall and McGraw-Hill are among the best performers on the New York Stock Exchange. Furthermore, higher profits tend to be made from information services than from other communications businesses, and the Thomson empire is well positioned to be a major player because its professional publications are in fields where the demand for database information is exploding.

But the empire is not just looking outwards for its expansion. Opportunities within the empire for growth through cooperation are also being explored. For example, Thomson Books is now investigating the possibility of producing books for other divisions and doing projects in conjunction with Thomson Regional Newspapers. Such cooperation might, however, be tricky to achieve, because the divisions are accustomed to at least the illusion of decentralization and autonomy. In addition to these potential internal problems, the empire will want to avoid any charges of such shared effort being labeled as anticompetitive, especially as it has only recently brushed aside government charges in Canada over its newspaper division being engaged in restrictive business practices.

As the Thomson empire marks its golden anniversary, all its many contradictions remain. The big spending and decentralization are counterbalanced by stiff budget controls and stringent reporting procedures. The monopolies held by most of its newspapers conflict with the involvement in fiercely competitive businesses like travel, oil and gas, and book publishing. The passion for high profits is in contrast to new-product encouragement through the accelerated-development fund. The loathing of its small town North American papers for their content and antiunionism by many journalists and union leaders is offset by the respect of investment analysts for the fat profit margins. There continue to be both headlong, unplanned plunges into some businesses and long analyses of other ventures.

Finally, there is the paradox of the heads of the empire: the extroverted but steely Roy and the shy but steely Kenneth. But, as all the contradictions in their personalities, interests and activities have proved lucrative so far, there is little reason for the family or the empire to resolve the paradoxes in the future.

APPENDICES

A

THOMSON FAMILY'S HOLDINGS

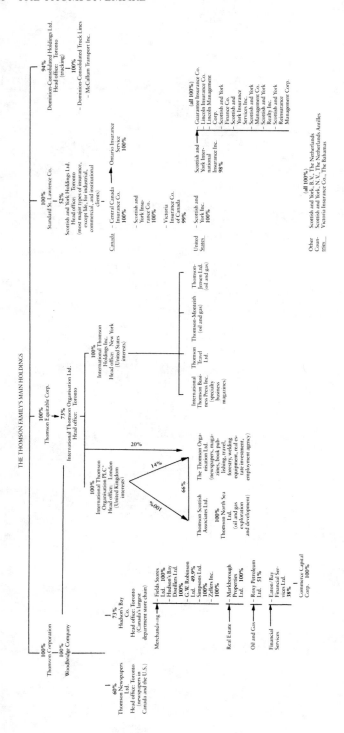

THE THOMSON FAMILY'S MAIN HOLDINGS

100%
Thomson Equitable Corp.

73%
International Thomson Organisation Ltd.
Head office: Toronto

100%
Thomson Corporation
100%
Woodbridge Company

60%
Thomson Newspapers Ltd.
Head office: Toronto
(newspapers in Canada and the U.S.)

73%
Hudson's Bay Co.
Head office: Toronto
(Canada's largest department store chain)

Merchandising
- Fields Stores Ltd. 100%
- Hudson's Bay Distillers Ltd. 100%
- G. W. Robinson Ltd. 49.9%
- Simpsons Ltd. 100%
- Zellers Inc. 100%

Real Estate
- Markborough Properties Ltd. 100%

Oil and Gas
- Roxy Petroleum Ltd. 51%

Financial Services
- Eaton/Bay Financial Services Ltd. 38%

- Commerce Capital Corp. 100%

100%
International Thomson Organisation PLC *
Head office: London (United Kingdom interests)

20%
The Thomson Organisation Ltd.
(newspapers, magazines, book publishing, travel, forestry, welding equipment, real estate investment, employment agency)

14%

66%

100%
Thomson Scottish Associates Ltd.

100%
Thomson North Sea Ltd.
(oil and gas exploration and development)

100%
International Thomson Holdings Inc.
Head office: New York (United States interests)

International Thomson Business Press Inc. (specialty business magazines)

Thomson Travel Ltd.

Thomson-Monteith (oil and gas)

Thomson-Jensen Ltd. (oil and gas)

100%
Standard St. Lawrence Co.

52%
Scottish and York Holdings Ltd.
Head office: Toronto
(most major types of insurance, except life, for industrial, commercial, and institutional clients)

Canada
- Central Canada Insurance Co. 100%
- Scottish and York Insurance Co. 100%
- Victoria Insurance Co. of Canada 99%

Ontario Insurance Service 100%

United States
- Scottish and York Inc. 100%

Scottish and York International Insurance Inc. 98%

(all 100%)
- Guarantee Insurance Co.
- Lincoln Insurance Co.
- Lincoln Management Corp.
- Scottish and York Finance Co.
- Scottish and York Insurance Services Inc.
- Scottish and York Management Co.
- Scottish and York Realty Inc.
- Scottish and York Reinsurance Management Corp.

94%
Dominion-Consolidated Holdings Ltd.
Head office: Toronto
(trucking)
100%
- Dominion-Consolidated Truck Lines
- McCallum Transport Inc.

Other Countries
(all 100%)
Scottish and York, B.V., The Netherlands
Scottish and York, N.V., The Netherlands Antilles
Victoria Insurance Co., The Bahamas

* PLC = Public Liability Co. The term means a company is listed on the Stock Exchange.) PLC replaced Ltd. after United Kingdom joined the European Economic Community to fit EEC practices.

B

CHRONOLOGY OF MAJOR EVENTS

Major Events in the Development of the Thomson Holdings

1894 • (June 5) Roy Thomson born

1923 • Kenneth Thomson born (Roy Thomson's only son)

1931 • Roy Thomson starts his first radio station (CFCH in North Bay, Ontario)

1934 • Roy Thomson starts his first newspaper (*The Daily Press* in Timmins, Ontario)

1951 • Roy Thomson enters insurance business

1952 • First U.S. newspaper bought (*The Independent* in St. Petersburg, Florida)

1953 • Fifty-nine-year-old Roy Thomson moves from Canada to the United Kingdom and starts building a global business with the purchase of *The Scotsman*, Scotland's leading newspaper

1957 • Roy Thomson obtains Scotland's first commercial television franchise

1959 • Acquisition of 18-paper Kemsley chain in the United Kingdom, including *The Sunday Times*, the leading Sunday newspaper

1960 • Thomson Organisation established: at first, to oversee newspaper and television interests; later expanded to travel, oil and gas, and forestry

1961 • Thomson Publications established (book and magazine publishing)

1964 • Roy Thomson becomes Lord Thomson of Fleet

1965 • Thomson Holidays established
       • Thomson Directories (Yellow Pages) started in the United Kingdom
       • Thomson Newspapers (Canadian and U.S. papers) goes public

1967 • *The Times* (of London) acquired

1971 • Roy Thomson invests in North Sea oil exploration

1976 • (August 14) Roy Thomson dies, age 82. His son, Kenneth, succeeds him

1978 • International Thomson Organisation (holding company for publishing, travel, natural resources businesses) formed
       • Final disposal of interest in Scottish Television

1979 • Hudson's Bay Co., Canada's largest department store chain, acquired for $640 million
       • Enters oil and gas industry in United States

1980 • Thomson Newspapers Ltd. pays $165 million to acquire FP Publications Ltd., a major chain of Canadian newspapers, including Toronto's *The Globe and Mail*
       • International Thomson Business Press Inc. formed in United States, as holding company for American business publications

1981 • Times Newspapers sold
       • Worldwide publishing interests of Litton Industries Inc. bought

C

PRINCIPAL INTERESTS: INTERNATIONAL THOMSON ORGANISATION LTD.

PUBLISHING

BOOKS

INTERNATIONAL THOMSON PROFESSIONAL PUBLISHING,
New York (books on finance, law, taxation, real estate, medicine)

American Banker Inc.;
The Bond Buyer Inc.
Information to the financial services community, primarily in the
banking, thrift, municipal and public finance industries

PUBLICATIONS:
American Banker; The Bond Buyer; The Weekly Bond Buyer;
Directory of Municipal Bond Dealers

INFORMATION SERVICES:
Inconet; Innerline; Munifacts

Callaghan & Company
Legal publishing; emphasis on corporation and commercial,
municipal and federal law, taxation, all aspects of trial and general
practice

RECENT TITLES:
Uniform Commercial Code Series; Federal Rules of Evidence Digest; Federal Grants and Cooperative Agreements; Proof of a Prima Facie Case; Defense of a Prima Facie Case; Fletcher Corporation Law Advisor; Law of Corporate Officers and Directors; New York Products Liability; Local Government Law

Clark Boardman Company Ltd.
Legal treatises, annual handbooks and monthly law reports, specializing in the law of immigration, antitrust, zoning, securities regulation, insurance, international transactions, criminal practice, licensing patents and trademarks, federal practice and entertainment

Warren, Gorham & Lamont Inc.
Professional books, looseleaf services, newsletters, journals and directories, primarily in taxation, banking, business law, real estate, accountancy and medicine

PUBLICATIONS:
Journal of Taxation; Federal Income Taxation of Corporations and Shareholders; Brady on Bank Checks; Real Estate Review; Journal of Business Strategy; Corporate Accounting; Accounting and Auditing Disclosure Manual; Truth-in-Lending; Thorndike Encyclopaedia of Banking and Financial Tables; Federal Taxation of Income, Estates and Gifts; Law of Real Estate Financing

SUBSIDIARY:
Auerbach Publishers Inc.
Professional books, looseleaf services, newsletters, journals and directories on computers and information management

THOMAS NELSON INTERNATIONAL, *Toronto*
(educational, trade, professional, and reference)

Delmar Publishers Inc.
Vocational and high-technology books

Nelson Canada
Educational, measurement and guidance

NFER—Nelson Publishing Company Ltd. *(50% holding)*
Measurement and guidance, psychological tests, educational research

Nelson Filmscan Ltd.
English-language teaching by video

Thomas Nelson Australia
Educational and trade publishing

Thomas Nelson and Sons Ltd.
Primary, secondary, and English-language teaching

Thomas Nelson Hong Kong Ltd.

Thomas Nelson Nigeria Ltd. *(40% holding)*

Professional Publishing Ltd.
SUBSIDIARIES:
Bondholders Register; Gee & Co. Ltd.; Laureate Press

THOMSON BOOKS LTD., *London*

Hamish Hamilton
SUBSIDIARIES:
Hamish Hamilton Children's Books; Elm Tree

General trade

Michael Joseph Ltd.
SUBSIDIARIES:
Mermaid Books; Pelham Books

General trade

Rainbird Publishing Group Ltd.
General trade book packager

Sphere Books Ltd.
SUBSIDIARIES:
Abacus; Celtic Revision Aids

Paperback

TBL Book Service Ltd.

Distribution

RICHARD DE BOO, *Toronto*
Law and taxation.

Canada Tax Service; Canada Corporation Manual; Canada Energy Law Service; Canadian Estate Planning Service; Canadian Mortgage Practice Reporter; Income Tax References

VAN NOSTRAND REINHOLD COMPANY INC., *New York*
(educational, professional and reference, college, trade and software)

SUBSIDIARIES:
CBI Publishing Co., Inc.; Compress; Hutchinson Ross Publishing Company; Science Books International (owns Heinle & Heinle Publishers)

WADSWORTH INC., *San Francisco*
(college textbooks and professional books)

SUBSIDIARIES:
Anaheim Publishing Company Inc.; Breton Publishers; Brooks/Cole Publishing Company; Kent Publishing Company; Lange Medical Publications, Inc.; Lifetime Learning Publications; PWS Publishers; Wadsworth Electronic Publishing Company; Wadsworth International Group; Wadsworth Publishers of Canada Ltd.; Wadsworth Publishers Company

BUSINESS MAGAZINES

INTERNATIONAL THOMSON PUBLISHING LTD., *London*
(a division of Thomson Information Services Ltd.)

BUSINESS PUBLICATIONS:
Big Farm Management; Big Farm Weekly; British Journal of Hospital Medicine; Building Trades Journal; Communications International; Construction News; Construction News Magazine; Construction News Products; Construction News Scotland; Drapers Record; Engineering Capacity; Fashion International; Hospital Development;

Hospital Equipment and Supplies; Meat; Meat Trades Journal; Men's Wear; New Electronics; Nursing Focus; Plant International; Remedial Therapist; Retail Jeweller; and Glass's Guide Service Ltd. (51%) publishes *Glass's Guide Car Magazine*

CONSUMER PUBLICATIONS:
Burlington Magazine; Cheshire Life; Circle Books; Family Circle; Gloucestershire and Avon Life; Illustrated London News; Lancashire Life; Living; Natural World; Pins and Needles; Political Quarterly; Warwickshire and Worcestershire Life; Yorkshire Life

INTERNATIONAL THOMSON BUSINESS PRESS INC., *Radnor, Pennsylvania*
(business and information sciences)

CES Publishing Corporation

Audio Times; Auto Sound and Communications; Computer Merchandising; Consumer Electronics Daily; Consumer Electronics Monthly; Consumer Electronics Show Daily; Video Business

Eastman Publishing, Inc.

Computer Merchandising; Software Merchandising

Huebner Publications, Inc.

Designfax; Fastener Technology; Machine Tool Specs Directories; Metlfax; Purchasing World; Tooling and Production; Wire Technology

International Thomson Transportation Information Services Inc.

Brandon's Shipper and Forwarder; Pacific Shipper; Coast Marine and Transportation Directory

Medical Economics Company Inc.

Clinical Laboratory Reference; Contemporary OB/GYN; Diagnosis; Diagnostic Magazine; Drug Topics; Drug Topics Red Book; MEDE Communications; Medical Economics; Medical Economics Books; Medical Economics for Surgeons; Medical Laboratory Observer; Medical Media International; Nursing Opportunities; Physicians' Desk Reference (PDR); PDR for Nonprescription Drugs; PDR for Opthalmology; PDR for Radiology and Nuclear Medicine; Red Book Data Services; RN

Med Publishing Inc.

Cardiovascular News; Practical Cardiology; Gastro-Intestinal Literature News; Geriatric Medicine Today; Internal Medicine; OB/GYN Literature News; Oncology Literature News; Pulmonary Diseases Literature News; Tuberculosis Literature News

Patient Care Communications Inc.

Patient Care

Redgate Publishing

Publications on computer software

Titsch Communications, Inc.

Broadcast Week; Cable File; Cable Vision; Communications Engineering Digest; International Communications Research; Mobile Radio Handbook; Radio Communications Report; Two-Way Radio Dealer

Veterinary Medicine Publishing Co.

Veterinary Economics; Veterinary Medicine/Small Animal Clinic; Veterinary Pharmaceuticals and Biologics

Ward's Communications Inc.

Ward's Auto Info Bank; Ward's Automotive Reports; Ward's Automotive Reports Index; Ward's Automotive Yearbook; Ward's Auto World; Ward's Engine Update

SUBSIDIARY:
Broad Run Enterprises Inc.

Tecfacts

THOMSON AUSTRALIAN HOLDINGS PTY LTD.
(business publications and trade fairs)

Thomson Publications Australia

Australasian Office News; Australian Advertising Rate and Data Service; Australian Electronics Engineering; Australian Mining; Australian Mining Year Book; b & t Advertising, Marketing and Media Weekly; b & t Year Book; Building Products News;

*Communications Australia; Construction & Road Transport;
Construction Equipment News; Cordells Building Publications;
Electrical Engineer; Factory Equipment News; Mingay's Electrical
Supplies Guide; Mingay's Price Service; Mingay's Retailer &
Merchandiser; Process & Control Engineering; Tenders; Thomson's
Electronics Data Book; Thomson's Industrial Products Registers;
Thomson's Liquor Guide; Thomson's Oil & Gas Year Book;* and
Glass's Guide Service (Australia) Pty Ltd. (51% holding) publishes
Glass's Guide Car magazine

THOMSON PUBLICATIONS S.A. (PTY) LTD., *Johannesburg*
(business publications and trade fairs)

BUSINESS PUBLICATIONS (37):
*Building Products News; Chemical Equipment News; Commercial
Transport; Computing SA; Daily Tender Bulletin; Electrical Engineer;
Electronics and Instrumentation; Food Industries Handbook; Food
Industries of South Africa; Freight World; Hospital and Nursing Year
Book of Southern Africa; Kontak; Materials Handling News;
Merkel's Builders Pricing Manual; Motor World; Natal Equipment
News; New Equipment News; New Equipment News, Cape and SW
Africa; New Retailer; Office World; Pack & Print; Plastics & Rubber
News; Power & Plant Engineering in South Africa; Professional
Caterer; Public Works; Railways of Southern Africa; S.A. Family
Practice; S.A. Mining Week; Shoes & Views; South African Fishing
Industry Handbook; South African Hardware; South African
Hospital Supplies; South African Industrial Week; South African
Journal of Hospital Medicine; South African Mining and Engineering
Journal; South African Mining and Engineering Year Book; Transport
Managers' Handbook*

SUBSIDIARIES:
The Pithead Press (Pty) Ltd.

BUSINESS PUBLICATIONS (6):
*Coal, Gold and Base Minerals of Southern Africa; Construction
Commercial News; Construction in Southern Africa; Export News;
Heating, Air Conditioning and Refrigeration; Production
Management*

Trade Fairs and Promotions (Pty) Ltd.; Mead and McGrouther (Pty)
Ltd. *(51% holding)*

INFORMATION AND PUBLISHING IN EUROPE

DENMARK:
Mostrups Forlag A/S
Thomson Communications (Scandinavia) A/S

FRANCE:
France SARL *(51% holding)*
Editions Professionnelles Glass

GERMANY:
Bertelsmann-Thomson Fachverlag GmbH
(44.8% holding)

HOLLAND:
Thomson Publications (Europe) BV

NORWAY:
Informasjonsforlaget A/S

NEWSPAPERS
Thomson Regional Newspapers*

*Canadian and U.S. newspapers owned separately from International Thomson Organisation
Limited by Thomson Newspapers Limited (see Appendix E).*

COMPUTER DATA SERVICES

UNITED STATES:
International Thomson Information Inc.
(data-base publishing and information services)

SUBSIDIARIES:
Carrolton Press Inc.
Publisher of "Remarc" computer data base

INACOM
Technical, scientific and engineering information services

Thomson & Thomson Inc.
Trademark search services

Research Publications Inc.
Micropublishing academic and professional reference materials, newspapers, U.S. and foreign patents

Research Publications Ltd.
(based in United Kingdom)

UNITED KINGDOM:
Thomson Data Ltd.
(a division of Thomson Information Services Ltd.)

Patent information, micropublishing, legal publishing and data marketing

SUBSIDIARIES:
Computacar Ltd.
Derwent Publications Ltd. *(92% holding)*
ESDU International Ltd.
European Law Centre Ltd.

Commercial Laws of Europe; Common Market Law Reports; European Commercial Cases; European Commercial Intelligence; European Human Rights Reports; European Law Digest; Fleet Street Reports

Eurolex
Legal database

DIRECTORIES

Thomson Directories, *United Kingdom*
(a division of Thomson Information Services Ltd.)
(50% partnership)

Local directory publishers

TRAVEL

UNITED KINGDOM:
Thomson Travel Ltd.
(package tours, aircraft charter and travel retailing)

SUBSIDIARIES:
Britannia Airways Ltd.; Lunn Poly Ltd.; Portland Holidays Ltd.;
Thomson Holidays Ltd.

UNITED STATES:
Thomson Travel Inc.
(package tours and travel retailing)

SUBSIDIARIES:
Club Universe; Specialised Travel Division; Unitours Inc.; and
Canadian subsidiary—Thomson Vacations

EUROPE AND NORTH AFRICA:
Malta: **Beauport Investment Trust Ltd.**
(49.1% holding) and hotels*

Tunisia: **RYM SA** *(45.5% holding)*

Hotels also in Italy and Spain.

NATURAL RESOURCES

UNITED KINGDOM:
Thomson North Sea Ltd.
(oil and gas development and forestry investment)

SUBSIDIARIES:
Thomson Scottish Petroleum Ltd.; Thomson Scottish Forestry Ltd.

UNITED STATES (DALLAS):
Thomson-Monteith Ltd.
(oil)

CANADA (CALGARY):
Thomson-Jensen Ltd.
(oil)

ASSOCIATED COMPANIES

UNITED KINGDOM:
The Solicitors' Law Stationery Society PLC *(39.1% holding)*

Wigham Poland Holdings Ltd. *(35% holding)*

APPENDIX

D

FIVE-YEAR RESULTS

INTERNATIONAL THOMSON ORGANISATION LIMITED

FIVE-YEAR RESULTS

(Results are reported in British pounds by ITOL; translated into Canadian and U.S. dollars at the average exchange rate for each year.)

	British Pounds (in millions)		Canadian Dollars (in millions)		U.S. Dollars (in millions)	
	Sales	Net Income	Sales	Net Income	Sales	Net Income
1983	1,503.5	72.0	2,808.9	134.5	3,461.8	165.7
1982	1,334.1	51.5	2,878.8	247.3	3,552.7	305.2
1981	1,180.7	43.5	2,867.6	275.9	3,438.2	330.8
1980	917.2	45.1	2,494.4	325.5	2,915.9	380.5
1979	687.1	55.2	1,707.8	304.7	2,000.7	357.0

THOMSON NEWSPAPERS LTD.

FIVE-YEAR RESULTS

(In millions of Canadian dollars)

	1983	1982	1981	1980	1979
Revenue	705.2	666.4	645.9	532.4	335.6
Profit	126.1	99.4	96.9	75.8	65.0

E

NEWSPAPER CIRCULATION

CIRCULATION OF THOMSON-OWNED NEWSPAPERS
(Canada and U.S. as of end of November 1983;
U.K. as of end of December 1983)

	Total Number of Papers	Number of Daily		Number of Weekly	Total Circulation	Smallest Daily	Biggest Daily	Biggest Weekly
Canada	52	39		13[a]	1,208,340 (paid)	5,780	315,643	8,269
		a.m.	3		40,131 (free)	The Evening	The Globe	The Yorkton
		p.m.	35			Patriot	and Mail	Enterprise
		a.m./p.m.	1			Charlottetown,	Toronto	Yorkton,
						Prince Edward		Saskatchewan
						Island		
United States	88	84		4	1,325,231	2,960	65,120	3,380
		a.m.	5			The Daily	The Reposi-	The McLeans-
		p.m.	78			Dispatch	tory	boro Times-
		a.m./p.m.	1			Douglas,	Canton, Ohio	Leader
						Arizona		McLeansboro,
								Illinois
United Kingdom	60[b]	12		47	1,483,141 (paid)	41,823 (paid)	152,802 (paid)	122,051 (paid)
		a.m.	6		1,203,857 (free)	Evening Post	Evening	Sunday Sun
		p.m.	6			Reading (near	Chronicle	Newcastle
						London)	Newcastle	

NOTES:
[a] Including 4 bi-weekly and 2 tri-weekly
[b] Including 1 monthly
SOURCES: Audit Bureau of Circulation,
Thomson Newspapers Limited,
Thomson Regional Newspapers

THOMSON NEWSPAPERS

Canada

(As of 30 November 1983)

Location		Name of Paper	Circulation	A.M. P.M. Weekly
Alberta:	Lethbridge	*The Lethbridge Herald*	28,269	p.m.
British Columbia:	Kamloops	*Kamloops Sentinel*	26,120 (free)	Tri-weekly
	Kelowna	*The Kelowna Daily Courier*	16,490	p.m.
	Nanaimo	*Nanaimo Daily Free Press*	9,061	p.m.
	Penticton	*Penticton Herald*	8,508	p.m.
	Vernon	*Vernon Daily News*	8,993	p.m.
	Victoria	*Times-Colonist*	78,939	a.m./p.m.
Manitoba:	Winnipeg	*Winnipeg Free Press*	191,871	p.m.
New Brunswick:	Bathurst	*The Northern Light*	8,078	W
Newfoundland:	Corner Brook	*The Western Star*	10,564	p.m.
	St. John's	*The Evening Telegram*	38,339	p.m.
Nova Scotia:	New Glasgow	*The Evening News*	11,387	p.m.
	Sydney	*Cape Breton Post*	31,560	p.m.
	Truro	*The Daily News*	8,601	p.m.
Ontario:	Barrie	*The Barrie Examiner*	12,728	p.m.
	Belleville	*The Intelligencer*	17,435	p.m.
	Brampton	*The Daily Times*	6,390	p.m.
	Cambridge	*Cambridge Daily Reporter*	13,570	p.m.
	Chatham	*The Chatham Daily News*	15,807	p.m.
	Collingwood	*Enterprise-Bulletin*	6,231	W
	Cornwall	*Standard-Freeholder*	17,010	p.m.
	Dunnville	*Dunnville Chronicle*	3,623	W
	Elliot Lake	*The Standard*	4,816	Bi-weekly
	Georgetown	*The Herald*	14,011 (free)	W
	Guelph	*The Daily Mercury*	17,676	p.m.
	Hanover	*The Hanover Post*	4,322	W
	Kirkland Lake	*Northern Daily News*	5,852	p.m.
	Leamington	*Leamington Post*	5,833	W
	Midland	*The Free Press*	6,039	Bi-weekly
	Niagara Falls	*Niagara Falls Review*	20,254	p.m.
	Orangeville	*The Banner*	6,176	Bi-weekly
	Orillia	*Daily Packet and Times*	9,827	p.m.
	Oshawa	*The Oshawa Times*	22,316	p.m.
	Pembroke	*The Pembroke Observer*	7,145	p.m.
	Peterborough	*Peterborough Examiner*	24,412	p.m.
	St. Thomas	*St. Thomas Times-Journal*	10,101	p.m.
	Sarnia	*The Sarnia Observer*	24,112	p.m.
	Simcoe	*The Simcoe Reformer*	9,696	p.m.
	Sudbury	*The Sudbury Star*	29,571	p.m.

Thunder Bay	*The Chronicle Journal*	28,457	p.m.
Thunder Bay	*The Times-News*	8,828	a.m.
Timmins	*The Daily Press*	13,725	p.m.
Toronto	*The Globe and Mail****	315,643	a.m.
Trenton	*The Trentonian and*		
	Tri-County News	7,827	Tri-weekly
Welland	*The Evening Tribune*	17,037	p.m.
Woodstock	*The Daily Sentinel-Review*	8,760	p.m.

Quebec**

Prince	Charlottetown	*The Morning Guardian*	17,426	a.m.
Edward	Charlottetown	*The Evening Patriot*	5,780	p.m.
Island:				

Saskatch-	Moose Jaw	*Moose Jaw Times-Herald*	9,930	p.m.
ewan:	Prince Albert	*Prince Albert Daily Herald*	10,179	p.m.
	Swift Current	*The Swift Current Sun*	4,877	Bi-weekly
	Yorkton	*The Yorkton Enterprise*	8,269	W

* *The Globe and Mail* started an afternoon edition in June 1984.
**Montreal Standard Printer (printing company—not included in total)
NOTE: Circulation calculated on all publishing days as per Audit Bureau of Circulation formula.
Based on Thomson Newspaper Ltd.'s figures.

THOMSON NEWSPAPERS

United States
(As of 30 November 1983)

Location		Name of Paper	Circulation	A.M. P.M. Weekly
Alabama:	Dothan	*The Dothan Eagle*	22,672	p.m.
	Enterprise	*The Enterprise Ledger*	6,950	p.m.
	Opelika	*The Opelika-Auburn News*	14,065	p.m.
	Phenix City	*The Phenix Citizen*	1,563	W
Arizona:	Douglas	*The Daily Dispatch*	2,960	p.m.
Arkansas:	Fayetteville	*Northwest Arkansas Times*	11,108	p.m.
California:	Barstow	*Desert Dispatch*	6,933	p.m.
	Eureka	*The Times-Standard*	20,564	p.m.
	Oxnard	*The Press-Courier*	20,058	p.m.
	West Covina	*San Gabriel Valley Daily*		
		Tribune	63,339	a.m.
	Whittier	*The Daily News*	16,669	p.m.
	Yreka	*Siskiyou Daily News*	5,190	p.m.
Connecti-cut:	Ansonia	*The Evening Sentinel*	17,310	p.m.
Florida:	Englewood	*Englewood Herald*	3,026	W
	Key West	*The Key West Citizen*	7,432	p.m.

	Marianna	*Jackson County Floridan*	4,962	p.m.
	Orange Park	*Clay Today*	4,809	p.m.
	Punta Gorda	*Daily-Herald News*	8,082	p.m.
Georgia:	Cordele	*The Cordele Dispatch*	5,302	p.m.
	Dalton	*The Daily Citizen-News*	12,422	p.m.
	Griffin	*Griffin Daily News*	12,369	p.m.
	Thomasville	*Thomasville Times-Enterprise*	10,895	p.m.
	Tifton	*The Tifton Gazette*	9,167	p.m.
	Valdosta	*The Valdosta Daily Times*	17,589	p.m.
Illinois:	Jacksonville	*Jacksonville Journal Courier*	15,781	a.m./p.m.
	McLeansboro	*The McLeansboro Times Leader*	3,380	W
	Mount Vernon	*The Register-News*	12,052	p.m.
Indiana:	Kokomo	*The Kokomo Tribune*	28,916	p.m.
	New Albany	*The Tribune*	10,760	p.m.
Iowa:	Council Bluffs	*Council Bluffs Nonpareil*	19,109	p.m.
	Oelwein	*The Oelwein Daily Register*	6,848	p.m.
Kansas:	Atchison	*Atchison Daily Globe*	5,729	p.m.
	Leavenworth	*The Leavenworth Times*	9,600	p.m.
Kentucky:	Corbin	*The Times-Tribune*	7,466	p.m.
Louisiana:	Lafayette	*The Daily Advertiser*	34,520	p.m.
Maryland:	Salisbury	*The Daily Times*	27,151	p.m.
Massachus- etts:	Fichtburg	*The Daily Sentinal and Leominster Enterprise*	24,050	p.m.
	Taunton	*Taunton Daily Gazette*	14,036	p.m.
Michigan:	Adrian	*Adrian Daily Telegram*	17,222	p.m.
	Escanaba	*The Daily Press*	10,384	p.m.
	Houghton	*The Daily Mining Gazette*	11,951	p.m.
	Iron Mountain	*The Daily News*	10,435	p.m.
	Marquette	*The Mining Journal*	17,568	p.m.
Minnesota:	Albert Lea	*The Evening Tribune*	10,138	p.m.
	Austin	*Austin Daily Herald*	9,853	p.m.
Mississippi:	Laurel	*Laurel Leader-Call*	10,313	p.m.
Missouri:	Cape Girardeau	*The Southeast Missourian*	14,912	p.m.
	Carthage	*The Carthage Press*	5,108	p.m.
	Sikeston	*The Daily Standard*	9,508	p.m.
New Hampshire:	Portsmouth	*The Portsmouth Herald*	15,792	p.m.
New York:	Herkimer	*The Evening Telegram*	7,124	p.m.
	Newburgh	*The Evening News*	17,101	p.m.
	Oswego	*The Palladium-Times*	8,019	p.m.
North Carolina:	Rocky Mount	*The Evening Telegram*	14,049	p.m.
Ohio:	Canton	*The Repository*	65,120	p.m.
	Coshocton	*The Coshocton Tribune*	7,887	p.m.

	East Liverpool	*The Evening Review*	13,678	p.m.
	Franklin	*The Franklin Chronicle*	2,482	W
	Greenville	*The Daily Advocate*	9,257	p.m.
	Lancaster	*Lancaster Eagle-Gazette*	17,875	a.m.
	Marion	*The Marion Star*	19,182	p.m.
	Middletown	*Middletown Journal*	24,242	p.m.
	Newark	*The Advocate*	22,186	p.m.
	Piqua	*The Piqua Daily Call*	10,788	p.m.
	Portsmouth	*The Daily Times*	19,441	p.m.
	Salem	*The Salem News*	9,995	p.m.
	Steubenville	*The Herald Star*	21,553	p.m.
	Xenia	*The Xenia Daily Gazette*	11,310	p.m.
	Zanesville	*The Times Recorder*	24,123	p.m.
Oklahoma:	Ada	*The Ada Evening News*	9,429	p.m.
Pennsylvania:	Connelsville	*The Daily Courier*	13,899	p.m.
	Easton	*The Express*	47,278	p.m.
	Greenville	*The Greenville Record-Argus*	5,184	p.m.
	Hanover	*The Evening Sun*	22,309	p.m.
	Kittaning	*The Leader-Times*	11,659	p.m.
	Lock Haven-Jersey Shore	*The Express*	11,585	p.m.
	Meadville	*The Meadville Tribune*	17,277	a.m.
	Monessen-Charleroi-Donora	*The Valley Independent*	17,077	p.m.
South Carolina:	Florence	*Florence Morning News*	32,058	a.m.
South Dakota:	Mitchell	*The Daily Republic*	12,527	p.m.
Utah:	St. George	*The Daily Spectrum*	12,979	p.m.
Virginia:	Petersburg	*The Progress-Index*	20,433	p.m.
West Virginia:	Fairmont	*The Times-West Virginian*	15,586	a.m.
	Weirton	*The Weirton Daily Times*	7,740	p.m.
Wisconsin:	Fond du Lac	*The Reporter*	20,363	p.m.
	Manitowoc	*Herald-Times-Reporter*	17,066	p.m.
	Waukesha	*Waukesha Freeman*	23,425	p.m.
	Wisconsin Rapids	*The Daily Tribune*	12,979	p.m.

NOTE: Circulation calculated on all publishing days as per Audit Bureau of Circulation formula. Based on Thomson Newspaper Ltd.'s figures.

UNITED KINGDOM NEWSPAPERS
(As of 31 December 1983)

Location	Name of Newspaper	Circulation	W = (Weekly)
ENGLAND			
Berkshire County *(Near Windsor, about 30 miles west of London)*	Ascot Times Bracknell Times Crowthorne Times Wokingham Times }	12,570 (paid for)	W W W W
Cheshire County *(About 40 miles southeast of Manchester)*	Chester Chronicle	36,159	W
	Crewe Chronicle Nantwich Chronicle }	26,610	W W
	Middlewich Chronicle Northwich Chronicle Winsford Chronicle }	10,214 (paid for)	W W W
	Runcorn Weekly News	9,500	W
	Widnes Weekly News	10,000	W
	Chester Mail	40,045	W
	Ellesmere Port Mail	22,381	W
	Frodsham and Helsby News	5,000 (free)	W
	Penketh and Great Sankey News	10,000	W
Lancashire County *(About 30 miles northwest of Manchester)*	Evening Telegraph	47,725 (paid for)	
	Blackburn and Darwen Mail	56,871	W
	Burnley and Padiham Mail	35,559 (free)	W
	Pendle Mail	34,250	W
Middlesbrough *(40 miles south of Newcastle)*	Evening Gazette	81,568 (paid for)	
	Teesside Advertiser	173,000 (free)	W
Newcastle	Evening Chronicle	152,802	
	Sunday Sun	122,051 (paid for)	W
	The Journal	69,222	
	The Advertiser	150,756 (free)	W
Reading *(50 miles west of London)*	Evening Post	41,823 (paid for)	
	Reading Standard	80,000 (free)	W
Shropshire County *(Official name, Salop) (Borders on Wales, about 50 miles from Birmingham)*	Whitchurch Herald	5,806 (paid for)	W

NORTHERN IRELAND

Belfast	*Ballymena Observer*	14,061 ⎫	W
	Belfast Telegraph	150,402 ⎬ (paid	
	East Antrim Times	15,932 ⎭ for)	W

SCOTLAND

Aberdeen	*Evening Express*	82,475 ⎫ (paid	
	The Press and Journal	112,080 ⎭ for)	
	The Citizen	84,133 ⎫	W
	Scene	40,000 ⎭ (free)	W
Edinburgh	*Evening News*	123,827 ⎫ (paid	
	The Scotsman (national circulation)	92,963 ⎭ for)	
	Edinburgh Advertiser	161,911 (free)	W

WALES

Cardiff	*South Wales Echo*	102,452 ⎫ (paid	
	Western Mail	79,435 ⎭ for)	
	Barry Post	16,490 ⎫	W
	Caerphilly Post	36,520 ⎬	W
	Cardiff Post	101,320 ⎬ (free)	W
	Penarth Post	11,244 ⎭	W
Southern Valleys	*Aberdare Leader* ⎫	11,703	W
	Mountain Ash Leader ⎭		W
	Glamorgan Gazette	21,307 (paid	W
	Gwent Gazette	8,282 for)	W
	Llantrisant Observer ⎫		W
	Pontypridd Observer ⎬	23,886	W
	Rhondda Leader ⎭		W
	Merthyr Express ⎫	18,286	W
	Rhymney Valley Express ⎭		W
	Abergavenny Gazette	12,500	W
	Bridgend Star	12,366	W
	Merthyr Star	17,500	Monthly
	Neath Guardian ⎫	46,000 (free)	W
	Port Talbot Guardian ⎭		W
	Newport and Cwmbran Post	56,111	W

APPENDIX

F

DIRECTORS: THOMSON COMPANIES

DIRECTORS
Major Thomson Companies

International Thomson Organisation Ltd.

Senior Officers and Directors

NAME	POSITION	OTHER AFFILIATIONS
Kenneth Roy Thomson *Title:* Right Honorable Lord of Fleet of Northbridge in the City of Edinburgh *(Toronto)*	*Chairman:* International Thomson Organisation Ltd. (parent company—Canada) International Thomson Organisation PLC (United Kingdom) International Thomson Holding Inc. (United States)	Director Abitibi-Price Inc.; Toronto-Dominion Bank Art collector
John A. Tory, Q.C. *(Toronto)*	*Deputy Chairman:* International Thomson Organisation Ltd.	Director Abitibi-Price Inc.; Royal Bank of Canada

	International Thomson Holdings Inc.	Honorary Solicitor, Canadian Mental Health Association
	Director: International Thomson Organisation PLC	
Gordon C. Brunton *(London, England)*	*President:* International Thomson Organisation Ltd.	Director and Past Chairman: Sotheby Parke Bernet Group PLC
	Managing Director and Chief Executive: International Thomson Organisation PLC	
	President and Chief Executive Officer: International Thomson Holdings Inc.	
W. Michael Brown *(New York)*	*Executive Vice-President:* International Thomson Organisation Ltd.	
	Executive Vice-President and Chief Operating Officer: International Thomson Holdings Inc.	

OTHER DIRECTORS

International Thomson Organisation Ltd.

W. J. Des Lauriers *(Toronto)*	Partner, law firm of Tory, Tory, Des Lauriers & Binnington

Charles Edward (Ted)
  Medland
(Toronto)

*Chairman, President
  and Chief Executive
  Officer:*
Wood Gundy Ltd.

Board of Governors:
Wellesley Hospital
  (Toronto)

James Whittall,
  D.S.O.
*(Distinguished Service
  Cross) (Toronto)*

Chairman:
Reed Stenhouse Inc.

Member and
  Associate: Insurance
  Institute of America

International Thomson Organisation PLC

Claude Neville David
  Cole
*(Westminster,
  England)*

*Joint Deputy
  Managing Director:*
ITOL, PLC

Chairman:
Thomson Books Ltd.

*Chief Executive and
  Chairman:*
Thomson Information
  Services

Court of Governors
  and also Council:
  University of Wales

Author of several
  volumes of poetry

James Donald Evans
(Darlington, England)

*Joint Deputy
  Managing Director:*
ITOL, PLC

*Chairman and Chief
  Executive:*
Thomson Regional
  Newspapers Ltd.

Joseph Darby
(London, England)

Managing Director:
Thomson North Sea
  Ltd.

Roger Davies
(London, England)

Managing Director:
Thomson Travel Ltd.

M. D. Knight
(London, England)

Company Secretary:
International
  Thomson
  Organisation Ltd.

M. S. Mander
(London, England)

Managing Director:
Thomson Information
  Services

A. J. B. Mawdsley
(London, England)

Financial Director:
International
   Thomson
   Organisation PLC

J. H. Sauvage
(London, England)

Chairman:
Thomson Travel Ltd.

Note: As of the end of 1984, Gordon Brunton will retire. Michael Brown
will succeed him as president of International Thomson Organisation
Ltd., and James Evans will become managing director of International
Thomson Organisation PLC and executive vice-president of
International Thomson Organisation Ltd.

Thomson Newspapers Ltd.

NAME	POSITION	OTHER AFFILIATIONS
Kenneth Thomson	*Chairman and President*	
John Tory	*Deputy Chairman*	
Brian W. Slaight *(Toronto)*	*Executive Vice-President*	
Peter T. Bogart *(Toronto)*	*Vice-President, Finance and Treasurer*	
John H. Coleman *(Toronto)*	*President:* J.H.C. Associates Ltd.	Director of 20 companies, including Chrysler Corporation, Imasco Ltd., Royal Bank of Canada, Xerox of Canada Ltd.
John S. Dewar *(Toronto)*	*Chairman and Chief Executive Officer:* Union Carbide Canada Ltd.	Board of Trustees, Queen's University (Kingston, Ontario)

Lorne K. Lodge *(Toronto)*	*Chairman and Chief Executive Officer:* IBM Canada Ltd.	
St. Clair McCabe *(Clearwater, Florida)*	*President:* Thomson Newspapers Inc. (U.S.)	
Douglas J. Peacher *(La Jolla, California)*	*Former President:* Simpsons-Sears Acceptance Co.	Honorary Trustee, Concordia University (Sir George Williams) (Montreal)
David C. H. Stanley	*Past Vice-President:* Wood Gundy Ltd.	Past President, Canadian National Institute for the Blind

Hudson's Bay Company

NAME	POSITION	OTHER AFFILIATIONS
Kenneth Thomson	(See International Thomson and Thomson Newspapers)	
John Tory	(See International Thomson and Thomson Newspapers)	
Donald S. McGiverin *(Toronto)*	*Governor and President:* Hudson's Bay Co. *Chairman:* Simpsons Ltd. *Deputy Chairman:* Markborough Properties Ltd.	
Alexander J. MacIntosh *(Toronto)*	*Deputy Governor:* Hudson's Bay Co. Partner, law firm of Blake Cassels & Graydon	Vice-Chairman, John Labatt Ltd. Trustee, Brock University (St. Catharines, Ontario)

Ian A. Barclay
(*Vancouver*)

Chairman:
British Columbia
  Forest Products Ltd.

Governor, British
  Columbia Lions
  (football club)

Marcel Bélanger, O.C.[1]
(*Quebec City*)

President:
Gagnon & Bélanger
  Inc.

C. W. (Wally) Evans
(*Toronto*)

President:
The Bay

G. Richard Hunter,
  Q.C., M.B.E.[2]
(*Winnipeg*)

Partner, law firm of
  Pitblado & Hoskin

Martin W. Jacomb
(*London, England*)

Vice-Chairman:
Kleinwort, Benson
  Ltd.

Josette Leman
(*Montreal*)

Travel Consultant:
McGregor Travel Co.

Director, Research
  Fund, Montreal
  Heart Institute

**W. Donald C.
  Mackenzie**
(*Calgary*)

President:
W. D. C. Mackenzie
  Consultants Ltd.

Dawn R. McKeag
(*Winnipeg*)

President:
Walford Investments
  Ltd.

Registered nurse;
  married to former
  Lieutenant
  Governor of
  Manitoba and
  daughter of former
  Manitoba Premier
  Douglas Campbell

John H. Moore
(*London, Ontario*)

Chairman:
Executive committee,
  board of directors,
  London Life
  Insurance Co.

Past Chairman and
  President, John
  Labatt Ltd.
Past President: Brascan
  Ltd.

George T. Richardson
(*Winnipeg*)

President:
James Richardson &
  Sons Ltd.
Past Governor:
Hudson's Bay Co.

Director, Canadian
  Imperial Bank of
  Commerce

Rt. Hon. Lord Trend
(*Oxford, England*)

Rector:
Lincoln College,
  Oxford

Pro-Vice-Chancellor,
  Oxford University
Former Secretary
  (1963–73) of the
  British Cabinet

Donald O. Wood *(Toronto)*	*Vice-President,* *finance:* Hudson's Bay Co.	Board member: Toronto Arts Productions; Winnipeg Ballet
Peter W. Wood *(Toronto)*	*Executive* *Vice-President:* Hudson's Bay Co.	National Director, Canadian Cancer Society

[1] O.C. = Officer of the Order of Canada
[2] M.B.E. = Member of the Order of the British Empire

Scottish and York Holdings Ltd.

NAME	POSITION	OTHER AFFILIATIONS
Kenneth Thomson	(See International Thomson and Thomson Newspapers)	
John Tory	(See International Thomson and Thomson Newspapers)	
R. W. Broughton *(Toronto)*	*Chairman and Chief* *Executive Officer:* Scottish and York Holdings Ltd.	
R. D. Abbot *(Toronto)*	*Vice-President and* *Secretary-Treasurer:* Scottish and York Holdings Ltd.	
Sidney Chapman *(Toronto)*	*Retired chief financial* *officer and director:* Thomson Newspapers Ltd.	Co-founded Scottish and York Holdings Ltd.
Ian Croft *(Toronto)*	*Vice-President and* *Treasurer:* The Woodbridge Co.	
St. Clair McCabe	(See Thomson Newspapers Ltd.)	

A. D. McEwen
(Toronto)

Chairman:
McEwen Easson Ltd.
(Investment dealer)

Two Main Thomson Family Holding Companies

Thomson Equitable Corporation
OFFICERS:
Chairman: **Kenneth Thomson**
President: **John Tory**

Vice-President and Treasurer: **Ian Croft**
Vice-President and Secretary: **James Melville**
Assistant Secretary: **Miyoko Okino** *(John Tory's secretary)*

Board of Directors: **Kenneth Thomson, Phyllis Audrey Campbell** *(Kenneth Thomson's sister),* **John Tory, Ian Croft**

The Woodbridge Company
OFFICERS:
Chairman: **Kenneth Thomson**
President: **John Tory**

Vice-President and Treasurer: **Ian Croft**
Vice-President and Secretary: **James Melville**
Vice-President: **Peter Mills**
Controller: **William Dodds**
Assistant Secretary: **Miyoko Okino**

Board of Directors: **Kenneth Thomson, John Tory, Ian Croft, Peter Mills**

INDEX

HUDSON'S BAY CO.   SCOTTISH & YORK
TRUCK LINES SIMPSONS LTD. MARKB
THE CANTON, OHIO RESPOSITORY   BEL
WALES ECHO   AMERICAN BANKER   TH
DRAPERS RECORD   FAMILY CIRCLE
MERCHANDISING . PACIFIC SHIPPER   F
VETERINARY ECONOMICS   WARD'S AU
& DATA SERVICE   AUSTRALIAN MINING
AFRICAN FISHING INDUSTRY HANDBOO
COMMUNICATIONS (SCANDINAVIA)A/S
HOLIDAYS LTD.   THOMSON HOLIDAYS
TRAVEL INC.   THOMSON VACATIONS
HAMILTON   MICHAEL JOSEPH LTD.
INSURANCE CO.   DOMINION CONS
MARKBOROUGH PROPERTIES LTD.
RESPOSITORY   BELFAST TELEGRAPH
AMERICAN BANKER   THE BOND BUYE
RECORD   FAMILY CIRCLE   I
MERCHANDISING PACIFIC SHIPPER
VETERINARY ECONOMICS   WARD'S
RATE & DATA SERVICE   AUSTRALIAN
SOUTH AFRICAN FISHING INDUSTRY H
THOMSON COMMUNICATIONS (SCAND
PORTLAND HOLIDAYS LTD.   THOMSO
THOMSON TRAVEL INC.   THOMSON
HAMISH HAMILTON   MICHAEL JOSE
& YORK INSURANCE CO.   DOMINION C
MARKBOROUGH PROPERTIES LTD.